Department of the Environment

Department of Health

Cryptosporidium in Water Supplies

Report of the Group of Experts

Chairman - Sir John Badenoch

(July) 1990
London: H M S O

First published 1990

ISBN 0 11 752322 4

The Rt Hon Christopher Patten MP
Secretary of State for the Environment
2 Marsham Street
LONDON SW1P 3EB

The Rt Hon Kenneth Clarke QC MP
Secretary of State for Health
Richmond House
79 Whitehall
LONDON SW1A 2NS

18 July 1990

Dear Secretaries of State.

I have pleasure in submitting the Report of the Group of Experts on cryptosporidium in water supplies set up in March 1989 in an urgent response to public concern resulting from an outbreak of cryptosporidiosis in Swindon and Oxfordshire. You will recall that I submitted our interim Report on 25 July 1989.

In this Report, we have attempted to set out what is known about the organism, its occurrence in the environment and its importance as a waterborne infection for man.

Although the number of cases of cryptosporidiosis appears to be increasing, it remains small in relation to the total number of cases of diarrhoeal illness. However, should mains water become contaminated, many people in the area of supply may become ill giving rise to great public concern.

It seems probable that the organism is present from time to time in all water sources in low numbers. Current water treatment processes are quite effective in dealing with these low numbers but should exceptional contamination of the source water occur, however carefully these processes are supervised and operated they cannot be guaranteed to prevent cryptosporidium getting through into the treated drinking water supply. We hope that as a result of a national programme of research initiated by the Group, more effective control of cryptosporidium in water supplies will become possible.

In the interim, until the results of this programme are known, we have outlined a code of best practice to be followed by health authorities, local authorities and water companies acting in close collaboration, to minimise the risk of an outbreak of cryptosporidiosis. We have also laid down guidelines for the control of an outbreak should one nevertheless occur.

I am most grateful to my colleagues who have willingly given up so much time to the Group's work; to Mr Mike Healey of the Drinking Water Inspectorate for much helpful advice; to the secretaries, Dr Ann Dawson, Department of Health, and Dr Derek Miller, Water Research Centre and to the two administrative secretaries, Mr Chris Whaley who helped us initially and Mrs Karin Cavill who has worked tirelessly and most effectively on the production of this Report.

As in the case of the interim Report, I am copying this letter to the Secretary of State for Scotland and am also sending copies to the Secretary of State for Wales, the Secretary of State for Northern Ireland and to the Minister of Agriculture Fisheries and Food.

John Badenoch.

SIR JOHN BADENOCH

i

GROUP OF EXPERTS ON CRYPTOSPORIDIUM IN WATER SUPPLIES

Chairman

Sir John Badenoch DM FRCP FRCP (Ed)

Members

Dr C L R Bartlett MSc MB FFCM Deputy: Dr Rachel Joce MBBS MFCM DCH	Communicable Disease Surveillance Centre, Public Health Laboratory Service
Dr Catherine Benton BSc PhD CBiol MIWEM	Strathclyde Regional Council
Dr D P Casemore PhD	Public Health Laboratory Service, Rhyl
Dr R Cawthorne BVM & S DipBiol PhD MRCVS	Ministry of Agriculture Fisheries and Food
Mr F Earnshaw FICE MIMechE FIWEM Deputy: Mr B R E Pound LRSC MIWEM	Severn Trent Water Ltd
Professor K J Ives DSc(Eng) FEng FICE	University College London
Mr J Jeffery MSc FIWEM FRIPHH	North Surrey Water Company
Dr H V Smith BSc PhD	Scottish Parasite Diagnostic Laboratory, Stobhill General Hospital
Dr M S B Vaile MB BS MRCGP FFCM	Maidstone Health Authority
Professor D A Warrell MA DM DSc FRCP	Nuffield Department of Clinical Medicine, University of Oxford
Dr A E Wright TD MD FRCPath DPH DipBact	Regional Public Health Laboratory, Newcastle upon Tyne (retired)

Observers

Mr R Cunningham	Department of Health
Mrs Anne Dennison Deputy: Mr R Walsh	Department of Health
Dr G I Forbes FRACMA FACOM FREHIS MFCM	Environmental Health (Scotland) Unit
Mr A C Paton BSc CEng FICE MIWEM	Scottish Development Department
Mr M G Healey BSc(Eng) AKC DPA MICE MIWEM	Drinking Water Inspectorate

Assessor

Dr D C Warhurst PhD MRCPath	London School of Hygiene and Tropical Medicine

Secretariat

Dr Ann Dawson BA MSc MRCP   Department of Health
Medical Secretary

Dr D Miller BSc PhD FIWEM MIChE   Water Research Centre
Technical Secretary

Mr C Whaley   Department of the Environment
to 25 September 1989 Administrative Secretary

Mrs Karin V Cavill   Department of the Environment
from 25 September 1989 Administrative Secretary

Contents

Part III: References, bibliographies, glossaries, abbreviations

Tables

Figures

Photographs

1. Three sporozoites of cryptosporidium on the surface of an enterocyte. Mouse ileum, 3 hours after infection with oocysts.
2. Low power view of lamb ileum 10 days after experimental infection with 10^6 cryptosporidial oocysts.
3. Higher magnification of lamb ileum (photograph 2), showing developing stages of cryptosporidium.
4. Scanning electron micrograph of developmental stages of cryptosporidium bulging from the microvillous surface of infected enterocytes.
5. Two cysts of *Giardia intestinalis* and two oocysts of *Cryptosporidium parvum* in an environmental sample, photographed under bright-field microscopy.
6. Two cysts of *Giardia intestinalis* and two oocysts of *Cryptosporidium parvum* in an environmental sample, stained with fluorescein labelled monoclonal antibodies and viewed under dark field epifluorescent microscopy.
7. Oocysts of *Cryptosporidium parvum* stained with fluorescein labelled monoclonal antibody.
8. A portable apparatus used for taking water samples for the isolation and detection of cryptosporidial oocysts.

Acknowledgements:

1–3 Moredun Research Institute, 408 Gilmerton Road, Edinburgh EH17 7JH. With thanks to Dr D A Blewett.

4 Reprinted with permission from ASM News, Washington DC, USA, Vol 54 No 11 (1988).

5–8 Scottish Parasite Diagnostic Laboratory, Stobhill General Hospital, Glasgow G21 3UW. With thanks to Dr H V Smith.

Summary

1.   Cryptosporidium is a protozoan parasite which has only been recognised relatively recently as a cause of diarrhoea in man. There are numerous species which affect mammals, birds, fish and amphibians but the only species known to infect man is *Cryptosporidium parvum*. In normally healthy individuals, cryptosporidiosis is usually characterised by an acute self-limiting diarrhoeal illness, commonly of 2–3 weeks duration, from which the patient recovers fully. In patients who are immunosuppressed, including those with AIDS, the disease is likely to much more serious. As yet there is no effective specific treatment.

2.   Initially, cryptosporidiosis was thought to be a zoonosis which spread directly from animals to man but it is now recognised that it spreads readily from person to person. Water is also emerging as an important vehicle for the transmission of infection and in the UK and the USA there have already been several outbreaks in which water has been implicated. The prevalence of cryptosporidium in livestock makes it likely that most oocysts in the environment derive from agricultural sources. All types of environmental water can become contaminated and the parasite may be present in low numbers in most waters from time to time.

3.   In Britain, the number of reported cases of cryptosporidiosis has been increasing but whether this is a true increase or whether it reflects to a considerable extent greater public awareness and improved detection methods is not known. In 1989, about 9,000 cases were reported. The number of cases resulting from waterborne infection must be less because of other means of spread. When viewed nationally, these waterborne cases represent only a very small fraction of all cases of diarrhoea but their importance lies in the fact that should the mains water become contaminated, many cases of illness may occur in the local area of supply.

4.   The water treatment processes in current use were not designed to deal specifically with the problem of cryptosporidial oocysts which are also unaffected by chlorine in the concentrations that can be used. Although treatment processes cannot be relied upon to prevent all oocysts from entering mains water, they are quite effective in dealing with low numbers of the parasite. However, if a water source should exceptionally become heavily contaminated with cryptosporidium, by accidental agricultural pollution or as the result of heavy rainfall and the resultant run-off from agricultural land, or from the discharge of sewage effluent, significant numbers of oocysts may pass into the treated water supply.

5.   Efforts are being made to develop a safe and effective disinfectant capable of killing cryptosporidium during the water treatment process. In the meantime, the risk of oocysts passing into the treated supply must be minimised by careful control of catchment areas and by ensuring that current water treatment processes are operated as efficiently as possible.

6.   Until more is known about the occurrence of cryptosporidium in the water environment and techniques for its isolation and identification are improved, routine monitoring of treated water for the parasite is not advocated. However, monitoring should be carried out if there has been exceptional contamination of the water source, if there has been a variation from normal operation in the water treatment works or if an outbreak of cryptosporidiosis is suspected in the community. It follows that water companies should develop the capacity to sample and test for cryptosporidium.

7.   Even if water treatment processes are operated in accordance with best practice there can be no absolute guarantee that cases of waterborne cryptosporidiosis will not occur. Health authorities, local authorities and the water companies should therefore develop together a clear strategy and contingency plans for the recognition and management of an outbreak of the disease.

8.   As a result of the Group's work, a national research programme on cryptosporidium has been established. This should lead to more effective control of cryptosporidium in water supplies. A further Report will be appropriate on the completion of this programme.

1 Introduction

Establishment of Expert Group

1.1 On 2 March 1989 following an outbreak of cryptosporidiosis in Swindon and Oxfordshire, the Rt Hon Michael Howard, QC MP, then the Minister for Water and Planning, announced that an expert group had been set up, in consultation with the Department of Health, under the chairmanship of Sir John Badenoch, to advise the Government on the significance of cryptosporidium in water supplies. The names of the members of the Group are listed on pages (ii) and (iii).

1.2 The Group was given the following terms of reference:

i to examine the occurrence and extent of cryptosporidium in water supplies;

ii to assess the significance for public health of cryptosporidium in water supplies;

iii to assess methods of monitoring for cryptosporidium and to formulate advice to water companies upon monitoring strategies;

iv to consider and formulate advice upon the protection of water supplies, treatment processes and the maintenance of distribution systems;

v to report jointly to the Secretary of State for the Environment and the Secretary of State for Health and to produce an interim report by the end of July 1989.

Interim Report

1.3 The Chairman of the Group wrote to the Secretary of State for the Environment and the Secretary of State for Health on 25 July 1989 to present the Group's Interim Report, (copy at Part III(I)). The Interim Report contained preliminary guidance on measures that could be taken to safeguard water supplies and information on public health aspects of infection with cryptosporidium.

1.4 Since that Report, the Group has considered detailed scientific and other evidence from many sources, the principal ones of which are listed in selective bibliographies at Part III(III and IV) and has also received reports on other waterborne or suspected waterborne outbreaks of cryptosporidiosis. The Group's earlier views are broadly consistent with this further information except in one important respect, namely, that contaminated drinking water must now be regarded as a cause of primary cases of cryptosporidiosis in the community, as well as infection through contact with the faeces of an infected animal. Secondary cases of cryptosporidiosis may occur from person to person spread if hygiene standards are not maintained.

Current Report

1.5 This Report now sets out to provide a comprehensive review of the current state of knowledge on cryptosporidium as an organism and its occurrence in the environment; its significance as a cause of infection in animals and man and the extent to which current water treatment processes can deal with the problems posed by contamination with the organism. The specialist reader may wish to consult the supporting scientific and technical data contained in Part II of the Report for more detailed information.

1.6 The Report also contains, in Chapter 9, an account of the main documented outbreaks of cryptosporidiosis which have been associated with water supplies. Chapter 10 identifies lessons that may be learned from these incidents and from consideration of cryptosporidium in relation to water treatment processes and sets out the situations in which water companies should consider monitoring for cryptosporidium. Most importantly, since the Group considers as yet best practice cannot wholly remove the risk of cryptosporidium occurring in drinking water supplies, Chapters 11 and 12 set out for health authorities, local authorities and water companies in England and Wales, a framework within which they should formulate plans to deal with the investigation and management of an outbreak of cryptosporidiosis. While much of this advice will be relevant also in Scotland, Part II(XI) gives an account of the different administrative arrangements that apply there.

1.7 During its deliberations, the Group identified many gaps in the knowledge of the organism itself, its occurrence and survival in the environment, its capacity to infect man, and the effectiveness of methods of water treatment in dealing with it. Together with the Water Research Centre, the Department of the Environment and the Department of Health, members of the Group were able to assist in the formulation of a national research programme into cryptosporidium which is now underway. Chapter 13 outlines this programme and identifies some areas for further research.

1.8 Chapter 14 contains recommendations based on the current state of knowledge. The Group believes that, if implemented, these will minimise the risks to the community from cryptosporidium and will improve the management of an outbreak of cryptosporidiosis should one nevertheless occur.

1.9 This Report is only a first step. It should be followed in one to two years' time by a further report assessing the results of the national research programme. At that time, it will be important to review the continuing relevance of the current recommendations and to propose new initiatives.

2 Cryptosporidium – The Organism

Introduction

2.1 Cryptosporidium is a protozoan parasite found in man, many other mammals and also in birds, fish and reptiles. In the infected animal, the parasite multiplies in the gastrointestinal tract. The animal then excretes oocysts of the parasite in its faeces. These oocysts are tiny spore-like organisms 4–6 microns in diameter which carry within them the infective form, the sporozoites. When ingested by another animal they can transmit the disease and set up a new cycle of infection.

Table 2 Documented Thermotolerance of Cryptosporidial Oocysts.

Temperature	Time (mins)	Excystation* (approx %)
40°C	5	92%
45°C	5	90%
50°C	5	19%
55°C	5	7%
60°C	5	0%
65°C	5	0%

*Excystation percentage =

$$\frac{\text{Nos of empty oocysts}}{\text{Nos of empty oocysts + nos of intact oocysts}} \times 100\%$$

Data extrapolated from: Blewett, D. A. (1989) Disinfection and Oocysts. In: Cryptosporidiosis: Proceedings of the First International Workshop. (eds. Angus, K. W. and Blewett, D. A.) Animal Diseases Research Association, Edinburgh. 107–115

2.2 Infection with the parasite does not always give rise to any symptoms. In very young animals, such as calves and lambs, it may cause a self-limiting illness with diarrhoea. In man, children are most commonly affected but the illness is not usually serious except in the immunosuppressed patient or in the tropics where malnutrition can contribute to a severe and protracted illness.

Identification

2.3 Cryptosporidium is a protozoan of the suborder *Eimeriina* which includes *Toxoplasma gondii* and *Isospora belli* that also infect man and *Eimeria* which produces disease in birds and mammals. Different species of cryptosporidium have been recorded, including *C.muris* and *C.parvum*, which are known to infect mammals and *C.meleagridis* and *C.baileyi* which cause disease in birds. However, the only species that is believed to be an important cause of disease in man and livestock is *C.parvum*.

2.4 The existence of different species of cryptosporidium presents problems in identification when oocysts are observed in environmental samples since it is not yet possible to differentiate between oocysts of different species. This potential for confusion may arise where contamination of a water supply is suspected.

| Lifecycle | 2.5 Cryptosporidium has a complicated lifecycle which may be completed within 1–8 days and which, unlike other members of the suborder, takes place within the body of a single host and can include repeated cycles of autoinfection in the host intestine (figure 2.1). |

2.6 The oocysts are shed in the faeces of an infected host in very large numbers. For example, it is known that infected calves excrete approximately 10^{10} oocysts daily for up to 14 days and it is likely that humans shed a similar number.

2.7 In the small intestine (duodenum) of an infected host, under the influence of bile salts and digestive juices such as tryspin, the oocysts splits along a suture line to release four sporozoites. The head (or apical complex) of these banana-shaped sporozoites contains binding proteins which attach it to the surface of the epithelial cells (enterocytes) lining the small intestine. The sporozoite then enters the epithelial cell and grows into a rounded trophozoite inside the cell membrane without entering the cytoplasm of the cell (ie, it is intracellular but extracytoplasmic).

2.8 The trophozoite, otherwise known as a Type 1 meront, undergoes asexual reproduction (merogony) to form up to eight merozoites. These first generation merozoites either invade other cells to become trophozoites and so reinfect the host or may, along with some second generation merozoites, develop into Type 2 meronts. A Type 2 meront undergoes asexual reproduction to form four merozoites which, on entering further cells, may develop into either a male microgamont or a female macrogamont. The microgamont produces 16 microgametes which on release fertilise the macrogamete (the mature macrogamont) to form a zygote which develops into the oocyst.

2.9 About 80 per cent of the zygotes develop into environmentally resistant thick-walled oocysts containing four sporozoites at the time they are released from the host cells. These oocysts are the forms that transmit the infection from one host to another. The remaining 20 per cent of the zygotes do not form a thick, two-layered oocyst wall but only have a unit membrane surrounding the four sporozoites. These thin-walled oocysts disrupt within the intestine of the host, the sporozoites invading further host cells leading to perpetuation of the infection without the need for ingestion of further thick-walled oocysts from the environment.

| Characteristics | 2.10 The oocysts of cryptosporidium are very resistant to adverse factors in the environment and can survive dormant for months in a recognizable form in cool, dark conditions in moist soil or for up to a year in clean water. However, no method has yet been discovered for determining the viability of individual oocysts recovered from environmental samples and it is therefore very difficult to interpret the significance of environmental data with any confidence. |

2.11 The oocysts are unaffected by chlorine in the concentrations that can be used in the treatment of drinking water and are resistant to the effects of 60 per cent alcohol and to many disinfectants commonly used domestically or in animal husbandry. They may be killed by certain powerful disinfectants that are not in general use in water treatment. Infectivity appears to be lost if the oocysts are frozen or when heated to temperatures of 65–85°C for five to ten minutes or exposed to boiling water (table 2.1).

Infectivity and Associations with other Organisms

2.12   In man, in normally healthy individuals, cryptosporidium has not been linked with viral or bacterial infection although it has been reported in association with another parasite *Giardia intestinalis (Giardia lamblia)*. It is possible that both parasites may have originated from a common source. In the tropics, cryptosporidial oocysts are so common in the faeces of asymptomatic persons that their presence in faecal specimens from patients with diarrhoea does not necessarily incriminate cryptosporidium as the sole cause of the symptoms. In patients who are immunosuppressed or who suffer from AIDS, cryptosporidium is now recognised as one of a large group of infections which can contribute to a protracted and life-threatening diarrhoeal illness.

2.13   Originally, cryptosporidial oocysts isolated from different mammals were thought to be derived from separate species but it is now known that this is not the case. *C.parvum* oocysts infect man and other mammals. Transmission to man has been recorded from man, cattle, sheep and cats. There is no evidence to suggest the transmission of avian strains to mammals. Although cryptosporidial infections are widespread in the animal kingdom, outbreaks of infection usually involve either calves or lambs and it is these animals that are likely to form the most important reservoir of infection for man.

3 Methodology for the Detection of Cryptosporidial Oocysts in Water

Introduction

3.1 The identification of microorganisms including cryptosporidial oocysts is a matter of importance to workers in a number of different disciplines. Microbiologists and epidemiologists need to know the source of the organisms, the level of contamination and the reservoirs of infection. They require information about the relationship of a particular organism to more easily measured indicator organisms which are used to estimate the general level of bacterial contamination of water supplies. Engineers and others responsible for water supplies need to know how to remove or destroy the organisms by water treatment. Those who regulate drinking water quality require information about when and where the organism occurs in water, the efficiency and availability of the methods of monitoring for the organism and whether or not it is possible to lay down statutory limits to the level of contamination that is acceptable. The need for more information has been highlighted by recent outbreaks of cryptosporidiosis which have shown that the usual bacterial indicators of infection cannot be relied upon to alert water companies to the possibility of cryptosporidium being present in potable water supplies.

Table 3.1† Method for the Recovery and Detection of Cryptosporidial Oocysts from Water

Step	Procedure	Comments
Sampling	Up to 1000 litres of water passed through either a polypropylene yarn-wound or a pleated fabric cartridge filter, 1.0 micron nominal pore size	Volume processed influenced by water quality. 88–99 per cent efficient
Elution	Up to 4 litres detergent solution used to elute oocysts from filter matrix	Recovery efficiency of 16–78 per cent. (The latest filters may be somewhat more efficiently eluted)*
Clarification and concentration	Oocysts pelleted by centrifugation. Density gradients (1.18–1.29 g/ml) used to clarify sample. 'Tween' 80-Sodium dodecyl sulphate used to minimise aggregation	Balance sought between concentration of oocysts and removal of extraneous debris. Algal contaminants common. Recovery efficiency 66-77 per cent
Detection	Concentrate stained with fluorescent antibody stain examined using epifluorescence	Interfering debris can decrease fluorescence

N.B. Overall method recovery 9–59 per cent

†Data from Rose, J. B. (1989)
*Recent information from the SCA panel

3.2 Cryptosporidial oocysts occur in low numbers in the aquatic environment and it is therefore necessary to sample large volumes of water to detect their presence. The oocysts are 4–6 microns in diameter and cartridge filters with a nominal pore size of one micron are used to trap them. Other particles of a similar size are also trapped so the retained material is subjected to a clarification process which separates the oocysts from particles of a similar size but of different densities.

Table 3.2* Detection of Cryptosporidial Oocysts in Water-Related Samples

Four criteria are recommended for the identification of cryptosporidial oocysts in environmental samples by fluorescent antibodies:

1. characteristic fluorescence specifically around the oocyst wall

2. shape (spherical)

3. size (4–6 microns diameter)

4. characteristic folding (the suture) in the oocyst wall. (The suture may occur in 60 per cent of a well preserved control sample and be less apparent in environmental samples.)

If no oocysts are found in the sample, it may be appropriate to review the following:

1. the number of samples collected

2. the site of collection with the identification of point and non-point sources of pollution

3. the manner in which the sample was collected (Long term filtration at slower flow rates will increase the chances of obtaining a positive result)

4. the volume collected

5. water quality influencing the efficiency of recovery

6. the equivalent volume examined

*After data from Smith, H. V. and Rose, J. B. 1990

3.3   The only options available for the identification of cryptosporidium are animal feeding experiments or direct microscopic examination. Animal feeding experiments are time consuming and expensive. They lead to a multiplication of the organisms making detection easier and can demonstrate that the organisms are viable and capable of causing infection, but they do not provide any indication of the numbers present in the original sample. Microscopic methods of detection can be quicker but they are labour intensive and are extremely demanding of skill and experience.

Table 3.3† Reactivity of commercially available monoclonal antibody (mAb) kits with cryptosporidial oocysts

Cryptosporidium	Reactivity of oocysts with mAbs	
	Meridian*	Northumbria**
C.parvum	+	+
C.baileyi	−	+
C.muris	−	+
C.meleagridis	+	Not tested

*Meridian Diagnostics Inc., Cincinnati, Ohio, 45244, USA

**Northumbria Biologicals Ltd, Cramlington, Northumberland NE23 9HL, UK

†After data from Smith, H. V. and Rose, J. B. 1990

3.4   Because the minimum infective dose for man is thought to be small, it is important to be able to identify small numbers of oocysts accurately. For microscopic analysis, it is also important to have a preparation as free as possible from debris which might mask the presence of the organisms or interfere with the process of identification.

Methods Used for the Isolation and Detection of Cryptosporidial Oocysts

3.5   The Standing Committee of Analysts, (SCA), a committee of the Department of the Environment set up in 1972 to review standard methods for quality control of the water cycle, has published the current provisional recommended procedure for the detection of cryptosporidium.* This is summarised in table 3.1.

* "Isolation and Identification of Giardia cysts and Cryptosporidium oocysts and Free Living Pathogenic Amoebae in Water 1989", HMSO 1990

3.6 The process can be divided into several parts: sampling; elution; clarification and concentration; and identification.

Sampling

3.7 A portable apparatus is used for taking water samples (figure 3. 1). It consists of an inlet hose (A) with a flow restriction valve (B), a filter housing (C) containing the cartridge filter made of either polypropylene yarn or fine pleated fabric with a nominal pore size of one micron, together with an outlet hose (D) and a water meter (E). The volume sampled will depend on the type of water but large volumes of between 100 and 1000 litres are recommended. Smaller samples may be adequate for filter backwash water and sewage effluent which are likely to contain larger numbers of oocysts.

Elution, clarification and concentration

3.8 The filter is removed from its housing and is teased apart or opened out. The trapped particles are washed off with large volumes of dilute detergent. The use of the detergent minimises the chance of the oocysts sticking to other particules in the washwater. Particles of greater density than oocysts are separated by centrifugation through a sugar solution of carefully controlled specific gravity in which the oocysts float on the surface while the other more dense particles sink. The oocysts in suspension are washed free of the sugar solution and then centrifuged again to concentrate them into a smaller volume prior to examination under the microscope.

Identification

3.9 The microscopic identification of cryptosporidial oocysts depends on careful measurement of their size and the use of special stains which emphasise structural features.

3.10 The oocysts of *C.parvum* are thick-walled, colourless, spherical or slightly ovoid bodies. When fully developed they contain four elongated sporozoites. On the surface of the oocysts there is a fold through which the sporozoites are released. This fold or suture is an important diagnostic feature because it can be emphasised by appropriate staining techniques.

3.11 Under the microscope, the oocysts of cryptosporidium are identified by the use of fluorescent antibodies. In this technique an antibody to oocysts is produced which binds specifically to certain structures on the surface of the oocyst. The antibody is joined to a fluorescent substance (a chemical marker) so that it can be more easily visualised (table 3.2). Antibodies specific to cryptosporidium are commercially available and, by their use, not only can the dimensions and shape of the suspected oocysts be defined but also the diagnostic suture can be identified. Unfortunately none of the fluorescent antibodies currently available can distinguish the oocysts of *C.parvum* from the oocysts of other species of cryptosporidium which are not harmful to man or livestock (table 3.3). Species-specific antibodies and gene probes will undoubtedly be developed in the future which would aid the detection and identification of oocysts in water samples.

The limitations of the methods of recovery and detection

3.12 Most of the oocysts present in water samples may be retained on the cartridge filter but, in the process of washing them off and separating them from other particles, up to 90 per cent of these may be lost. Experiments have shown that sampling at high flow rates, for example at 37.8 1/min, leads to a lower recovery rate than at low flow rates such as 3.78 1/min. The efficiency of the recovery is affected by the quality of the water. Algae and other suspended solids interfere with this and make identification more difficult.

3.13 Because of technical limitations, methods in current use for the sampling, concentration and identification of oocysts are likely to lead to an underestimate of the numbers present in the original sample. There is also the possibility of confusion with the oocysts of species other than *C.parvum* which are not known to cause illness in man. The greatest limitation is imposed by the fact than none of the techniques of detection of oocysts with the exception of animal feeding experiments can distinguish between those which are viable and capable of causing infection and others which are dead and harmless. Until these limitations are overcome, it must be assumed that every oocyst detected in a potable water supply is potentially infective for man.

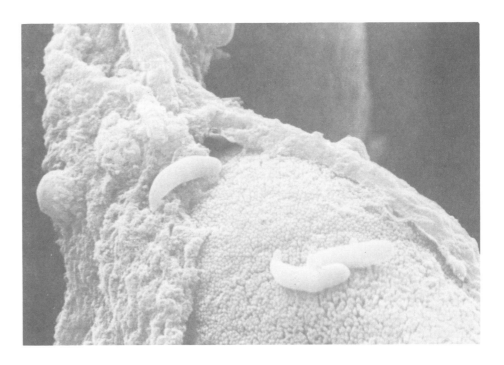

Three sporozoites of cryptosporidium on the surface of an enterocyte. The mucus layer is intact over most of the cell and an early trophozoite can be seen protruding through the mucus on the left hand edge of the cell. Mouse ileum, 3 hours after infection with oocysts.

Low power view of lamb ileum 10 days after experimental infection with 10^6 cryptosporidial oocysts. The normal gut architecture has been destroyed, the villi are stunted and fused and the normal absorptive epithelium has been lost. The entire mucosa is covered with endogenous stages of cryptosporidium.

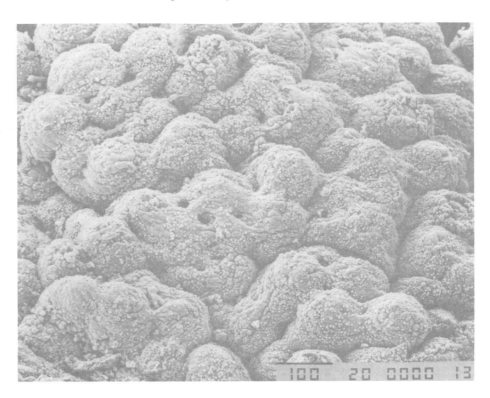

Higher magnification of lamb ileum (photograph 2) showing developing stages of cryptosporidium, some showing the outlines of maturing merozoites within.

Scanning electron micrograph of developmental stages of cryptosporidium bulging from the microvillous surface of infected enterocytes. In one of the parasites, some of the invasive merozoites can be seen because a portion of the host cell and parasite membranes was removed during processing. Note the craters that remain after the parasites rupture out of the vacuoles.

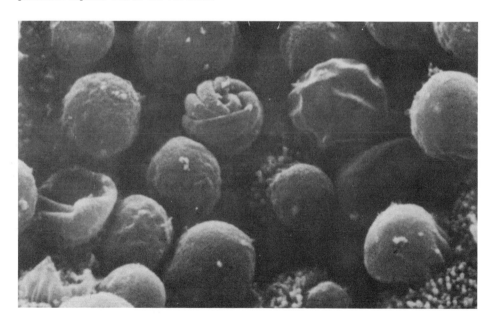

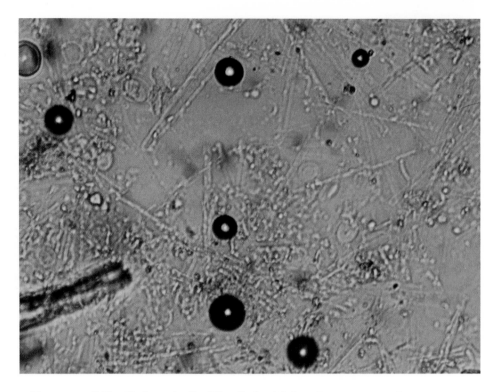

Two cysts of Giardia intestinalis (Giardia lamblia) and two oocysts of Cryptosporidium parvum in an environmental sample, photographed under bright field microscopy. Note difficulty in defining both cysts and oocysts in environmental samples using this technique. (Compare with photograph 6).

Two cysts of Giardia intestinalis (Giardia lamblia) and oocysts of Cryptosporidium parvum in an environmental sample. Cysts and oocysts are stained with fluorescein labelled monoclonal antibodies and viewed under dark field epifluorescent microscopy.

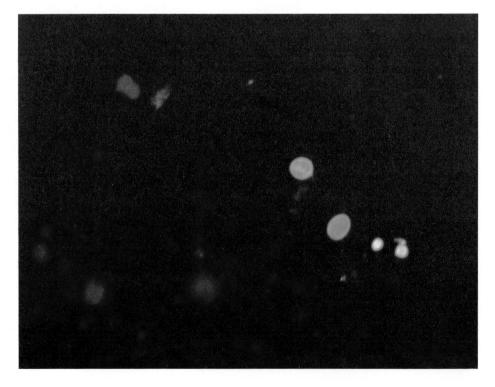

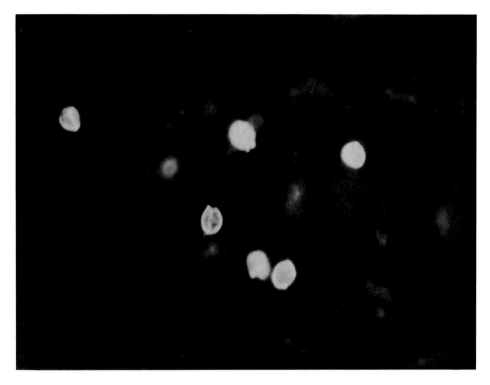

Oocysts of Cryptosporidium parvum stained with a fluorescein labelled monoclonal antibody. Note presence of diagnostic suture in the second oocyst from the left.

A portable apparatus used for taking water samples for the isolation and detection of cryptosporidial oocysts.

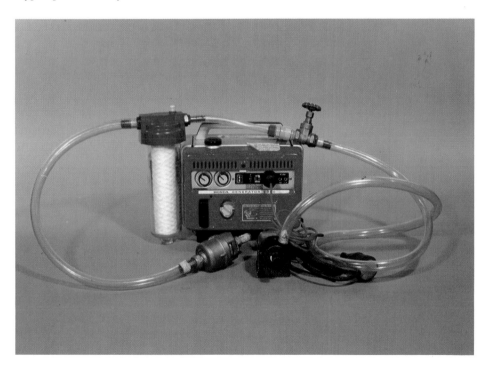

4 Occurrence of Cryptosporidial Oocysts in the Water Environment

Evidence

4.1 The occurrence of cryptosporidium in the environment has not yet been widely researched but limited samples from studies in the USA and UK found oocysts occurring commonly in all types of surface water (lakes, reservoirs, streams and rivers) including pristine waters with figures ranging from 0.006–2.5 oocysts per litre (o/l)*. Oocysts were found much less often in ground water samples. Only one of 13 ground water samples from the USA contained oocysts (0.005/l), and only two out of ten borehole samples from the UK contained oocysts (0.012/l) whereas four of seven samples taken from springs were positive (average 0.04/l). Surveys have found that oocyst concentrations were 1.5–1.9 times greater in waters where agricultural pollution seemed to be the major contaminating source, in contrast to discharges from sewage treatment works, which will also contain oocysts where infection exists in the community.

4.2 Considerable caution is needed in extrapolating from these data not only because of the small number of samples but also because of the inability to differentiate between species of cryptosporidium and to assess the viability of oocysts, (Chapter 2), and the shortcomings in current techniques for recovery of the oocysts from environmental samples (Chapter 3). Nevertheless, what is apparent from these surveys is that cryptospiridial oocysts can be found in very small numbers in all types of water source although they are likely to be more common in surface than ground waters. It also seems likely that there exists in many waters a background level of oocysts which may be suddenly increased by accidental pollution or by heavy rainfall especially if it follows shortly after the application of liquid or solid manure to the land.

Origins

4.3 From current knowledge of the organism and its close association with livestock (Chapter 5) it seems probable that most of the oocysts found in both surface and ground water derive from agricultural practices which can result in cryptosporidial oocysts from animal faeces entering water courses. Contamination can occur via several routes. Slurry stores can leak or burst. Through poor management they can overflow. The seepage from solid manure stores and the run-off from soiled yards (dirty yard water) may not be adequately collected and controlled, particularly in high rainfall areas. All these effluents which may contain cryptosporidial oocysts can find their way to water courses, either directly or via drains. Following landspreading of manure (either as solid manure or slurry), direct run-off of liquid may reach watercourses, perhaps exacerbated by rainfall or heavy dew. Alternatively, manure may percolate through soil

---

*Oocysts (or fractions thereof)/per litre is used to denote the mean number of oocysts present in each litre of the sample submitted for analysis. Because different volumes of water-related samples are submitted for analysis, it is necessary to standardise the results obtained, in terms of volume, and a standard volume of 1 litre is generally used.

to field drainage systems, for example, via cracks in dry soils and so pass to water courses. Finally, animal grazing near water courses may cause more direct contamination.

4.4 The Code of Good Agricultural Practice* and other guidance published by the Ministry of Agriculture Fisheries and Food (MAFF) highlights ways in which run-off from slurry can be minimised and the importance of keeping storage and landspreading operations away from waters. While comprehensive controls to remove animal grazing and manure spreading from catchment areas would be impracticable, consideration nevertheless should be given to ways of further limiting the amount of contamination from these sources, particularly close to water abstraction points.

4.5 In view of the high proportion of farm pollution incidents caused by slurry stores (and also silage effluent from silage stores), the Department of the Environment, in consultation with MAFF, is intending to introduce regulations to come into effect later this year to set minimum standards of construction for new slurry stores, silage stores and stores for agricultural fuel oil. It is proposed that the National Rivers Authority, which will enforce these regulations, will also have the power to require existing structures to be brought up to the requirements of the regulations if there is a significant risk of pollution. These regulations should reduce the number of farm pollution incidents in which cryptosporidial oocysts may pass into water courses and should facilitate early detection of seepage of contaminated material. However, neither these regulations nor close adherence to the Code of Good Agricultural Practice can remove the risk of oocysts entering water courses from farming practices.

4.6 The second main source of cryptosporidial oocysts in environmental waters, affecting principally surface water, arises from the disposal of the products of sewage treatment processes when infection exists in the community. Oocysts are excreted in the faeces by infected persons and will therefore occur in raw sewage from time to time.

4.7 Sewage treatment involves a number of processes to reduce the pollution from the discharge of effluent but these are not designed to remove pathogens or intestinal microorganisms. While some cryptosporidial oocysts are undoubtedly removed during these processes, it is certain that when present in the raw sewage, large numbers will pass through into the treated effluent to be discharged directly into water courses.

4.8 Oocysts are also likely to be present, although probably in smaller numbers, in sewage sludge which may be used in agricultural practice or deposited in designated land tip sites. Regulations** controlling the use of sewage sludge in agriculture were brought into effect in September 1989. However, because cryptosporidial oocysts remain viable in soil for months, adherence to these Regulations and the associated Code of Practice*** will not remove the possibility of contamination of water courses through the application of sludge to land.

---

*Code of Good Agricultural Practice (1985) Ministry of Agriculture Fisheries and Food.
**The Sludge (Use in Agriculture) Regulations 1989 (SI1263/89)
***Code of Practice for Agricultural Use of Sewage Sludge (HMSO 1989)

5 Cryptosporidiosis in Animals

5 Prevalence

5.1 Cryptosporidium species occur throughout the animal kingdom. They have been reported from mammals, birds, reptiles, amphibians and fish. There is, however, no evidence that cross-infection occurs between fish, reptiles and mammals.

5.2 *Cryptosporidium parvum (C.parvum)* appears to be the only species of clinical importance to domestic animals and man. Most livestock probably become infected before reaching adulthood although very few show signs of disease. Research is still at an early stage, but in small-scale surveys, cryptosporidial oocysts have been found in 10–80 per cent of calves with diarrhoea and in 0–14 per cent of healthy calves. They have also been found in 7–43 per cent of lambs with diarrhoea, and in healthy lambs, piglets and occasionally adult pigs and other species.

Sources of Infection and Infective Dose

5.3. Most animals probably acquire infection in infancy from their own species, either directly from faeces or through faecal contamination of the environment. The infective dose for livestock is unknown but is likely to be small.

Predisposing Factors

5.4 *C.parvum* appears to cause clinical disease in livestock only when the animal is heavily infected or when its resistance has been lowered. Animals less than one month old are most susceptible. Clinical illness in older animals is rare but may exceptionally occur through reactivation of previous infection. Resistance is normally acquired by the age of four weeks, but can be impaired by colostrum-deprivation, malnutrition, and any form of stress such as weaning, overcrowding, cold and intercurrent infections with other microorganisms such as rotavirus and *Escherichia coli.*

5.5 Calves are particularly susceptible to cryptosporidiosis. This may be because they tend to be weaned early. Several other organisms affect the gut of young calves and all contribute to the calf diarrhoeal syndrome which causes high mortality and enormous financial losses each year. The disease is apparently increasing in both calves and lambs although the increase may be due in part to better reporting.

Geographical Distribution

5.6 *C.parvum* infection occurs worldwide in livestock. Seasonal peaks tend to coincide with lambing and calving in the country concerned.

Cryptosporidiosis in Livestock in Great Britain
The disease in calves

5.7   In 1989, the MAFF Veterinary Investigation Service recorded 892* incidents of cryptosporidiosis in cattle in Britain compared with 853 cases in 1988 and 795 in 1987. In 1989, infection with *C.parvum* was reported as the fourth most prevalent pathogen causing diarrhoea in cattle, affecting both dairy and beef animals. Mixed infections of *C.parvum* with other pathogens are extremely common.

5.8   Seasonal peaks of disease coincide with birth peaks in spring and autumn. When the calving season begins, the first calves to be born often become infected with *C.parvum* mainly in the second week of life without showing any ill-health. In the these calves the parasite multiplies and vast numbers of oocysts are passed in the faeces, which contaminate the environment for the calves that follow. Infection spreads rapidly, and the later-born calves may become heavily infected and clinical disease results. After a period of severe watery diarrhoea, resulting in abdominal pain, dehydration and weight loss, they may recover, and thereafter remain immune to clinical attacks of the disease. They may, however, become asymptomatic carriers of the organism and pass small numbers of oocysts intermittently for the rest of their lives. Thus the parasite maintains its presence in the host population.

The disease in lambs

5.9   In 1989, the MAFF Veterinary Investigation Service recorded 157* incidents of cryptosporidiosis in sheep in Britain, compared with 162 incidents in 1988 and 88 in 1987. The disease is generally seen in one to two week old lambs, mainly in the spring. Symptoms are similar to those observed in calves except that diarrhoea is not a constant feature. Veterinary studies on cryptosporidial infection in lambs show that the severity of clinical disease decreases rapidly with age, and by the age of 30 days there may be no clinical signs of infection. Bottle fed lambs may be more prone to illness than naturally suckled lambs. Modern economic constraints are forcing farmers to time their lambing earlier so that more lambs are being born in the winter, in which case they must be reared indoors under conditions which increase the risk of infection with *C.parvum*.

The disease in other domestic animals

5.10   Cryptosporidiosis can occur in other domesticated animals including goats, deer, piglets and horses. It can also occur in pets such as cats, dogs, hamsters, guinea pigs and rabbits. However, clinical infection in all these other animals is rare and mainly occurs when there is some predisposing factor such as immunosuppression. These animals are not perceived as important sources of human cryptosporidiosis.

---

*Provisional figure

6 Cryptosporidiosis in Man

**Frequency of
Cryptosporidiosis in the
Community**
Great Britain

6.1   The diagnosis of cryptosporidiosis is made normally by the detection of cryptosporidial oocysts in the stools. In England and Wales, laboratories began to report the identification of cryptosporidium in 1983 and, in 1985, the Public Health Laboratory Service (PHLS) initiated a two year surveillance study. Since then the total number of cases reported to the PHLS has risen from 1,874 in 1985 to 7,904 in 1989 (table 6.1). The figures for Scotland also show an increase, from 265 in 1985 to 1,243 in 1989 (table 6.2). Figures 6.1 and 6.2 show that in 1989, among those cases of gastrointestinal infection where the diagnosis was confirmed by examination of the stools, cryptosporidium was the fourth most commonly identified cause, accounting for about 8 per cent of all cases in England and Wales and about 13 per cent in Scotland.

Table 6.1   Cases of Gastrointestinal Infection Reported following Examination of the Stools:

England and Wales[+] 1985–1989

Year	Total reports of gastrointestinal infection	Number due to cryptosporidium	Percentage of total
1985	63,752	1,874	2.9%
1986	68,217	3,560	5.2%
1987	72,047	3,277	4.5%
1988	80,608	2,750	3.4%
1989	96,111*	7,904	8.2%

*Provisional figure
+Based on preliminary analysis of voluntary reports from laboratories to the Communicable Disease Surveillance Centre

6.2   It is important to put these figures into context. In the majority of specimens sent to laboratories, no causal organism for the diarrhoea can be identified. In the PHLS study, cryptosporidial oocysts were identified in only about 2 per cent of specimens submitted for laboratory examination. The actual percentage of all cases of diarrhoea caused by cryptosporidium is likely to be even lower than this because most diarrhoeal illnesses are self-limiting and medical intervention is not required. Even where medical assistance is sought, stool specimens are not always sent for examination.

Table 6.2   Cases of Gastrointestinal Infection Reported following Examination of the Stools:

Scotland[++] 1985–1989

Year	Total reports of gastrointestinal infection	Number due to cryptosporidium	Percentage of total
1985	8,053	265	3.3%
1986	7,781	414	5.3%
1987	8,274	493	6.0%
1988	8,779	545	6.2%
1989	9,776	1,243	12.7%

++Based on reports to the Communicable Disease (Scotland) Unit

6.3 A further difficulty arises from the fact that since cryptosporidium has only been recognised relatively recently as pathogenic for man, the number of laboratories testing for the organism is still increasing and testing policies are not yet standardised. Inevitably, this will have contributed in part to the increase in detection of cryptosporidium over the past five years.

Other countries

6.4 Cryptosporidium is found worldwide and has been reported as a cause of diarrhoeal illness in many countries. In cases of diarrhoea where the stools have been examined, it has been found in 0.6–4.3 per cent of specimens in the USA, 13.1 per cent in Lahore, India and 16.5 per cent in Haiti.

Seasonal trends in cryptosporidiosis

6.5 Seasonal trends in the occurrence of cryptosporidiosis have been recorded in many countries: in the rainy season in Central America, in the summer in Australia, in the late summer in North America, and in the spring and late autumn in the UK. The reason for these peaks is unclear but may be related to changes in rainfall or to events in the farming year.

The Spread of Infection in the Community

6.6 Cryptosporidiosis is normally acquired by the faecal-oral route whereby oocysts excreted in the faeces by an infected animal or human are ingested by a susceptible person. The oocysts are capable of infecting a new host immediately they are released into the environment but can also survive outside a host for a considerable period. There are a number of ways in which the disease can be spread.

From animals

6.7 Direct transmission from animal to man (ie zoonotic transmission) was initially thought to be the main means of spread of the disease. Those at risk include agricultural workers and veterinarians working with livestock who should take special care over personal hygiene. The increasing trend towards lambing in deep litter sheds close to the farm house has also increased the risk of exposure of family members and visitors to infection with cryptosporidium. In particular, children may come into contact with farm animals during farm visits or when young animals such as lambs are taken to schools and nurseries to be shown to the children.

6.8 Pet animals such as dogs and cats have been shown to be infected and have sometimes been implicated in human cases. However, these do not appear to be an important source of infection.

Person to person

6.9 Person to person spread is now recognised to be an important means of transmission of cryptosporidiosis. Transmission of the disease occurs easily within families and in playgroups, nursery schools, day care centres, hospitals and other institutions unless precautions are taken.

Waterborne

6.10   Although it is now certain that cryptosporidiosis can be contracted from contaminated water, the proportion of the total number of cases of cryptosporidiosis which are waterborne is unknown. Since both zoonotic and person to person spread are important, only a proportion of the 9,000 cases reported in Britain in 1989 can be linked with water. When viewed nationally, the number of waterborne cases of cryptosporidiosis comprises only a very small fraction of all cases of diarrhoea. Their significance lies in the fact that should the mains water become contaminated, many cases of illness may occur in the area of supply and give rise to great public concern. Such an event is not common but, nonetheless, since March 1989 when the Group began its work, there have been two major outbreaks of cryptosporidiosis in which waterborne spread was suspected. Chapters 7–12 address in detail the problems posed by the risk of contamination of drinking water supplies.

6.11   Since all types of water sources in the environment may be contaminated at some time with cryptosporidial oocysts, it is generally inadvisable to drink any water not specifically intended for public consumption. There must also be a slight risk of contracting crypto-sporidiosis from the accidental ingestion of contaminated water by recreational users of rivers, reservoirs and inland waterways.

Other

6.12   Cryptosporidiosis is emerging as an important cause of travellers' diarrhoea although such patients may have mixed infections.

6.13   There have been a few reports of infection following consumption of raw milk and raw sausages but there is no evidence that such contamination is a significant source of infection.

Clinical Features of Cryptosporidiosis
The disease in man

6.14   In the past decade cryptosporidiosis has been recognised as an important cause of self-limiting but unpleasant diarrhoeal disease in normally healthy individuals. The first reported human case was diagnosed in 1976 by rectal biopsy in a 3 year old girl from Tennessee and, at about the same time, a severe diarrhoeal illness due to crypto-sporidium was diagnosed in an immunosuppressed patient who was later shown to have AIDS. At first, the organism was regarded as an opportunistic pathogen as the disease was almost only recorded in immunosuppressed patients. However, cases of cryptosporidiosis were soon identified among normally healthy people.

6.15   The disease is most prevalent in young children aged one to five years, especially those in nurseries, schools, or day care centres who are likely to acquire infection if they come into contact with infected animals or from person to person spread. Others at risk are those working with livestock, hospital personnel, travellers to areas of high prevalence and male homosexuals. Infants below six months of age are less commonly affected possibly because of transfer of maternal antibodies or because young babies have less contact with their environment. Where infection is waterborne, a substantial number of adults in the general population are likely to contract the illness.

Pathology

6.16   The pathogenic mechanisms which cause the symptoms in man have not yet been identified. The stools are watery and usually do not contain pus cells or red blood cells which suggests that a toxin or toxin-like substance induces increased secretion of water from the intestine. There is also evidence of malabsorption, especially of water. Loss of some digestive (brush-border) enzymes responsible for the break-down of sugars leads to bacterial fermentation of the sugars and this in turn causes an increased loss of fluids into the lumen of the intestine by osmotic effect.

Infective dose and incubation period	6.17 Although the infective dose of cryptosporidium is not known for certain, it is probably small. There have been no feeding experiments in human volunteers but some experimental research in non-human primates shows that as few as ten oocysts may cause infection. The figure may be even lower in man. This correlates well with the infective dose of another protozoan parasite, *Giardia intestinalis (Giardia lamblia),* in which as few as 10–100 cysts have been known to give rise to clinical infection in man. More research is required to establish the actual infective dose of cryptosporidium.

6.18 In cases where the time of infection can be assessed, the incubation period has ranged from 2–14 days.

Clinical features in immunocompetent (normally healthy) patients

6.19 In normally healthy people the disease begins with the sudden onset of gastrointestinal and sometimes "flu-like" symptoms; diarrhoea occurs in 80–90 per cent of patients with frequent, watery, very offensive stools. Cramping abdominal pain, vomiting and loss of appetite are common. Some patients may lose a significant amount of weight. About half the patients complain of "flu-like" symptoms with headache, malaise, aching muscles, fever and prostration. The symptoms usually last for about two to three weeks, sometimes for as long as five to six weeks. Most affected persons continue to excrete oocysts for two to three weeks after their symptoms have subsided but some may do so for longer periods.

Clinical features in immunosuppressed patients (those with decreased immunity)

6.20 In patients with depressed immunity due to AIDS, congenital hypogammaglobulinaemia or severe combined immunodeficiency syndrome, and in those receiving drugs such as cyclophosphamide and corticosteroids and those with severe malnutrition, the disease is much more serious. These patients develop frequent watery diarrhoea and may have up to 25 bowel motions per day, passing up to 20 litres of stool daily. They may suffer from cramping, upper abdominal pain often associated with meals, profound weight loss, weakness, malaise, anorexia and low grade fever.

6.21 In immunosuppressed patients, infection with cryptosporidium can involve the pharynx, the bronchial tree and the entire gastrointestinal tract including the gall bladder, bile duct and pancreas. Cryptosporidial cholecystitis (inflammation of the gall bladder) occurs in about 10 per cent of patients with AIDS and presents with right upper quadrant abdominal pain, persistent nausea and vomiting and usually severe diarrhoea. Except in those patients in whom suppression of the immune system can be reversed, for example by stopping the immunosuppressant therapy, these distressing symptoms may persist unabated until the death of the patient.

Laboratory investigations in patients with cryptosporidiosis

6.22 The condition may be diagnosed by finding cryptosporidium in the stool, in aspirates from the duodenum or jejunum or in biopsies from the bowel mucosa. In affected persons, IgG, IgM, IgE and IgA antibodies are produced after infection and these can be detected by immunofluorescent methods (IFA) or enzyme linked immunosorbent assay (ELISA). In immunocompetent persons, a rise in the blood white cell count or a disturbance in plasma electrolytes are unusual unless the patient becomes severely dehydrated. Radiography of the bowel shows prominent mucosal folds, thickening of the wall and abnormal motility and the changes may also involve the biliary system. Histological changes in the bowel mucosa include villous blunting and inflammatory cellular infiltration of the *lamina propria.*

Immunity, reinfection and reactivation

6.23   Little is known about reactivation and reinfection but in most patients one attack probably confers resistance to further symptomatic infection. However, there are a few cases on record of immunocompetent patients who have had more than one episode of infection. Asymptomatic infection probably occurs infrequently.

Differential diagnosis of cryptosporidiosis

6.24   In immunocompetent people, the condition must be differentiated from any acute diarrhoeal illness with associated abdominal pain and "flu-like" symptoms. Contact with farm animals or recent travel abroad or in the case of a child, the presence of other cases in the same school, nursery or day care centre should suggest the possibility of cryptosporidiosis.

6.25   An incubation of more than one week should also suggest the possibility of cryptosporidiosis but it is generally difficult or impossible to establish with certainty the time of infection. There is considerable overlap in incubation periods between different infections and, while cryptosporidiosis generally appears to have a longer incubation period than viral and many bacterial gastrointestinal infections, this cannot be relied on in differential diagnosis.

6.26   In immunocompetent patients, the most common differential diagnosis will be from giardiasis, an infection caused by *Giardia intestinalis (Giardia lamblia)*. Compared with giardiasis, the duration of acute symptoms in cryptosporidiosis is longer, intense abdominal pain and cramps more common but bloating anorexia and weakness less common. Occasionally patients may be infected with both cryptosporidium and giardia. In immunosuppressed patients, the differential diagnosis must be made from a number of other opportunistic intestinal infections which commonly occur.

Treatment of cryptosporidiosis

6.27   Over 40 antimicrobial agents have been tested against cryptosporidium in animals and man but to date no effective specific treatment for cryptosporidiosis has been found. In immunocompetent patients, the infection is self-limiting and requires supportive treatment only to prevent significant dehydration.

6.28   Immunosuppressed patients with severe diarrhoea and symptoms of malabsorption may require fluid, electrolyte and nutrient replacement. As lactose intolerance may develop, milk should be avoided. Antispasmodics may increase abdominal pain and bloating. If biliary obstruction occurs, temporary relief may be obtained by endoscopic papillotomy.

7 Water Treatment Processes and Removal of Cryptosporidial Oocysts

Introduction

7.1   The average household in the UK uses about 150 litres of water per person per day. In addition, water mains supply industrial and commercial premises. The amount of water which is treated and put into public supply totals about 15,000 million litres per day. This amount of water is drawn in almost equal proportions from aquifers (paragraphs 7.3–7.6), from lakes and reservoirs in upland areas and from lowland rivers. It is evident that all these sources of water are open to the possibility of contamination by cryptosporidial oocysts from time to time (Chapter 4).

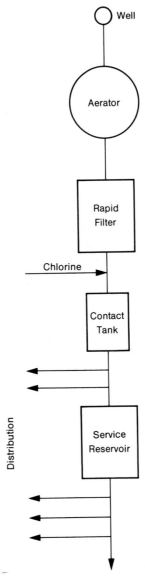

Figure 7.1 Possible sequence of ground water treatment

7.2 A number of surveys of treated drinking water have shown the presence of cryptosporidial oocysts. In western USA, 28 per cent of 23 samples contained oocysts (range 0.002–0.009/1), and in a series of 107 samples from the UK, 61 per cent were found to be positive (range 0.006–2.5/1). Although these surveys were limited and not representative of supplies generally, it is clear that current water treatment processes cannot be relied upon to remove all cryptosporidial oocysts. This Chapter examines the different sources of water and the treatment processes available. It also discusses ways of minimising the risk of oocysts passing into drinking water supply.

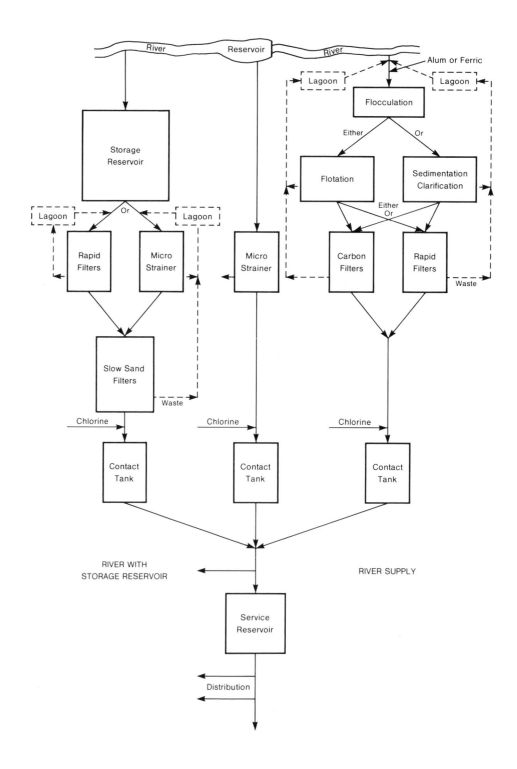

Figure 7.2 Possible sequences of surface water treatment

Ground Water

7.3 Water from wells and boreholes derives from rainfall percolating through the soil into porous rock called aquifers (such as limestone, chalk and sandstone). The process of percolation generally provides a considerable cleansing action with the result that water from many aquifers has traditionally been regarded as being of very high quality, free from microbiological contamination. The deeper the borehole the more likely it is that water will be of high quality. Some aquifers are overlain by an impervious layer of clay (for example London clay over the chalk) which prevents direct ingress of water from the surface above. Rain water has to enter the aquifer via remote outcrops of rock (the Chilterns and North Downs in the above example) and percolation follows a considerable pathway, up to several kilometres in some cases. Such aquifers, known as confined aquifers, provide some of best quality water in the country.

7.4 However, all aquifers contain fissures which allow some water to pass through faster than the rest. As this water is not subjected to the same cleansing action, the possibility of oocysts reaching the acquifer by this route must be recognised. Also, aquifers, including confined aquifers, may be penetrated by deep structures which provide a pathway for water to move rapidly downwards from the surface. A water supply borehole could be such a structure were it not standard practice to line boreholes and provide seals at the surface to guard against contamination.

7.5 Although many ground water sources will be free from cryptosporidial oocysts, the greater the extent of fissuring of the aquifer and the more construction work that has taken place over or actually within the aquifer, the greater must be the possibility of oocysts reaching the ground water. Under these circumstances, water companies should take special care to minimise contamination and to maintain borehole linings and seals to a high standard.

7.6 Ground water is treated by adding chlorine as a disinfectant but frequently this is no more than a precautionary measure against bacterial contamination. Some ground water may also be aerated and filtered through sand to remove iron and manganese. The water may sometimes be softened by lime precipitation or by ion-exchange or it may have nitrate removed also by ion-exchange. As these treatment processes will not kill oocysts, some risk of contamination of water supplies must exist. This risk in most cases will be small although, as yet, it has not been assessed (figure 7.1).

Upland Surface Water

7.7 A few upland waters draining from sparsely populated catchments into lakes or reservoirs are of such high quality that they have required no more than microstraining followed by chlorination. However, the grazing of sheep and cattle in the catchment must put these sources at some risk of contamination from cryptosporidial oocysts. As the oocysts are resistant to the doses of chlorine normally used in waterworks practice, there must be a possibility of viable oocysts passing into supply (figure 7.2).

7.8 Many upland waters, especially those gathered from peaty catchments, being highly coloured, require intensive treatment. In most cases, a coagulant is added to the water, usually aluminium sulphate (alum), which precipitates as aluminium hydroxide flocs, about 1–2 mm in diameter. These flocs capture the fine particles which impart colour to the water, but the resulting floc particles are weak and easily ruptured and must therefore be handled with care. The flocs can be removed by filtration through sand, a process which is often preceded by settlement or flotation. It seems likely that oocysts will be caught by the floc and removed at the settlement or filtration stage. However, some oocysts, possibly a very small number, may pass through these treatment stages especially if the flocs are ruptured. A final stage of disinfection with chlorine, as mentioned previously, will not destroy these oocysts which will pass forward into supply.

Lowland Surface Water

7.9 Lowland waters can receive agricultural drainage and sewage effluents both of which can be expected, on occasion, to contain large numbers of oocysts. Many lowland waters are hard, containing a high level of calcium bicarbonate, and are rich in nutrients and organic matter which encourage aquatic growths. After rainfall, lowland rivers are often turbid with fine, suspended particles. Most lowland waters, being polluted to some degree, contain high levels of pathogenic and other bacteria. In consequence, water derived from lowland sources requires intensive treatment before it can be put into public supply (figure 7.2).

7.10 In some cases, water is taken directly from rivers into treatment works which are therefore required to deal with wide variations in river water quality. In other cases, the abstracted river water is pumped into large open storage reservoirs, containing several weeks' supply. This stored water serves as a contingency against drought and provides a buffer against pollution, enabling river intakes to be closed for a short period if a pollution incident has led to the passage of dangerous material down the river. Long term storage encourages natural purification processes to come into play.

7.11 During reservoir storage, turbidity is reduced and the number of coliform bacteria generally declines but growths of planktonic algae may proliferate. Reservoir managers tend to induce mixing of the water to avoid stratification and discourage algal growth which interferes with treatment processes. Such mixing inhibits the settlement of oocysts. Even without this mixing the settlement rate of oocysts is so low that significant removal is unlikely.

7.12 It has been calculated that in a reservoir with a depth of 20 metres with no currents to disturb quiescent conditions, an oocyst will take 463 days to settle to the bottom. If the oocysts were aggregated into clumps, their settling rate would still be small, for instance, a 10-oocyst aggregate would take 145 days to settle the 20 metres. Natural aggregation is therefore unlikely to contribute to the removal of oocysts and, in any case, no evidence of natural aggregation has been advanced. It is possible that some oocysts may be removed by predation by aquatic organisms, but, again, no observations exist to support this possibility. As oocysts have been shown to survive several months in water it is evident that reservoir or lake storage which may bring about some reduction in oocyst numbers, cannot be expected to provide a total barrier.

7.13 Two principal forms of treatment are used for lowland water whether taken directly from rivers or following reservoir storage. These are: chemical coagulation with rapid filtration; and pre-filtration followed by slow sand filtration (figure 7.2).

Chemical coagulation

7.14 The addition to water of certain metallic salts, for example aluminium sulphate, poly-aluminium chloride, ferric sulphate and ferric chloride, as described earlier (paragraph 7.8), produces hydroxide precipitates, which aggregate under controlled chemical conditions. These fluffy precipitates enmesh particles in the water together with some of the dissolved and organic matter. All natural particles in water carry a small, negative electrical potential on their surfaces of approximately −20 mV. Since the hydroxide flocs carry a small positive electrical potential there is mutual attraction with particulate matter in the water which augments the physical bonding and enmeshment described above. Laboratory measurements have shown that cryptosporidial oocysts also are negatively charged and it has been postulated that this charge could be exploited in water treatment processes.

7.15   In most situations, aluminium and ferric salts have been found to be equally effective provided they are used under optimal conditions. There is no evidence to indicate that the one might be more effective than the other in removing cryptosporidial oocysts. In some circumstances, flocs generated by both aluminium and ferric salts can be strengthened or improved by the addition of coagulant aids. These are organic polymers, long-chain molecules, many of which carry electrical charges, either positive or negative. It may be that such aids could enhance the removal of cryptosporidial oocysts.

7.16   The levels of aluminium and ferric salts remaining in the water are strictly controlled. Most of the flocs produced by the addition of these salts are removed in sedimentation tanks. The most common form of tank in the UK is the floc blanket tank, in which the flocs are suspended as a cloud (the "blanket") as water flows upwards. The flocs are drawn from the cloud as watery sludge. Less common are horizontal flow tanks, in which the flocs settle to the bottom. Where the flocs are very light, fine air bubbles may be used in a flotation process to carry the flocs to the surface from which they can be skimmed to form a frothy sludge. These different types of sludge are handled by water companies as discussed below (paragraphs 7.27–7.29).

Rapid filtration

7.17   Rapid filters are deep beds (0.6–1.0 metres) of sand, or anthracite plus sand, or a similar material such as granular activated carbon. The particle size chosen is usually about 1 mm diameter. Operated at flow velocities of about 5–10 metres per hour, a rapid filter operates at about 50 times the rate of the historical slow sand filter discussed later. It retains most of the flocs and other particles which escape chemical coagulation and sedimentation. It does not act as a strainer as such, but retains material within the pores of the sand bed by a mechanism which has been described as "defence in depth".

7.18   Flocs and particles in suspension encounter a sequence of 1,000 grains as they flow through the pores of a 1.0 metre deep bed and so have very many chances of adhering to a grain. If oocysts are enmeshed in the residual flocs, then it can be expected that they will be filtered out along with those flocs. However, although the filter is extremely effective, it does not retain all particles and some, including oocysts if present, are carried forward in the filtrate and hence into supply.

7.19   The theory of water treatment technology suggests that single oocysts or even clumps, will be poorly retained owing to their small size, low density and spherical shape. This theory finds support from small-scale studies in the USA of the filtration of water following flocculation and sedimentation. Although the evidence is inconclusive, these studies suggest that the passage of oocysts through various filters is principally dependent on the number of oocysts in the raw water.

7.20   A rapid filter is stopped and backwashed periodically according to a time cycle (typically 24 hours), when it is too clogged to allow flow to continue, or when the turbidity of filtrate is too great for public supply purposes. The washwater which flushes out the deposits by upward flow represents typically 1–2 per cent of the flow. The handling of washwater, is discussed below (paragraphs 7.27–7.29).

7.21   If filtration is disturbed by any change in the rate of flow, particularly by a surge, deposits may be dislodged from the filter pores, because they are held in precarious equilibrium with the flowing water. These dislodged deposits may pass into the filtrate and hence to supply.

7.22   Turbidity monitoring can indicate changes in the quality of filtered water. Although modern nephelometric turbidimeters are not particularly sensitive to particles in the 1–10 micron range, which includes oocysts (about 4–6 microns), a continuously monitoring turbidimeter in each filter should detect any significant dislodgement of particles. If, however, only one turbidimeter monitors a combined works filtrate, any individual dislodgement may be hidden by dilution from other filters. While low turbidity itself does not indicate the absence of oocysts, even a small deviation from an expected pattern of turbidity readings can be an indication that filtration has been disturbed. Water companies should consider whether a change, taken together with other factors affecting water quality and conditions at the works, is sufficient to warrant monitoring for cryptosporidium. (For further discussion of the need for monitoring see Chapter 10).

Slow sand filters

7.23   About 20 per cent of the water supplied in England and Wales is treated on slow sand filters which are the oldest form of filter used for public water supplies. Typically, a slow sand filter covers about 0.4 hectares and has a depth of about 0.7 metres of fine sand. The size of the sand grains is about 0.3–0.4 mm in diameter and the rate of flow passing through the bed about 0.1–0.2 metres per hour.

7.24   Because of the fineness of the sand which could become rapidly clogged, particularly with certain algae, water is pre-filtered through coarse (1–3 mm) rapid sand filters or through stainless steel woven mesh microstrainers with openings of about 25 microns. As chemicals are generally not added and therefore no flocs are formed, it is unlikely that these pre-filtration units significantly retain particles as small as cryptosporidial oocysts.

7.25   The slow sand filter with its fine sand and slow flow rate offers considerable opportunity for small particles to be retained. However, the smallest pores in the sand bed are still about 60 microns in size, so removal of cryptosporidial oocysts and similar small particles by straining is most unlikely. The significant feature of a slow sand filter is the formation of a bacterial and algal slime in the top 10–20 mm of the sand. This biological layer, called *schmutzdecke* (German: dirt-layer), contributes greatly to the filter's efficiency by capturing very small particles. Some of these may be ingested by protozoa, larvae and other microorganisms which proliferate in the *schmutzdecke*. After cleaning, which removes the *schmutzdecke*, filters are brought into service very slowly to allow redevelopment of an active biological layer. This "ripening period" is extremely important. Slow sand filters are known for their high efficiency in removing coliforms (1–2 microns) yet some pass through; the same is probably true of cryptosporidial oocysts (4–6 microns).

7.26   When a filter is too clogged to pass the required flow, usually after several weeks of operation, the filter is drained and the top 10–30 mm scraped off by mechanical means. This skimmed sand is taken to washing machines where sand and dirt are separated by vigorous hydraulic agitation. Handling of the washwater is discussed below (paragraphs 7.27–7.29).

Sludges and Washwater

7.27   At any one treatment works, sludges from settlement and flotation tanks, the backwash water from rapid filters and water used for washing the layer of sand removed from slow sand filters, typically represent 4–6 per cent of water treated and put into supply. This is a significant volume and because only a fraction of it represents impurities removed in the treatment works, water companies attempt to reclaim as much as possible. This augmentation of the water source by reclaimed water is valuable, especially in times of drought.

7.28   Reclamation is achieved by separating out the impurities, for example, by settlement in lagoons. The clarified water is returned to the treatment works inlet and recycled through the various stages. The sludge "cake" is deposited on a designated waste disposal site or is distributed on agricultural land. If the treatment works is known to be contaminated with cryptosporidial oocysts, water companies should make special arrangements to dispose of the "cake", which may contain large numbers of oocysts, to a designated waste disposal site rather than to agricultural land.

7.29   Similarly, if oocysts are present in the raw water, the water recycled during the treatment process may contain large numbers of oocysts. In this way, oocysts which have been removed by water treatment may be given a further opportunity to penetrate the water treatment process. At present there is no method of treating water before it is recycled so as to guarantee the removal or inactivation of cryptosporidial oocysts. It is therefore important that water companies should develop contingency plans which avoid the recycling of water when the water treatment works is found to be contaminated. Discussions should be held with the National Rivers Authority if those plans entail the discharge of the water to rivers. Water companies should also be ready to monitor recycled water as discussed in Chapter 10. Provided personal hygiene is maintained, waterworks staff are under no risk from the handling of material potentially contaminated with cryptosporidium.

Disinfection

7.30   In the UK, water for public supply is routinely disinfected, mainly by chlorination at concentrations less than 5 mg/1. Chlorine is a powerful disinfectant and after 30 minutes of contact it can be expected that no detectable coliforms will remain and only a very small number of other bacteria. Sometimes ammonia is added to the chlorine to form chloramine, which although not such a powerful disinfectant, persists longer in the water mains. Since chlorination produces some undesirable substances when reacting with organic compounds in water, there is a practical limit to the amount of chlorine that can be applied to water for human consumption.

7.31   Whereas most other microorganisms are susceptible to chlorine at the concentrations used for water treatment, cryptosporidial oocysts are not. Concentrations of chlorine between 8,000 and 16,000 mg/1 have been found necessary to kill the oocysts. These levels are far in excess of the range that could be used in water treatment processes.

7.32   Since standard filtration methods cannot be guaranteed to remove oocysts and as chlorination is not effective, a search is underway to identify an alternative disinfectant. One possibility is ozone which is already used as a disinfectant in continental Europe, particularly in France and Switzerland. Recent laboratory reports of the efficacy of ozone to reduce excystation and also to reduce infectivity of oocysts in mice have been encouraging. Further, the use of ozone at concentrations that could be applied in water treatment processes has been shown to inactivate 99 per cent of oocysts.

7.33   However, although the use of ozone as a disinfectant for cryptosporidium merits further study, it has its disadvantages. It breaks down organic molecules and the resulting products are biodegradable by bacteria and may encourage bacterial regrowth in the water mains. It may also react with the constituents of water to create organic by-products which may be toxic. If it is applied before coagulation, undesirable organic by-products may be removed by flocculation or by filtration but further study is needed to evaluate this.

7.34   Other disinfectants such as chlorine dioxide and hydrogen peroxide and the use of ultraviolet irradiation may be technically feasible, but they would be expensive, particularly for large-scale supplies. Hydrogen peroxide has been shown in laboratory applications to require doses of more than 1,000 mg/1 to kill oocysts and this is not a practicable concentration for use in drinking water treatment. The effect of ultraviolet radiation on oocysts is as yet unknown.

Distribution of Water

7.35   After leaving the treatment works with a small residual content of chlorine the water should not be exposed to the open air until it emerges at consumers' taps. Bacteria and some very small aquatic animals can flourish in water mains, but as cryptosporidial oocysts are dormant in water, they will not multiply and are unlikely to collect in properly maintained pipe systems.

7.36   Contamination of treated water may nevertheless occur since in long delivery mains with large networks of distribution pipes, leaks are inevitable. Most are small and undetected, but even these can lead to a loss of 10–20 per cent of the water. If the pipes remain under pressure, the leaks are outwards and the water quality is not compromised. If pressure falls, due to exceptional demand, for example, as a result of fire-fighting or a burst in the main, then surrounding water in the ground, including sewage (because sewers also leak) may seep in. When pipes are repaired the danger of infection has to be recognised. A strict protocol* has been developed by the water industry for protecting pipes from microbiological contamination, but as it relies upon the use of chlorine as a disinfectant it cannot be totally satisfactory in guarding against contamination by cryptosporidial oocysts.

7.37   Most water distribution systems contain covered service reservoirs. Because the water level rises and falls in these structures air vents must be provided. Poor air vents, the means of access and structural cracks can all be sources of contamination but, properly constructed and maintained, service reservoirs should not represent a danger to water supply. Some service reservoirs are covered with grass which is grazed by livestock to keep it under control. In view of the possibility of cryptosporidial infection in livestock this practice should be discouraged as advised in the current protocol.*

---

* Operational Guidelines for the Protection of Drinking Water Supplies (WAA Sept. 1988).

8 Private Water Supplies and Point of Use Devices

Introduction

8.1 Over 99 per cent of the population of the UK are supplied with mains water using the methods of treatment described in Chapter 7. However, some households do receive private supplies, derived principally from wells or boreholes but occasionally from springs and streams. Some of these supplies will be treated by conventional methods including chlorination while others receive little or no treatment. Private supplies may become contaminated with oocysts but this is only one of the hazards to which they may be subject.

8.2 One option open to such householders seeking to improve the quality of their water supply is to install a point of use device for treating the drinking water. Although initially such devices were designed for private and possibly impure supplies, increasingly they have been advertised to the public for improving the quality of mains water. Indeed, it is not now unusual to find suppliers or retailers suggesting these devices as a final defence for all drinking water against all contaminants including cryptosporidial oocysts.

8.3 Reliable data on the efficiency and safety of these devices are lacking, although some research is to be undertaken as part of a project sponsored by the Department of the Environment. Comprehensive tests are needed both to establish the efficiency of devices in removing potential contaminants, including cryptosporidial oocysts, and to assess the potential risks that may exist from concentrating oocysts or other potentially harmful organisms or substances in the unit or the reject flow. In the absence of such information, the following paragraphs can only summarise the types of point of use devices available and draw attention to some of the possible advantages and disadvantages in their use.

Types of Unit

8.4 There are several different types of unit available which are either intended to produce a physical barrier against impurities or a treatment stage for specific removal of certain substances. Some units are plumbed into mains supplies; other are simply jugs fitted with filters. In other cases, small treatment processes may be installed.

Mechanical filters

8.5 Mechanical filters which may be constructed of wound textiles, microporous plastics or porous ceramics can be effective for removing particulate matter but the removal of oocysts will depend upon the pore size used. Sometimes units are impregnated with silver which can limit growth of bacteria but this is unlikely to be effective for killing oocysts.

8.6 The filters need to be replaced or cleaned regularly. In view of the possible concentration of materials removed which could present a health hazard, disposal of the used elements should be undertaken with care.

Activated carbon

8.7   Activated carbon is commonly used in a cartridge form to improve the organic quality of water, including taste. Water treatment experience suggests that the type of shallow bed used would not be effective in removing oocysts. Since the organic material retained on the carbon filter can provide a growth medium for bacteria, it may make the water bacteriologically less pure. Silver may be incorporated to prevent bacterial growth but again this is unlikely to be effective against oocysts.

Ion exchange

8.8   These units employ a cartridge containing ion exchange resin beads. They are intended for softening water and removing minerals particularly nitrate. It is unlikely that the cartridge itself or the resin beads would provide an effective barrier against oocysts.

Reverse osmosis

8.9   Reverse osmosis units effect a demineralisation of water using a membrane which allows the passage of water but rejects dissolved salts and suspended material which pass into the drain. To be effective the membranes in these units need to be replaced at intervals according to manufacturers instructions.

8.10   The pore size used would undoubtedly retain oocysts but tests with bacteria show that the integrity of the membranes and the seals used to allow the membranes to work under a high differential pressure cannot be guaranteed and penetration can occur. It is difficult to assess the risk especially considering the low concentration of oocysts likely to be present.

Distillation

8.11   Water stills are likely to be effective both in terms of killing oocysts at the temperature of boiling water and in the effectiveness of separation created by steam removal and condensation. Such units are more commonly used in hospitals, laboratories and commercial premises but not usually in domestic properties. In any case, the regular use of distilled water for drinking is not desirable on health grounds.

Ultraviolet radiation

6.12   Some small private supplies are disinfected using ultraviolet radiation. To ensure safety in disinfection, a high quality water containing only low levels of suspended matter is required. This may necessitate pre-filtration of the supply. Regular maintenance is also required. Little is yet known about the effectiveness of ultraviolet radiation against cryptosporidium.

9 Outbreaks of Cryptosporidiosis

Introduction

9.1   Several outbreaks of cryptosporidiosis have now been documented both in the USA and UK. This Chapter focuses on those incidents where contamination of drinking water was seriously considered as a possible route of infection, even if oocysts were not detected in the mains supply to the community. This Chapter also summarises some less well documented outbreaks of cryptosporidiosis which later analysis has suggested may have been associated with water supply. Finally, it includes for completeness a note on outbreaks linked with contamination of recreational waters, although these are outside the remit of the Group.

Documented Outbreaks in the USA
Braun Station, Texas

9.2   The first documented waterborne outbreak of cryptosporidiosis occurred in Texas in a community of about 6,000 persons in July 1984. The incidence of diarrhoea was 12 times that of the neighbouring communities and oocysts were detected in 47 of 79 individuals with diarrhoea. A second pathogen, the Norwalk virus, was also detected among the infected population and uncertainty therefore exists as to the amount of illness attributable to cryptosporidium. In a control group not exposed to the community water supply, 12 of 194 people were found to be excreting cryptosporidial oocysts.

9.3   The water supply was an artesian well and chlorination was the only treatment. No cryptosporidial oocysts were detected in the treated water but this may have been because methods for the recovery and identification of oocysts were not well developed at the time. Tests showed that dye introduced into the community's sewage system appeared in the well water.

9.4   *Comment:* Although no oocysts were detected in the drinking water, the cause of the outbreak was presumed to be sewage contamination of the supply, possibly following the treatment stage.

Carrollton, Georgia

9.5   In January 1987, an outbreak of waterborne cryptosporidiosis occurred in Carrollton, Georgia. The incidence of diarrhoeal illness peaked in the last two weeks of January and the first two weeks of February. An estimated 13,000 people were affected, giving an overall attack rate of 40 per cent but the rate was significantly higher in those who consumed water from the city's supply than in those who used water from wells. Cryptosporidial oocysts were found in 39 per cent of the 147 stool specimens examined. No other pathogen was isolated.

9.6   The drinking water treatment plant took its water from a river fed by a lake and a number of streams in the vicinity. There was a sewage outflow upsteam of the catchment area. The water was treated conventionally by coagulation, sedimentation, rapid sand filtration, and disinfection with chlorine. No recycling of backwash water was carried out.

9.7   In late January, samples of treated water were found to contain particles as large as 100 microns and cryptosporidial oocysts were detected. Seven of nine samples collected in early February were positive for oocysts and concentrations averaged 0.63/1 (oocysts per litre) within the distribution system, the highest level being found in a 24-hour sample taken post-filtration (2.2/1). By February 11, samples of treated water were negative for oocysts.

9.8   Samples taken from the source waters were either negative or revealed low levels of oocysts (0.08/1). On February 5, raw sewage from the effluent above the catchment area contained 34/1 and on March 20, 1.2/1.

9.9   Investigation of the working of the treatment plant revealed that throughout the period, the treated water had met USA primary drinking water standards of less than one nephelometric turbidity unit (NTU) and less than one coliform per 100 ml. Chlorine concentrations were 1.5 mg/l after disinfection and 0.5 mg/l within the distribution system. The average turbidity for the previous 12 months had ranged from 0.4–0.8 NTU.

9.10   Although all statutory standards were met, operational irregularities were identified. The impellers of the mechanical agitators required to effect coagulant dispersion had been removed in December 1986 and their replacements had not been fitted. The absence of the agitators led to inadequate chemical mixing and impaired removal of particulate matter. In addition, the efficiency of filtration was impaired by failure not only of the equipment but also of procedures used to control the flow of water through the filters and to monitor turbidity. It was found that some individual filters were passing water with a turbidity as high as 3.2 NTU although once blended with water from other filters, the turbidity of the water overall had fallen to less than 1 NTU, thus satisfying the USA standards.

9.11   Other suspect operational procedures included the shutdown of filters when demand was low and the start-up of dirty filters without backwashing. This could have led to the discharge of dirt, flocculant particles and microorganisms including oocysts from the filter beds. Although such a procedure is uncommon in the UK, it is not unusual in the USA. During the Christmas and New Year holidays, however, the demand for water at Carrollton had been particularly low, increasing the number of individual filters which had been shut-down. Thus, in the first week of January, the number of filters restarted without undergoing backwashing increased to 38 from the usual weekly average of 22. Whereas three filters properly washed and restarted produced water with a turbidity ranging from 0.07–0.18 NTU, three filters restarted without backwashing produced water with a turbidity ranging from 0.2–3.2 NTU. In February, the water treatment process was improved and continuous monitoring showed turbidity of 0.2 NTU or less.

9.12   Although no outbreaks of diarrhoeal disease had been reported in any livestock in the area, cryptosporidial oocysts were detected in the faeces of three of 56 cattle tested from nine farms in the watershed, but none was pastured in the area where oocysts were found in the source waters. No major rainfall occurred in early January, but more than 250 mm of rain and snow fell from January 15–22.

9.13   In mid-February, after the outbreak had subsided, a blockage of a major sewer was discovered which had led to an overflow of sewage in an area above the water treatment intake. Dye tracer studies indicated that discharge from the point of sewage overflow could reach the river and the water treatment plant in approximately six hours. Although this overflow could have augmented the oocyst load reaching the plant, it was not possible to ascertain whether the overflow had occurred prior to, during or after the outbreak.

9.14 *Comment:* There is strong evidence that this was a waterborne outbreak of cryptosporidiosis. The source of the contamination was never established. It is possible that at some time the lake or the river became heavily contaminated with oocysts but that at the time the outbreak reached its peak and the source water was sampled, only residual numbers of oocysts remained. The sewage spill and the increased rainfall just after the onset of the outbreak may have increased the number of oocysts reaching the works. A follow-up survey of the affected population suggested that there may have been a low level of infection with cryptosporidium prior to the actual outbreak. What does seem likely, however, is that the changes in water treatment around the holiday season, perhaps especially the shutdown and the start-up of the filters without backwashing, allowed oocysts to pass into the treated water in sufficiently high numbers to cause widespread illness.

Documented Outbreaks in the United Kingdom
Saltcoats and Stevenston, Ayrshire

9.15 The first outbreak of cryptosporidiosis in the UK in which cryptosporidial oocysts were detected in treated water occurred in Ayrshire in April 1988. At the time, there had been a sharp outbreak of diarrhoeal disease in the area and enquiries to local general practitioners suggested that the incidence of diarrhoeal disease in two towns which had the same drinking water supply was two to five times the expected rate. Twenty seven people who were either resident in the area served by that supply or who had drunk the water were diagnosed as suffering from cryptosporidiosis, strongly suggesting that the water was the source of the infection. Ten of the 27 were over 18 years of age.

9.16 The water supply for this area came from the Camphill works where it underwent coagulation, flocculation, rapid sand filtration and chlorination. The treated supply was routed through a break-pressure tank to storage tanks at another works.

9.17 Oocysts were detected in the treatment works, 300/l in the filter backwash water and 3 per gram in the pressed sludge "cake" but not in samples either from the raw water entering or the final water leaving the works. Nevertheless, two of seven water samples from the mains supply were positive for oocysts (0.04/l and 4.8/l) and post-treatment contamination was suspected. The break-pressure tank within a trunk main contained 0.04/l and inspection of the tank revealed an old 520 mm fire-clay pipe, the records for which had shown incorrectly that it has been disconnected. This pipe was found to be discharging run-off from the surrounding catchment area into the break-pressure tank. Samples from this tank, the neighbouring stream and soil and grass collected from the immediate vicinity of the fire-clay pipe were all positive for oocysts.

9.18 Cattle slurry and dung had been sprayed on the land in the neighbourhood of the fire-clay pipe just before the outbreak. For some time there had been little or no rainfall but three very wet days occurred just prior to the beginning of the outbreak.

9.19 *Comment:* Cryptosporidial oocysts appear to have been introduced into the break-pressure tank containing chlorinated water for distribution via an old, fire-clay pipe, which collected run-off from the surrounding catchment area during heavy rainfall. The source of the oocysts was not identified, but as the contaminated soil and grass also contained traces of muck it is possible that the practice of slurry or muck spreading on the catchment could have either added to intermittent low grade contamination or caused the contamination event.

Swindon/Oxfordshire

9.20 The second UK outbreak of cryptosporidiosis where oocysts were detected in treated water occurred in Swindon and parts of Oxfordshire. The first cases probably occurred in December 1988 but the outbreak peaked in February and March 1989. Over 500 cases were confirmed by laboratory analysis and up to 5,000 people overall may have been affected. Attack rates were highest among children under the age of five although people of all ages were affected.

9.21 Attack rates were generally higher in Swindon than in Oxfordshire. In each of the two health authority districts, attack rates were significantly higher for those communities receiving water from the Farmoor reservoir than those receiving water from other sources. The second highest attack rate occurred in a small community in Oxfordshire which received its waters from a surface waterworks at Worsham which abstracted water from the River Windrush, a tributary of the River Thames located upstream of the Farmoor reservoir.

9.22 An impoundment reservoir at Farmoor supplied water to both the Farmoor and Swinford water treatment works and, from there, treated water was distributed to a large area of Oxfordshire. Treatment was by conventional rapid sand filtration followed by disinfection with a final dose of chlorine of 1.5 mg/1 free chlorine over two hours. The final water had a turbidity of 0.2–0.4 NTU with a free chlorine residual of 0.4–0.5 mg/1. Whereas Worsham works employed alum as the coagulant, at Farmoor and Swinford alum was used in the summer but when the reservoir water quality deteriorated due to algal activity, polyaluminium chloride was used. This had been normal operational practice since 1986. Short trials of iron coagulates were carried out at each works in June and October 1988.

9.23 Initial investigations revealed the presence of oocysts in backwash water from a rapid gravity sand filter (10^4/1), in water leaving the Farmoor treatment plant (0.1/1) and at the end of the distribution system in Swindon (24/1). At the peak of the outbreak, 30 per cent of water samples from the distribution systems in the outbreak area contained oocysts (range 0.002–77/1). Raw water from the reservoir contained 0.002–14/1 whereas treated water leaving the treatment works contained 0.002–5/1. The highest counts were obtained from in-process samples at the works with up to 10^6/1 in samples of settled backwash water from filters.

9.24 During the investigation the capability of the Farmoor works to remove oocysts was assessed. Whereas the rapid sand filters reduced the numbers of oocysts by over 99 per cent, the settlement process for treating the filter backwash water and sludge achieved a reduction of only 83 per cent. As a result, the supernatant fluid from the settlement tanks which was returned to the head of the works (the start of the treatment process) contained 10^3/1 and this combined with numbers in the raw water entering the works (up to 10/1) resulted in an average daily load of 10^9

oocysts on each filter. The relative inefficiency of the settlement process to reduce the number of oocysts prolonged the time when they penetrated the treatment process into supply. Extensive washing (twice in 24 hours) after cessation of the recycling of the backwash water and operation on reduced filter run times (24 hours) resulted in the treated water leaving the works being free from oocysts within a week.

9.25   No oocysts were detected in sediment taken from the raw water reservoir, or in the disinfection contact tank or the distribution system in Oxfordshire. In Swindon, sediment in an underground treated water reservoir receiving Farmoor water from the trunk main contained 100 oocysts per gram. The flow to this reservoir had been unusually high to cope with high water demand during the autumn and winter. Oocysts were not detected in samples from the trunk main itself.

9.26   Throughout the period October 1988 to April 1989, treated water was free from coliform bacteria and monitoring of turbidity, chlorine demand, coagulant residuals and bacterial plate counts did not reveal any adverse changes in the quality of the treated water.

9.27   As far as is known, symptomatic cryptosporidiosis was not present in farm animals in the catchment area, although it was diagnosed in three dairy herds well above the source of the River Thames. However, during October 1988, severe diarrhoea occurred in cattle at a farm located adjacent to the River Windrush above the intake to Worsham works. River flows were exceptionally low due to unusually warm weather. The only significant rainfall causing a noticeable rise in river flow occurred over a few days at the end of November.

9.28   *Comment:* The rapid decline in positive samples in the distribution system following remedial action at the works (paragraph 9.24) points to contamination in the source water. The findings of the epidemiological and environmental investigations are consistent with an episode of contamination whereby animal waste containing high numbers of viable oocysts was washed into the River Windrush at the end of November. Whilst low levels of oocysts were found in other surface water sources in the Thames catchment, these findings were not associated with a rise in disease in the human population, and in late spring oocysts disappeared from most surface sources in the catchment.

Loch Lomond

9.29   During the period January to June 1989, 442 cases of cryptosporidiosis were reported in Scotland. A detailed investigation was carried out in the three health board areas with the highest incidence, Argyll and Clyde, Lanarkshire and Lothian, where 244 cases were reported. Follow-up questionnaires returned on 206 of these cases showed that 54 per cent were under 10 years of age, with 41 per cent in the age group 1–4 years, and that 22 per cent had been admitted to hospital during the course of their illness. In the majority of cases, the onset of symptoms was in April or May. The outbreak tailed off after May when the incidence of disease returned to background levels, although in Lothian, the outbreak began earlier and went on longer.

9.30   A questionnaire revealed that 98 (39 per cent) of those who were found to have cryptosporidial oocysts in their faeces were supplied at home with water from Loch Lomond. Statistical analysis confirmed a higher incidence of cryptosporidiosis in persons who were supplied with Loch Lomond water compared to persons residing in the same areas who were supplied with water from other sources. However, the range of incidence rates in different districts all supplied by the same Lomond water implied that other factors could also be important. In the two weeks preceding the onset of the illness, 37 per cent of cases had contact with people with similar symptoms, suggesting a high incidence of person to person spread; 32 per cent had travelled away from their home town although only two people had been abroad; and 49 per cent had contact with farm animals or pets but there were few reported cases of illness among the animals.

9.31   Water is abstracted from Loch Lomond at Ross Priory and pumped through two mains, one leading to Blairlinnans treatment works for distribution to the north bank of the river Clyde and Renfrewshire, and the other to the Balmore treatment works for distribution into Lanarkshire and West Lothian. Abstracted water is passed through coarse and mechanically operated fine screens before being chlorinated and pumped to the treatment works, where it is passed through stainless steel microstrainers (nominal pore size 23 microns). The pH is raised to reduce plumbosolvency and a further dose of chlorine added. Analyses of water samples were instigated in April 1989 and oocysts were detected in both the raw water sampled at the Ross Priory inlet (range 0.01–2.3/1) and in treated water in the distribution system (range 0.008–0.4/1) on sporadic occasions thereafter.

9.32   *Comment:* The results of the investigation indicate that an outbreak of cryptosporidiosis occurred in April and May 1989 in people living in the area supplied by the water from Loch Lomond. The finding of small numbers of cryptosporidial oocysts in the Loch Lomond water supply taken with the epidemiological evidence does point to an association between Loch Lomond water and the incidence of disease. However, the evidence is not conclusive as to the source of infection contributing to the spread of cryptosporidiosis, and other factors, including post-treatment contamination, cannot be ruled out at this stage. A further study is under way to continue to monitor closely the incidence of cryptosporidiosis in these areas.

North Humberside

9.33   An outbreak of cryptosporidiosis began in North Humberside in late December 1989. By the end of May when the outbreak was over, cryptosporidial oocysts had been detected in the faeces of 477 persons. The age of persons affected varied from three months to 95 years. Preliminary epidemiological studies suggested that the route of infection was mains water supplied from the treatment works at Barmby-on-the-Marsh (Barmby), 25 miles west of the city of Kingston-upon-Hull (Hull).

9.34   The Communicable Disease Surveillance Centre (CDSC), in collaboration with Hull Health Authority and Hull Public Health Laboratory, carried out a case control study which showed a statistically significant association of illness with consumption of water from the Barmby works. Studies of 85 of the primary cases showed that most patients suffered diarrhoea, loss of appetite and abdominal pain and many also had other symptoms. The duration of illness ranged from 2–31 days with a median value of 13 days. Nine of the 85 were admitted to hospital.

9.35   Barmby Works abstracts water from the River Derwent which has a rural catchment to the north with extensive arable farming and grazing. Unless its turbidity exceeds 20 NTU, river water is normally abstracted continuously through screens into a large storage reservoir with a holding capacity of up to 15 days. The outflow from the reservoir is taken from one of three points, with either the top or middle draw-off pipes normally in use. The outflow from the reservoir passes through rapid gravity sand filters and slow sand filters before chlorination. The treated water is then stored in a reservoir for approximately nine hours at normal works output before being partially dechlorinated and pumped into the distribution system.

9.36. Yorkshire Water Services initiated a programme of monitoring for cryptosporidium in June 1989 following a decision to by-pass part of the flow past the slow sand filters to boost supplies to Hull, where prolonged drought had decreased ground water and river water supplies to a critically low level. Positive results for cryptosporidium were obtained from samples of raw water leaving the reservoir on 20 June 4 oocysts in 2 litres) and on 28 June (1 oocyst in 1.5 metres). From the beginning of November to the end of December a substantial number of samples of raw water leaving the reservoir were taken and all were negative except for that on 11/12 December when a reading of 2 oocysts in 17 litres was obtained. Samples were also taken from major stages in the treatment works, and treated water in the distribution system was also sampled but only two of these samples were positive.

9.37 For most of November and December, a proportion of the water flow at Barmby by-passed the slow sand filters. From 8–14 December, the percentage by-passing peaked at 30 per cent. There was a further by-passing (24 per cent) from 6–8 January 1990. There are a number of other operational aspects of relevance to the period of by-passing in December. From 1 June 1989 to 25 January 1990, the intake pumps from the river continuously abstracted water except for a few days in November and from 16–21 December. The closure of the intake pumps in these periods was in line with standard practice following a high and rising turbidity level in the river. On 18 December, the bottom draw-off point from the reservoir was brought into action. The draw-off point was returned to the middle level on 22 December.

9.38 During the period 8–28 December 1989 the values for turbidity, algal count and *E coli* content of raw water, water in process and treated water were normal for the plant, with the exception of the figures for algal count and turbidity of the final treated water on 18 December which were high. There were no positive coliform counts in the final water leaving the works.

9.39 Although rainfall had been low for several months in the River Derwent catchment area, there was heavy rainfall between 10–20 December 1989, with a peak from 13–16 December. Up to 20.2 mm were recorded in a single day in an area with an annual rainfall of some 600 mm. Further periods of heavy rainfall occurred on 2, 5–8 and 23–29 January 1990.

9.40 At the time of writing, the Drinking Water Inspectorate was conducting an investigation into the outbreak, following the receipt of a draft final report from the CDSC. The CDSC's epidemiological studies provided support for the view that the outbreak was initiated by contamination of drinking water and that this was followed by a community outbreak resulting from person to person spread. However, these results had been challenged by Yorkshire Water Company on the basis of expert epidemiological advice.

9.41 A possible explanation of the outbreak put forward by CDSC was that a brief intermittent contamination of the supply occurred which could not be detected by the level of sampling undertaken. Any residual organisms were then quickly flushed through the system and did not settle. The apparent absence of oocysts in drinking water and the low numbers detected in filter backwash and filter core samples might have reflected the transient nature of the event and/or failure to sample at an appropriate time and place. That does not explain why no similar outbreaks of cryptosporidiosis occurred in Hull in June 1989 when oocysts were detected or in December 1989/January 1990 in areas of West and South Yorkshire which also received small amounts of water from the Barmby Works.

9.42 *Comment:* No conclusion can be drawn about this outbreak pending the completion of the Drinking Water Inspectorate's report. The relative importance of operating conditions in December 1989 and of the exceptionally heavy rainfall following a period of drought needs to be assessed. In particular, while by-passing of sand filters, closure of the intake pumps, use of bottom draw-off point and turbidity readings higher than normal are all signs of sub-optimal working of a treatment works, these factors may not have been significant in bringing about the outbreak of cryptosporidiosis in this case.

Other Outbreaks
Cobham, Surrey

9.43 Two outbreaks of cryptosporidiosis which occurred in Cobham, Surrey, in 1983 and 1985 may have been waterborne although the epidemiological evidence was not conclusive. The water originating from a spring and river was treated by liming, filtration and chlorination. It was suggested that oocysts penetrated the treatment and that, at least in the case of the second outbreak, run-off following rainfall contributed to the contamination of the water source.

Holywell, North Wales

9.44 Between March and May, 1984, 19 cases of cryptosporidiosis occurred in people either living in or having direct connection with the town of Holywell. Examination of upland river feeder streams revealed the presence of cryptosporidial oocysts, but methods were not available to test the treated water at that time. All the cases and the controls used the same water supply, and although a waterborne source was suspected no evidence to implicate the water supply was found. No common source could be determined, but person to person, zoonotic and foodborne transmission were all considered to be likely routes of infection.

Sheffield, Yorkshire

9.45 A possible, but unconfirmed waterborne outbreak occurred in Sheffield, between April and October 1986. Of 104 patients with cryptosporidiosis, 81 per cent drank water supplied from the same reservoir complex, an association that was found to be statistically significant compared with people whose water came from other sources. Oocysts were detected in faecal samples from cattle on farms adjoining the reservoir area, in surface waters from the reservoir and feeder streams, and from brown trout caught from the reservoir.

Bernalillo County, New Mexico

9.46 Waterborne cryptosporidiosis has also been tentatively identified in New Mexico. Since 1984, laboratories had been reporting cases of cryptosporidiosis to the New Mexico Office of Epidemiology. From July to October 1986, 76 cases of cryptosporidiosis were found through laboratory identification of oocysts in stools. An investigation was initiated to determine the source of infection and the risk factors associated with the illness. Using matched controls it was found that there was a statistically significant association between drinking untreated surface water and illness, but an increased risk of infection was also related to camping in the area, swimming in surface water, attending day care centres, or possessing a pet which was young or ill.

Recreational Waters
Doncaster

9.47   Between August and October 1988, a steep rise in the number of cases of cryptosporidiosis, many in young children, occurred in the Doncaster area. A case control study showed a statistically significant association between illness and head immersion while swimming in the learner pool at Armthorpe leisure complex. Investigation revealed that pipes serving the filtration plant to the pool had been disconnected in several places. There had been a blockage in the sewage system at the premises and this had caused a backflow and allowed sewage containing oocysts to be sucked into the water treatment system. 500/1 were detected in samples taken from the water of the learner pool and 76 oocysts per gram were found in samples of sand from the associated filter.

Scotland

9.48   Oocysts have also been detected in at least four swimming pools in Scotland (range 0.005–2.8/1) since July 1989. Analyses were undertaken because of an epidemiological association between cryptosporidiosis in the community and the swimming pool in question, but on none of these occasions did the treated water source supplying the pools under investigation contain oocysts.

10 Lessons: Water Treatment Processes; Monitoring; Epidemiology

Introduction

10.1 A number of common features can be identified in the outbreaks of cryptosporidiosis described in Chapter 9. This Chapter concentrates on the lessons which can be learned from these outbreaks and from consideration of cryptosporidium in relation to water treatment processes and sets out the circumstances in which monitoring of water supplies for oocysts may be advisable. It also considers the value of epidemiological studies.

Water Treatment Processes

10.2 The outbreaks of cryptosporidiosis described in Chapter 9 demonstrate that conventional water treatment processes cannot guarantee the safety of drinking water supplies at all times. However, the evidence suggests that certain practices are more likely to facilitate the passage of oocysts through a water treatment works. In particular, the evidence from Carrollton suggests that the shutdown of filters and their restart without being backwashed can contribute to the oocyst load in the treated water supply. These practices, which are not common in the UK, should be avoided. This outbreak also highlights the importance of having a system whereby the turbidity on each filter can be measured individually to assist the early detection of conditions which may favour the breakthrough of oocysts into the treated water.

10.3 No conclusion can yet be drawn about the significance of the partial by-passing of the slow sand filters in the suspected waterborne outbreak of cryptosporidiosis in North Humberside. But any major change in normal operations at a water treatment works must increase the risk that cryptosporidial oocysts will pass through into the treated public supply if they are present in the source water.

Monitoring for Cryptosporidium

10.4 When operated optimally and assuming no more than background levels of oocysts in raw water sources, current water treatment processes appear able to prevent contamination of water supplies by cryptosporidial oocysts. However, evidence from the documented outbreaks points to an increased risk of oocyst contamination either following accidental agricultural pollution of source water or following a period of exceptionally heavy rainfall after a dry spell, especially when associated with recent spreading of slurry on agricultural land in the catchment area. Slight peaks have been noted in the spring and autumn which may be linked to seasonal farming practices.

10.5 It also seems likely that water supplies may be more susceptible to oocyst contamination when there has been a major planned change in a water treatment process or when a normal treatment process (such as a slow sand filter) has to be by-passed for operational reasons. In either situation, waterworks can effectively be considered to be operating sub-optimally.

10.6 Most water companies do not monitor treated drinking water supplies routinely for cryptosporidial oocysts. Even where some monitoring is undertaken, the current provisional method is too inefficient and unreliable particularly at low levels for the results to be interpreted with confidence (Chapter 3). Furthermore, it is not yet possible to distinguish the different species of cryptosporidium or to determine the viability of any oocysts detected. Given these shortcomings in the methodology and until more information is available from current research studies about the occurrence of cryptosporidium in water sources, the Group does not feel able to recommend that water companies should undertake routine monitoring of treated water for cryptosporidium. Each water company should, however, develop a strategy which sets out when and how often monitoring will be undertaken in the light of the known risks (paragraphs 10.4–10.5) and local circumstances. The strategy should be reviewed regularly.

10.7 In formulating a monitoring strategy, water companies should take into account the desirability of monitoring treated water for cryptosporidial oocysts in the following circumstances:

following exceptional contamination of water sources by agricultural pollution of sewage;

for a transitional period when a significant planned change in a water treatment process or distribution network takes place;

when, for exceptional operational reasons, the water treatment process is operating abnormally;

when turbidity readings or levels of indicator or other organisms deviate from the normal ranges;

if an outbreak of cryptosporidiosis in the community is suspected as being linked to a water supply.

10.8 If a waterborne outbreak of cryptosporidiosis is suspected, water companies will need to establish an investigative programme of monitoring for cryptosporidial oocysts covering source waters, the water treatment works and the distribution system. Evidence from the Swindon/Oxfordshire outbreak suggests that the most likely place in which oocysts may be detected is in the backwash water from filter beds but samples should be taken from:

the source waters;

the surrounding catchment areas and mud deposits in reservoirs if there is evidence of the spreading of manure;

treatment works including backwash water, sludge, filter beds and any recycled water;

pipelines and service reservoirs especially if the information on the geographical spread of the disease indicates an affected area smaller than the total area served by the water supply;

points in the distribution network where contaminated water may still remain even after it has been flushed out of the rest of the system.

10.9 There is no doubt that early detection of cryptosporidial oocysts in water supplies would facilitate the management and control of a suspected waterborne outbreak of cryptosporidiosis. With the exception of the Ayrshire and Swindon/Oxfordshire incidents, little evidence of oocyst contaminaton of water supplies was obtained during the investigation of the suspected waterborne outbreaks. This may be due in part to shortcomings in the methodology and to the fact that peak contamination may have passed before sampling was instituted.

10.10   It is clear that water companies need to have available the trained personnel and appropriate equipment to implement immediately a sampling programme when either an outbreak of cryptosporidiosis is suspected as being waterborne or when a decision is taken for other reasons to initiate monitoring for cryptosporidial oocysts. They should also make arrangements in advance so that samples can be examined expeditiously when required. Because of the complexities of the sampling and examination procedures, these arrangements must include provision for independent sampling and for cross-checking of the results of examination by independent laboratories with specialist experience. The PHLS has in operation a quality control scheme for analysing the microbiological quality of drinking water and this is available to all laboratories and water companies from the Newcastle Regional Public Health Laboratory. It is anticipated that this programme will be extended to include cryptosporidium.

Epidemiological Studies

10.11   The value of epidemiological studies in focusing on possible causes of an outbreak has been clearly demonstrated in the incidents reported in Chapter 9. The same basic principles should be followed in the epidemiological investigation of cryptosporidiosis as for other outbreaks of communicable disease. In general, the sudden onset of widespread gastroenteritis affecting people of all ages is typical of a waterborne outbreak. Evidence from the outbreaks of cryptosporidiosis shows that a waterborne outbreak tends to be associated with a higher number of adult cases than would otherwise be expected. However, current laboratory practice generally involves the screening only of stool samples from children for cryptosporidial oocysts. It is important, therefore, that early consideration should be given to screening all stool samples for cryptosporidial oocysts when an outbreak of cryptosporidiosis is suspected. It needs to be recognised that if the pattern of screening changes, more cases are likely to be detected.

10.12   At the earliest possible stage of a suspected waterborne outbreak, it is important to compare the geographical distribution of cases with water supply zones. Initial epidemiological investigation should establish age/sex distribution, sources of water at home and work and volumes consumed, contact with other persons with diarrhoea, with animals and farms and the use of swimming pools and other water. It should also take account of history of travel, food consumption and cooking methods.

10.13   Where the epidemiological survey establishes a link with pet animals, it is advisable to take specimens from these animals to ensure that they are not a source of infection. Similarly, Veterinary Investigation Centres should be consulted to establish information on significant recent diarrhoeal disease in livestock on farms within the local water supply catchment or upstream of an abstraction point.

10.14   The usefulness of case control studies has been well demonstrated in investigations of outbreaks of cryptosporidiosis. They can help to establish whether there is an association between the consumption of water from a particular supply and the development of cryptosporidiosis and whether the risk of developing the illness increases in proportion to the volume of that water consumed.

11 Roles of Public and Private Bodies Involved in a Suspected Waterborne Outbreak of Cryptosporidiosis in England and Wales

Introduction

11.1 Experience from the documented outbreaks of cryptosporidiosis suggests that the respective roles and responsibilities of the organisations and individuals concerned are not always clear in practice and that this confusion and overlap could hamper the effective management of an outbreak. This Chapter therefore attempts to set out for England and Wales the roles and responsibilities of the key organisations and individuals involved and their inter-relationships. Similar information for Scotland is contained in Part II(XI).

Public and Private Bodies in England and Wales

11.2 The principal public and private bodies concerned in the recognition and control of suspected waterborne outbreaks of disease are listed below.

Department of the Environment and Welsh Office

11.3 Ministers of the Department of the Environment and the Welsh Office are answerable to Parliament for drinking water quality in England and Wales and for administering the relevant legislation in the Water Act 1989 and the Water Supply (Water Quality) Regulations 1989. The Departments give advice to water companies and local authorities and maintain close liaison with the National Rivers Authority.

Drinking Water Inspectorate

11.4 The Drinking Water Inspectorate was established in January 1990 to check upon the quality of drinking water. It will advise the Secretaries of State for the Environment and for Wales liaising as necessary with local authority environmental health officers and with the Department of Health. It will assess the adequacy of arrangements made by water companies for monitoring the water they supply and the progress they have made on remedial programmes of work.

Water companies

11.5 Water companies have a statutory duty to supply wholesome water for domestic purposes and to implement the Water Supply (Water Quality) Regulations 1989. They also have a statutory duty to notify the local authority and district health authority and the Department of the Environment or the Welsh Office of any event which is likely to give rise to a significant risk to the health of the people residing in the companies' area.

11.6 Structures and organisational responsibilities of water companies vary so much that responsibilities for emergency planning will tend to be allocated differently in each company. In general, the Technical Director or the Director of Operational Services is likely to be the senior accountable officer.

National Rivers Authority

11.7 The National Rivers Authority (NRA) is responsible for monitoring, maintaining and improving the quality of "controlled waters" (rivers, canals, lakes, estuaries, coastal waters and underground water) in England and Wales. It regulates discharges to such waters made by water and sewerage undertakers, industrial or commercial businesses and agriculture. The NRA also carries out preventative and remedial measures in relation to pollution incidents.

Ministry of Agriculture Fisheries and Food (MAFF)	11.8 The Veterinary Investigation Service is an integral part of the MAFF State Veterinary Service and comprises a network of 19 Veterinary Investigation Centres in England and Wales. It provides facilities for the diagnosis and investigation of diseases in agricultural livestock and maintains close liaison with local health authorities where zoonotic diseases are concerned.
Department of Health	11.9 The Department of Health has a leading role in developing policy to promote and safeguard the health of the public. In pursuing these objectives much of the responsibility is laid on a wide variety of other governmental and non-governmental agencies.
	11.10 The Chief Medical Officer, Department of Health, and the Chief Medical Officer, Welsh Office, provide medical advice to government departments in England and Wales. There is a statutory requirement for the "proper officer" (paragraph 11.11) to inform the relevant Chief Medical Officer concerned, of any serious outbreaks of infectious disease, including waterborne outbreaks.
Health authorities and local authorities	11.11 District health authorities have general responsibility for the prevention, diagnosis and treatment of illness in their localities. The present statutory provision regarding the control of outbreaks of communicable disease is complex and under review (paragraphs 11.16–11.23). It gives a variety of control powers to a "proper officer" of a local authority who for this purpose is usually a public health physician employed by the health authority, until quite recently called the Medical Officer for Environmental Health (MOEH).
	11.12 District and borough councils have a statutory duty under section 56 of the Water Act 1989 to keep themselves informed about the wholesomeness and sufficiency of drinking water supplies in their areas, including private water supplies, and to take steps to secure that remedial action is taken if defects are detected. In practice it is the Chief Environmental Health Officer (CEHO) who assumes this responsibility and who may exceptionally require a water company to provide an alternative supply. The CEHO is directly accountable for his actions to the environmental health (or equivalent) committee of his local authority.
	11.13 Environmental health officers cooperate regularly with health authority personnel on the prevention, investigation and control of infectious disease. They also have an important role in educating the public.
Laboratory services	11.14 The Public Health Laboratory Service (PHLS), through its 52 constituent laboratories around the country, together with other NHS and private laboratories, provides microbiological diagnostic facilities for specimens from patients both in hospital and in the community and may be the first to identify an outbreak of cryptosporidiosis. The PHLS also offers a service for microbiological examination of environmental samples including food and water.
Communicable Disease Surveillance Centre	11.15 The Communicable Disease Surveillance Centre (CDSC), which is part of the PHLS, is responsible for the surveillance of communicable disease in England and Wales. It obtains, collates and analyses data and distributes information on infections to those concerned with prevention and control of communicable disease. It may be involved in the recognition of outbreaks of disease and, in a major outbreak, can be called upon for assistance to undertake epidemiological studies.

New Public Health Arrangements in England and Wales 1989/90

11.16   In recent years the public health function has undergone a number of changes following Ministers' acceptance of the main recommendations of the Report "Public Health in England; Report of the Committee of Inquiry into The Future Development of The Public Health Function" (Cmd 289). This Inquiry was set up in response to two major outbreaks of communicable disease – salmonella food poisoning in the Stanley Royd Hospital in Wakefield and Legionnaires' disease at Stafford – which had both resulted in public inquiries. These reports pointed to a decline in available medical expertise in environmental health and in the investigation and control of communicable disease and recommend a review of the public health function in England. As a result, a Committee was set up under the Chairmanship of the Chief Medical Officer, Sir Donald Acheson, which made a number of recommendations which are currently being implemented. These recommendations are of relevance to a waterborne outbreak.

11.17   Department of Health circular HC(88)64 emphasises the public health functions of a district health authority and requires each authority to appoint a Director of Public Health (DPH). The DPH has overall responsibility for reviewing the health of the population within the district and for identifying potential causes of ill health. Thus, the DPH will be the chief source of public health advice to the health authority. He will also act as a source of public health medical advice to the relevant local authority.

11.18   Other steps are being taken to ensure that communicable disease is controlled more effectively. Regional health authorities have been asked to review their existing provision for the surveillance, prevention and control of communicable disease and infection and to put forward proposals for handling the transition to new arrangements. These arrangements involve the appointment of Consultants for Communicable Disease Control (CCDCs) in district health authorities. These posts will eventually cover the whole of England and Wales.

11.19   Although the DPH is the chief source of public health advice to a health authority, it is the CCDC who will have executive responsibility for the surveillance, prevention and control of communicable disease within a health district. He will eventually take over the infectious disease duties which are now, with few exceptions. carried out by the MOEH who is appointed by the local authority as the "proper officer" for infectious disease control.

11.20   The CCDC will be responsible for drawing up the health authority's own contingency plan, which will come into effect should an outbreak of cryptosporidiosis be suspected and for coordinating the necessary action. He is also best placed, in consultation with the local authority, the water company and other appropriate agencies, to formulate the overall outbreak control plan for the investigation and management of waterborne outbreaks. In addition, he will be responsible for coordinating work on the control of infection between hospitals and between hospitals and the community.

11.21   Some district health authorities have already appointed a CCDC while others have retained the post of MOEH for the time being. It is important to note that the CCDC is a specialist in his own right and not the deputy of the DPH; however, like the MOEH, he will normally be directly accountable to the DPH in management terms.

11.22 It is expected that a CCDC will be appointed as "proper officer" by the corresponding local authorities while existing statutory provisions for the control of communicable disease remain in force. These provisions are currently being reviewed in order to clarify, among other issues, the relationship between district health authorities and local authorities in respect of infectious disease control and the role and accountability of current MOsEH or future CCDCs.

11.23 Currently, therefore, the DPH is responsible for ensuring effective arrangements for the control of communicable disease are in place but responsibility for taking action is in some districts the responsibility of the newly appointed CCDC, while in others it remains for the time being that of the MOEH. In a few districts, the DPH may also be the CCDC. However, because of his overall responsibilities for public health, it is with the DPH that water companies and local authorities should establish and maintain links.

12 Investigation and Management of a Suspected Waterborne Outbreak of Cryptosporidiosis

Introduction

12.1   In an outbreak of cryptosporidiosis, most of the agencies described in Chapter 11 will be involved but the key roles will be those of the district health authority, the district or borough council and the water company concerned. Local authorities and health authorities will already have policies and plans for the recognition and control of outbreaks of communicable disease and these will include arrangements to be made when water is suspected as the cause of infection in the community. Water companies also have emergency plans which include arrangements to be made in the event of microbiological contamination of water supplies. Taken together, these emergency plans form the basis of the Outbreak Control Plan. The overall Plan must coordinate these three plans and make arrangements for the establishment of an Outbreak Control Team with representatives from each of the organisations concerned to manage and control an outbreak should one occur.

Table 12.1

Remedial action to remove cryptosporidial oocysts from water treatment processes

Checklist of steps to be considered

Reservoir supply
— Change draw-off level.
— Revert to direct river supply.
— Use alternative sources.

Direct river abstraction
— Check catchment control measures.

Ground waters
— Check catchment control measures. (In the longer term, it may be necessary to deepen borehole linings to preclude surface water penetration and to give additional protection to spring source collecting chambers).

Microstrainers
— No effective remedial measures available.

Coagulation/flocculation
— Optimise coagulant dose.
— Optimise pH for coagulation and choice of coagulant. Include temporary plant for acid or alkali addition.
— Include flocculant aids.
— Ensure stirred flocculators are operational.
— Ensure adequate flocculation time.

Sedimentation/clarification/flotation
— Check operation of sludge bleed systems.
— Avoid sludge blanket disturbance whether by throughput changes or wind disturbance.

— Downrate plant if possible to ensure best possible particle entrapment.

Filtration
— Backwash rapid gravity filters as frequently as possible consistent with maintenance of throughput.
— Ensure depth of media maintained above the minimum level, particularly on slow sand filters.
— Control carefully filter start-up procedures. Run filters on slow start after return to service, or preferably run to waste until filtrate turbidity satisfactory.
— Ensure part-used filters (both rapid gravity and slow sand filters) are never returned to service without cleaning.
— Measure continuously or very regularly turbidity of water from individual filters.
— Achieve consistently lowest possible turbidity since this will minimise oocyst breakthrough.
— Monitor filter headloss.
— Control filter backwash cleaning cycle to ensure maximum headloss or turbidity of filtrate allowable are not exceeded before cleaning.
— Consider conditioning of water before filtration with a polyelectrolyte (rapid gravity filters only).
— Consider pre-conditioning of filter bed by addition of polyelectrolyte to final rinse of backwash water (rapid gravity filters only).

Filter backwash water
— Divert filter backwash water and other process waste water so that it is not returned to the works without special treatment. (Conventional backwashing water management will allow such water to provide a substantial additional oocysts load to the treatment system).
— Ensure that the disposal of waste process water is carried out in accordance with statutory requirements and contingency arrangements made with the NRA for disposal of waste process water during periods of oocyst challenge to a works.

Upland supplies without filtration
— Introduce a filtration step using improvised equipment. (May be appropriate for small sources).

Contact tanks
— Inspect, clean out, ensure removal of all sludges.

Service reservoirs
— Inspect, clean out, ensure removal of all sludges.
— Repair roofs (e.g. by fitment of butyl rubber sheets) if rain water can seep in.

Distribution systems
— Introduce programme of flushing and/or scouring to remove suspect water and any contaminated mains deposits from system.

Disinfection
Conventional disinfection by chlorine in ineffective and other methods of disinfection are not yet proven to be effective in removing oocysts from water supply.

However, where the necessary back-up systems are already in place, consideration may be given to:
— the addition of ozone, post filtration. This could only be used where a suitable contact tank is available and with an absorption step for organic compounds post application, for example granular activated carbon;

— the application of chlorine dioxide in process;

— the use of ultra-violet irradiation. The dose requirement is likely to be high, precluding this as a possibility except on very small sources.

12.2   This Chapter sets out for England and Wales the common elements which should appear in all the plans and identifies specific items relating to each. It also provides a framework for the overall Outbreak Control Plan. Some of the advice may be helpful in Scotland particularly to water authorities but readers concerned in the management of an outbreak of cryptosporidiosis in Scotland should also refer to Part II(XI).

Plans:
Liaison and Lines of
Communication
Co-ordination

12.3   Responsibility for the co-ordination of the emergency plans and for the establishment of an Outbreak Control Team is not formally assigned. Subject to the outcome of the current review of the law on infectious disease control, the Group suggests that the responsibility for initiating and co-ordinating action should be placed on the district health authority.

12.4   The Report "Public Health in England" (Cmd 289) recommended that each health district should have an advisory multi-disciplinary District Control of Infection Committee. Where this committee is in place, it seems sensible that the health authorities, local authorities and water companies should meet under its umbrella for contingency planning. Where these committees have not been established, effective local arrangements will have to be agreed.

12.5   The water sub-committee so formed will need to co-ordinate the constituent emergency plans and the overall Outbreak Plan and to ensure that all procedures and measures for action are regularly tested. The sub-committee should have responsibility for seeing that the plans are kept up to date and that any action recommended following an outbreak is carried out.

Responsibilities

12.6   Each of the emergency plans will need to set out clearly the statutory duties of the organisation and the responsibilities of named individuals in the management structure and how these relate to the responsibilities of those in other organisations. All staff should have clear instructions as to their role in an outbreak.

12.7   Specified officers should be identified to serve on the water sub-committee of the Control of Infection Committee and some of these officers should be members of the Outbreak Control Team. They should be of such seniority and expertise that they are able to commit the organisations they represent to appropriate action.

Liaison and
communication links

12.8   Each of the emergency plans should set out the communication network between the health authority's Director of Public Health (DPH), the Chief Environmental Health Officer (CEHO) of the local authority and the water company's Technical Director (or Director of Operational Services or equivalent) and their departments. Communication channels should include other organisations such as the National Rivers Authority (NRA), the MAFF Veterinary Investigation Service and the Public Health Laboratory Service (PHLS) including its Communicable Disease Surveillance Centre (CDSC).

12.9 A particularly important part of the plans should be the establishment of a permanent 24 hour communication system known to all, including secretaries and switchboard operators, and involving, for example, stand-by rotas of staff and radiopagers. These links must be regularly tested and updated (paragraph 12.5).

12.10 Recognition of a waterborne outbreak of cryptosporidiosis requires close liaison at all times between health and local authorities and water companies. The plans therefore need to set out in some detail how and by whom information is to be passed from one organisation to another on a regular basis, for example, water companies should notify the health and local authorities if cryptosporidial oocysts are detected in the treated water supply.

**Outbreak Control
Team**
Establishment

12.11 The Outbreak Control Plan should provide for the establishment of an Outbreak Control Team, to be called into being by the DPH should he suspect an outbreak (paragraph 12.3). For this purpose, a useful working definition of an outbreak of cryptosporidiosis is when observed rates of infection exceed the background level.

12.12 The Consultant for Communicable Disease Control (CCDC), the Medical Officer for Environmental Health (MOEH) or a local microbiologist either in the NHS or the PHLS will probably be the first to recognise an outbreak. Alternatively, evidence of an outbreak may become apparent to the CDSC. Indications that the outbreak may be waterborne are likely to come from the geographical distribution of the cases and from the fact that a significant number of primary cases are occurring in adults. Confirmation that water is the source of the infection may come from the identification of cryptosporidial oocysts in the mains water supply. It is unlikely that without access to the necessary epidemiological data, a water company will be the first to warn of a possible outbreak although it may be the first to be aware of a potential risk from oocysts in the water supply.

12.13 The members of the Outbreak Control Team should include the DPH and/or the CCDC or the MOEH whoever is in post, medical microbiologists from the NHS and the local PHLS, the CEHO and senior representatives from the water company involved including the Technical Director (or Director of Operational Services or equivalent). During the course of an investigation, other members may have to be co-opted from the hospital and community health services, for example, representatives of the health authority management team, the hospital infection control team and a general practitioner. Other members may include the regional epidemiologist if in post, epidemiologists from the CDSC, and microbiologists with particular expertise in identifying cryptosporidium.

12.14 Since water distribution systems are not co-terminous with the areas of district health authorities or local authorities, co-operation between neighbouring authorities is essential and it is recommended that only one Outbreak Control Team should be established by local agreement. The lead would usually be assumed by the DPH or the CCDC in the authority which first suspected an outbreak or in which most cases of illness were identified.

Terms of reference

12.15 The terms of reference of the Outbreak Control Team should include the following:

i to review the evidence for an outbreak and the results of epidemiological and microbiological investigations;

ii to decide on control measures and to determine the necessary commitment of personnel and resources;

iii to make on-going arrangements for informing the public;

iv to decide when the outbreak has finished;

v after the outbreak, to prepare for submission to the Drinking Water Inspectorate and the Department of Health and to the health authorities, local authorities and water companies concerned, its report of the outbreak containing recommendations for further action.

12.16 Arrangements should be made for the Team to meet frequently and regularly throughout the course of the outbreak. Full administrative and secretarial services must be provided to support the Team. There should be an agenda for each meeting. Confidential minutes should record all decisions taken.

Control measures

12.17 The Outbreak Control Team has a major role in co-ordinating the action taken by the health and local authorities and the water companies in the context of their own plans and in agreeing, for example, epidemilogical studies or microbiological sampling programmes. Although health and local authorities and water companies all have statutory duties regarding the health and safety of the population and the provision of alternative water supplies, they should act together through the Outbreak Control Team to decide on appropriate control measures.

12.18 If a water supply is found to be contaminated by cryptosporidial oocysts, one course of action open to the water company would be to turn off the mains supply. A decision to turn off a supply would be taken only in the most extreme of circumstances because of the danger to public health and the potential fire hazard. Without water on tap, hygiene would be neglected, toilets would not be flushed because families could not carry sufficient water to their homes in buckets and similar containers, and domestic appliances would not work. Moreover, although water companies have a capacity to supply some water by tanker and bowser, the total volume they could supply to a town or conurbation would only be a small fraction of that used normally. Much industrial and commercial activity would come to a halt and life in the community would be extremely difficult.

12.19 As cryptosporidial oocysts can be destroyed by high temperatures, an alternative course of action would be to maintain the mains supply but advise consumers to bring to the boil all water used for drinking and culinary purposes. A decision to give such advice should be taken in the light of all the circumstances which can best be assessed by the Outbreak Control Team. It is important to note that a 'boil water notice' or 'order' has no statutory basis or authority, so for that reason, the terms are avoided in this Report.

12.20 A decision by the Outbreak Control Team to advise consumers to boil their water needs to be taken in the context of the known and potential risks to different groups posed by the level of contamination and the range of alternative supplies available. Risk assessment, for example, might suggest that while risks to the community as a whole were small and that general advice was not justified, advice to specific, high-risk groups might be appropriate. Alternatively, supplies in bags or bottles might be provided for those groups. It should be recognised, however, that generally there would be little advantage in providing alternative supplies from tankers and bowsers because water supplied in this way is subject to contamination as it is carried to and stored in the kitchen and, hence, has to be boiled before use.

Information to the public 12.21 It is essential that the interface with the media should be controlled from one location to be agreed by the Outbreak Control Team. In practice, this means that there should only be one designated spokesman for the Team.

12.22 The Outbreak Control Plan itself should contain guidelines on supplying information to the public and have set in place practical arrangements to facilitate speedy action by the Outbreak Control Team. During an incident, the Team will need to decide:

i the information to be made available to the press and public — there are advantages in providing a once daily update for the press at an agreed time;

ii the way in which information should be released for example by leaflets, letters, use of television, radio, newspapers and loudspeaker vans;

iii whether to establish a telephone information service for the public on both health and water matters.

12.23 In reaching decisions on these issues, the Team should be alert to the importance of providing early and clear information on the nature and scale of the problem and on the action recommended, if any, and of updating this information regularly. Such information should not, of course, compromise patient confidentiality.

12.24 Before advice is given to consumers, for example to boil their water, the Team would need to identify the target population and to formulate special advice for hospitals, schools and residential homes and for the food and catering industry. Announcements by means of radio, television, the press and loudspeaker are very effective, but experience reveals that not every consumer is reached by them. It is not only ethnic minorities and those who are deaf or who cannot read who are missed. It is therefore important to repeat announcements so long as the emergency lasts and to distribute leaflets to homes at a very early stage. Consumers must be told when the emergency is over. The logistics of giving advice can be seen to be extremely complicated so it follows that to be effective, it must be pre-planned and periodically tested and these tests should be reviewed and evaluated.

Health Authority Plan 12.25 The CCDC or MOEH (whoever is in post) has responsibility for drawing up the district health authority's own emergency plan to come into effect when an outbreak occurs, for coordinating all necessary action during the outbreak and for reviewing the action taken. He should notify the Chief Medical Officer of all major outbreaks, keep him informed of progress and make a final report to him incorporating the Outbreak Control Team report. The CDSC should also be kept informed.

12.26 In addition to the common elements referred to in paragraphs 12.3-12.10 above and the duties of the Outbreak Control Team (paragraphs 12.11–12.24), the health authority plan should include:

i an enhanced surveillance system for the early detection of cases of cryptosporidiosis in the community, based on reports from laboratories;

ii arrangements to be made to alert general practitioners of a suspected outbreak, with the request that they inform the CCDC of all cases of diarrhoea and that they promote high standards of hygiene in the community, especially in the affected families to prevent secondary spread from person to person;

iii arrangements to inform and advise the staff of NHS hospitals and other NHS premises, private hospitals and nursing homes and the support teams for immunosuppressed persons in the community, such as those with AIDS and those on renal dialysis;

iv arrangements for additional medical and nursing staff to be made available and beds designated in the event that significant numbers of patients need to be admitted to hospital in a large community outbreak;

v a review of the implications for NHS hospitals and other health premises of advice to boil water. A survey will need to be carried out in advance to ensure that adequate supplies of boiled water or safe alternative supplies can be provided if necessary.

Local Authority Plan

12.27   The local authority's emergency planning procedures will include action in the event of an outbreak of waterborne disease. District and borough councils are under a statutory duty to take such steps as they consider appropriate to keep themselves informed about the wholesomeness and sufficiency of water supplies within their areas. They may examine and sample the water supply and have a power of entry for the purpose of investigation. They may also require a water company to provide information.

12.28   The environmental health department has a major role in the education of the public and will wish to issue advice and guidance in the event of an outbreak of cryptosporidiosis. The local authority plan should therefore set out arrangements to inform and advise the public, the institutions for which it is responsible including schools and residential homes, the food and catering industry and other commercial organisations. It should include guidance on the action to be taken following the issue of advice to boil water.

12.29   The CEHO would be expected to prepare a report on a contamination incident for the environmental health or equivalent committee of the local authority. The authority could then consider the need for a formal submission through the Drinking Water Inspectorate to the Secretary of State for the Environment or the Secretary of State for Wales.

Water Company Plan

12.30   In common with the emergency plans of the health authority and local authority, the water company plan will need to set out individual responsibilities, communication routes within the water company and with other organisations and its role in the Outbreak Control Team (paragraphs 12.3–12.24). In addition, it should address three particular areas: monitoring and sampling procedures; action to deal with contamination and the provision of alternative supplies.

12.31   At present, routine monitoring of water supplies for the presence of cryptosporidial oocysts is not advocated. However, water companies may still become aware of potential contamination of supplies and are under a duty to notify the health authority, local authority and the Drinking Water Inspectorate of any incident likely to cause a significant health risk. If a waterborne outbreak is suspected, action should be taken:

i to establish the boundaries of the water supply zone under suspicion;

ii to provide the Outbreak Control Team with up to date information (including maps) on water sources and distribution to the affected population;

iii to investigate the possibility of source pollution, for example, by incidents of pollution upstream of the raw water intake, liaising with the NRA, the MAFF Veterinary Investigation Service, practising veterinary officers and farmers as appropriate, to establish what relevant farming practices have recently taken place and whether there has been an outbreak of cryptosporidiosis in livestock in the catchment area;

iv to establish whether any significant operational changes have taken place at the water treatment works, for example, by-passing of some element of treatment, or change in coagulant used;

v to establish, by scrutinising records, whether there have been any unusual variations from normal operating conditions, for example:

    a changes in raw water, for example, high turbidity, high colour, unusually high or low pH or changes in its microbiological quality;

    b coagulation control lost or difficult;

    c higher than usual turbidity of filtrate;

    d filter runs of abnormal length;

    e unusually high throughputs, or unusually rapid changes in throughput;

    f changes in the microbiological quality of treated water;

    g unusually high demands for chlorine;

vi to establish as soon as possible an investigative programme of monitoring for cryptosporidial oocysts.

12.32 The water company will undertake the programme of monitoring but because of the complexities of the sampling procedures and the need for cross-checking of results by independent laboratories with specialist experience, it is important to agree in advance with other members of the Outbreak Control Team how this should be organised. It would be advisable to monitor at the same time for other pathogenic microorganisms. Results of all tests should be made available immediately to the members of the Outbreak Control Team.

12.33 The water company will need to consider measures to eradicate cryptosporidial oocysts from the system. Action should be considered even if oocysts have not been detected in the water supply when initial descriptive epidemiology is suggestive of a waterborne source. Possible remedial measures associated with each stage are set out in table 12.1 although not all stages will be relevant in each case.

12.34 The water company's plan should also include details of how alternative supplies are to be proved to any priority groups identified by the health authority and local authority.

13 Research

**Development of a
National Research
Programme**

13.1 The gaps in the knowledge of cryptosporidium identified by the Group have been drawn together into a national research programme. The Department of the Environment (DoE) is funding the main laboratory work. The water companies, the Foundation for Water Research (FWR) and the National Rivers Authority (NRA) are providing additional funding for the surveys of occurrence. The programme is itemised in table 13.1 and the various elements discussed below.

Table 13.1 Elements of the National Research Programme:

Research Item	Investigators	Sponsors
Development of standard method of isolation and measurement	Standing Committee of Analysts	DoE
Novel methods of enumeration	Scottish Parasite Diagnostic Laboratory, Glasgow (SPDL)	DoE
Viability of oocysts	Scottish Parasite Diagnostic Laboratory, Glasgow (SPDL)	DoE
Specificity	Contract to be awarded	DoE
Infective dose	SPDL Glasgow	DoE
	Public Health Laboratory Rhyl PHLS/Moredun Institute Edinburgh	DoE
Survey of oocyst occurrence in water sources	Severn Trent Water Ltd, Thames Water Utilities Ltd, Anglican Water Services Ltd, Southern Water Services Ltd, Yorkshire Water Services Ltd, Water Research Centre	Severn Trent Water Ltd, Thames Water Utilities Ltd, Anglican Water Services Ltd, Southern Water Services Ltd, Yorkshire Water Services Ltd, Foundation for Water Research National Rivers Authority DoE
Epidemiology	Communicable Disease Surveillance Centre	DoE DH
Removal in water treatment	SPDL Glasgow Water Research Centre	Foundation for Water Research
	University College London	DoE SERC
Disinfection Studies	Water Research Centre	DoE
	Public Health Laboratory Rhyl	Industrial Sponsors
Quality Assurance	SPDL Glasgow Public Health Laboratory Rhyl	DoE
Coordination	Water Research Centre	DoE

Separation and
measurement of oocysts

13.2   The objective of sampling methods is to obtain effective removal of oocysts from large volumes of water within an acceptable period and to ensure that oocysts can subsequently be removed from the filter for laboratory counting. The present system employs a cartridge filter which is inefficient and gives variable results. Other filters have been tried which remove more oocysts from the water sample but it has then proved difficult to release the oocysts intact from the filters.

13.3   Subsequent separation, concentration and counting of the oocysts is time consuming, labour intensive and costly. In contrast to stool analysis, the procedure for environmental samples is more difficult because quantification is required, concentrations are low and other suspended matter in water can interfere with microscopic examination. The present procedure has been standardised in a provisional method published in May 1990 by the UK Standing Committee of Analysts (paragraphs 3.5–3.13).

13.4   One area of research concerns the method of concentrating the oocysts after their removal from the filter. A possible approach is by the use of magnetic particles and this is part of the research commissioned at the Scottish Parasite Diagnostic Laboratory (SPDL) at Stobhill Hospital, Glasgow.

13.5   A further subject for research concerns the staining techniques used as part of the microscopic examination. A number of different approaches are being tested in the research programme, also at SPDL.

13.6   The work set in hand should pave the way for improved measurement techniques which, it is hoped, will be adaptable to routine work in water company laboratories.

Specificity and viability

13.7   Present methods of detecting oocysts are as yet unable to distinguish the oocysts of *Cryptosporidium parvum* which can infect humans from oocysts of other species of cryptosporidium which are not known to infect man. Nor can they determine whether the oocysts are alive or dead.

13.8   Included in the national programme, therefore, is work at SPDL to develop laboratory tests of viability. Selected laboratories have also been invited to submit proposals for work on specificity, possibly involving the use of gene probes or monoclonal antibodies.

Occurrence of
cryptosporidium in
water; associated
epidemiology

13.9   A limited amount of survey work has been carried out by water companies following the waterborne outbreaks of cryptosporidiosis in England and Scotland, with some intensive work in the areas affected. The results showed that snapshot sampling was not very rewarding and the Group considered that a more detailed continuing examination of a few sources would give better information on the extent and pattern of occurrence and the likely origins of the oocysts.

13.10   In a programme lasting 12 months, three river stretches and six boreholes have been chosen for a study with the former sampled three times each week and the latter weekly. More intensive sampling will be instituted should significant numbers of oocysts be detected.

13.11   The river stretches have been selected in collaboration with Severn Trent Water, Thames Water Utilities and Yorkshire Water Services, with Anglian Water Services and Southern Water Services covering the boreholes. The companies are carrying out the sampling and providing half the cost of analysis with counterfunding from the FWR and the NRA. Quality assurance work is funded by DoE and carried out at SPDL and PHLS Rhyl.

13.12   In parallel with the sampling and analysis programme, epidemiological studies have been initiated under the direction of the PHLS Communicable Disease Surveillance Centre in the areas supplied with water from the sources included in the survey. By means of enhanced surveillance and the use of questionnaires, an attempt will be made to establish whether there is a relationship between the occurrence of oocysts in water and episodes of disease in the community. In this way, it is hoped to obtain more immediate data than that obtained by retrospective investigation of outbreaks of cryptosporidiosis where almost certainly any increases in the numbers of oocysts in the raw water are likely to have been missed.

Removal during water treatment

13.13   Comprehensive studies of the removal of oocysts in full scale water treatment works have not so far been carried out. Some studies have been undertaken in the course of investigation of potential contamination of works but there are difficulties with this type of study not least to be sure that oocysts will be found in the water once a comprehensive and costly system of sampling has been set up. Furthermore, during any such survey, conditions are likely to be changed in an attempt to minimise the passage of oocysts through the works. In spite of these difficulties, some work of this kind is included in the national research programme and also in some studies being carried out by SPDL for the Water Research Centre (WRc) with funds from the FWR.

13.14   Another approach is the use of a smaller scale pilot plant. This has the advantage of being separate from the normal supply system and, providing that adequate attention is paid to safety aspects, the plant can be seeded with oocysts on a trial basis. In such an experimental unit, all processes and chemicals applied can be varied. Some water companies are already undertaking small-scale pilot plant studies but the Group considered that an extension of this research should await the results of other studies already included in the programme.

13.15   The Group considered that some basic laboratory studies were needed to examine the removal of oocysts by conventional water treatment processes. In particular this should include the efficacy of coagulants and coagulant aids, and work on the basic electrical and surface properties of oocysts.

13.16   In the national programme, the main laboratory studies on these topics are being carried out by University College, London with DoE funding and grant aid from 1 October 1990 from the Science and Engineering Research Council (SERC). Additional items in this study include the use of surrogate organisms and the use of optical methods for monitoring the presence of oocysts in raw and treated waters. Work on electrical and other surface properties has also been included in the SPDL programme on the biology of the organism.

Disinfection

13.17   The Group regards research into disinfection as of paramount importance. It is clear from previous research that chlorine, at the concentrations which could be used in waterworks, is ineffective in killing oocysts. This has far-reaching implications for water companies because disinfection is used as the final barrier in treatment to prevent waterborne disease.

13.18   Work on alternative disinfectants is in progress in a number of laboratories including some in the UK and the USA. Studies in Brussels indicate that ozone and chlorine dioxide could be effective against oocysts with doses of ozone and contact times within practicable limits for water treatment. Further laboratory studies of ozone are being carried out at the WRc, funded by DoE and in pilot-scale work by the PHLS, Rhyl, in conjunction with industrial sponsors.

13.19   Apart from assessing the effectiveness of disinfectants using an acceptable test of viability, it is important to consider other aspects of safety in their use, for example the possible formation of hazardous by-products from organic materials in the water. The means of incorporating such processes in conventional treatment and the need to maintain a residual level of disinfectant in distribution systems are subjects which need further research.

Point of use devices

13.20   Little is known about the efficiency of point of use devices in removing oocysts or the potential risks in disposing of spent units which could contain high concentrations of oocysts. As part of a DoE sponsored project, the efficency of different types of unit will be investigated and protocols drawn up to assist in the further evaluation of such units, including any problems which they may pose.

Quality assurance

13.21   Much of the national research programme involves measurement of oocysts in a variety of water samples. In view of the complexity of the procedures and the inherent inaccuracies in measurement, the Group considered it essential that quality assurance procedures should be incorporated into the programme.

13.22   Important aspects are positive identification of oocysts and cross-checks on quantitative enumeration. This involves ensuring that laboratories carrying out evaluations have staff capable of using the complex standard procedures and the establishment of a system of reference to two specialist laboratories for duplicate analysis.

Medical research

13.23   Some elements of the research programme already discussed are of considerable interest to the medical profession, for example, the work on specificity of cryptosporidial oocysts and the epidemiological studies.

13.24   Little is known about the minimum infective dose of cryptosporidial oocysts to man and such information would be helpful in deciding on appropriate standards to be met in water supply. As part of the national programme, SPDL will be carrying out work funded by DoE on infectivity in mice and, in conjunction with an African laboratory, on infectivity in primates. Also as part of the programme funded by DoE, work will be carried out at the Moredun Research Institute, Edinburgh in collaboration with the PHLS Rhyl, to investigate infectivity in lambs.

Further Research

13.25   The ongoing research will not provide answers to all the problems relating to cryptosporidium. Further funding will be required to support work which will build upon the results from the present phase. The development of a disinfectant capable of killing cryptosporidial oocysts seems to be the priority and, in particular, it may be appropriate to devote additional funding to research into the use of ozone. Even if a disinfectant for cryptosporidium is found, this will not entirely eliminate the disease in the community and the development of a specific treatment is an urgent priority.

14 Conclusions and recommendations*

The Organism
Detection and viability

There are many gaps in the current state of knowledge about cryptosporidium which limit our ability to devise more satisfactory ways of controlling the impact of the organism on man. Current methods for the detection of oocysts in environmental samples are inefficient and unreliable and likely to lead to an underestimate of the numbers present. Furthermore, these methods are not yet able to distinguish between different species of oocysts or to determine whether the oocysts detected are viable and therefore capable of causing infection.

Recommendations

14.1   Research should be undertaken:

i to improve current methods for the isolation, identification and enumeration of cryptosporidial oocysts in environmental samples; (Chapter 3)

ii to develop methods (for example, specific antibodies and gene probes) for distinguishing the different species of cryptosporidium; (paras 2.3–2.4, 3.11)

iii on the viability of oocysts recovered from environmental samples and the survival of oocysts in the environment; (para 2.10)

iv on ways in which the oocysts may be killed or rendered non-infective. (para 2.11)

14.2   Because the techniques involved in analysing environmental samples for cryptosporidium are highly complex and specialised, research programmes should provide for results to be cross-checked with one of the specialist laboratories working in this field. (Chapter 3, paras 13.21–13.22)

Pathogenicity

Originally species of cryptosporidium were each thought to be confined to one host but this has been shown not to be the case. However, the only species that is believed to be an important cause of disease in man is *Cryptosporidium parvum*.

Recommendation

14.3   Research should be undertaken into the pathogenicity of different species of cryptosporidium for man. (paras 2.3, 2.13)

Control of Cryptosporidium in the Environment
Occurrence

Evidence on the occurrence of cryptosporidium in the environment is very limited. It does, however, seem likely that there exists in many waters a background level of oocysts which may be increased by heavy rainfall, agricultural contamination or possibly other factors.

---

* Most of the recommendations given in this Chapter apply to the whole of the UK but refer to the organisational arrangements which apply in England and Wales. The different bodies and their responsibilities in Scotland are outlined in Part II(XI).

Recommendation	14.4 Research should be undertaken to determine the levels of oocysts occurring in different types of water sources in the UK including ground water and to seek to determine the origin of these oocysts. (Chapter 4)
Catchment Control	Although small numbers of cryptosporidial oocysts may occur from time to time in most environmental waters, a risk to health is only likely to arise if an unusually high concentration of oocysts occurs in the water source. Should this happen, although water treatment processes will remove large numbers of oocysts, a significant number may still pass through into the final drinking water. Catchment control may reduce the risk of this occurring and is therefore of considerable importance. The prevalence of cryptosporidial infection in livestock makes it likely that the majority of oocysts found in both ground and surface water derive from agricultural sources. Contamination may also arise from the disposal of the products of sewage treatment processess when infection exists in the community.
Recommendations	14.5 The Ministry of Agriculture Fisheries and Food and the National Rivers Authority should review advice on the storage and disposal of animal manure in order to reduce further the contamination of water courses and ground water, particularly close to water abstraction points. (paras 4.3–4.5)
	14.6 The National Rivers Authority, water companies and those responsible for private supplies, should in collaboration with the Ministry of Agriculture Fisheries and Food, seek ways to reduce contamination of water sources, particularly close to water abstraction points including boreholes and wells. (Chapter 4)
	14.7 In the longer term, the Ministry of Agriculture Fisheries and Food should promote the development of safer methods for the use of manure (solid and liquid) as a fertiliser in agriculture. (paras. 4.3-4.5)
	14.8 The Department of the Environment and sewerage undertakers should consider ways of improving sewage treatment processes to effect a further reduction in the pathogens in sewage effluent and sewage sludge. (paras 4.6-4.8)
Cryptosporidiosis in Man Laboratory analysis and reporting	An accurate assessment of the incidence of cryptosporidiosis is difficult because laboratory policies for examining stools are not standardised and in England and Wales, laboratories are not required to report positive findings.
Recommendations	14.9 As soon as practicable, the Department of Health should designate cryptosporidiosis as a "reportable" disease as defined in the Review of Law on Infectious Disease Control (Department of Health, 1989). (paras 6.1-6.3)
	14.10 The Public Health Laboratory Service, in association with other NHS and private laboratories, should review and standardise policies for examining faecal samples for cryptosporidium. (paras 6.1-6.3)
Animals as a source of infection	Cryptosporidiosis is normally acquired by the faecal-oral route whereby oocysts excreted in the faeces of an infected animal are ingested by a susceptible person. Livestock are an important reservoir of cryptosporidial infection and direct transmission from animal to man is considered to be a major route of infection. Good personal hygiene can minimise the risk of acquiring the infection.

Recommendations	14.11 Environmental health officers should issue guidance to farmers, veterinarians, and others who come into contact with livestock on the importance of personal hygiene to protect themselves and their families from cryptosporidial infection. (para 6.7)
	14.12 Environmental health officers and health educators should issue guidance to schools on the particular importance of personal hygiene for children who are to go on farm visits or have contact with farm animals and on the need to report to the local Consultant for Communicable Disease Control or Medical Officer for Environmental Health any subsequent significant diarrhoeal illness among such children. (para 6.7)
Person to person spread of infection	Person to person spread is now recognised as a major route of transmission of cryptosporidiosis. Normal personal hygiene, including the washing of hands after using the toilet and before eating, reduces the risk of spread of secondary infection in this way. Such precautions are particularly important during an outbreak.
Recommendations	14.13. In an outbreak of cryptosporidiosis, those responsible should ensure that extra care is taken over personal hygiene, particularly:

i in playgroups, nursery schools and day care centres; (para 6.9)

ii in hospitals where infected patients and staff may transmit the illness to other patients and staff unless appropriate precautions are taken; (para 6.9)

iii in water treatment works which may be contaminated. (para 7.29) |
| | 14.14   In an outbreak of cryptosporidiosis, environmental health officers, health educators, general practitioners and others responsible, should actively promote high standards of hygiene in the community, especially in the affected families to prevent secondary spread from person to person. (paras 6.9, 12.26, 12.28). |
| Waterborne infection | Water is now known to be an important vehicle of transmission of cryptosporidial infection and several community outbreaks of cryptosporidiosis in the UK and the USA have been linked with mains water supply. Since both zoonotic and person to person spread are also important, only a proportion of the 9,000 cases reported in Britain in 1989 can be linked with water. When viewed nationally, the number of waterborne cases of cryptosporidiosis comprises only a very small fraction of all cases of diarrhoea. Their significance lies in the fact that should the mains water become contaminated, many cases of illness may occur in the area of supply. (Recommendations relating to contamination of mains water supply follow from Recommendation 19 onwards).

Since most environmental waters may be contaminated with low numbers of oocysts from time to time, there must also be a slight risk of infection directly from these waters. |
| Recommendation | 14.15   The appropriate Government departments should issue advice to the public that:

i water not intended for consumption should not be drunk (for example, by ramblers or campers) without first being boiled;

ii people who use rivers, reservoirs and inland waterways for recreational purposes may run a slight risk of contracting cryptosporidiosis from the ingestion of contaminated water. (para 6.11) |
| Travellers' diarrhoea | Cryptosporidiosis is emerging as an important cause of travellers' diarrhoea. |

Recommendation	14.16 The Department of Health should draw to the attention of doctors that cryptosporidium is a significant cause of travellers' diarrhoea. (para 6.12)
Clinical aspects	Cryptosporidiosis is an unpleasant diarrhoeal illness from which otherwise healthy people usually recover with supportive treatment in about two to three weeks, although the severity and duration of illness varies considerably. In immunosuppressed patients, particularly those with AIDS, the disease is much more serious and potentially life-threatening.
Recommendation	14.17 In view of the severity of cryptosporidiosis in immunosuppressed patients, the Department of Health should draw to doctors' attention the need to advise such patients on ways to minimise the risk of contracting the infection. (para 6.21)
Infective dose	Little is yet known about the infective dose of cryptosporidium for man.
Recommendation	14.18 Research should be undertaken into the minimum infective dose of cryptosporidium for man. (para 6.17)
Water Treatment and Distribution Current water treatment practices	Water treatment is an integrated operation, although it proceeds through a series of unit processes each of which contributes to the safety of the treated water supply. Each individual process has an essential and defined role, which cannot be changed or set aside without some risk of cryptosporidial oocysts passing into the public supply. Evidence from documented outbreaks of cryptosporidiosis suggests that the risk of oocysts penetrating the treatment works increases under certain circumstances.
Recommendations	14.19 To minimise the risk of cryptosporidial oocysts passing into public water supplies, water companies should pay particular attention to the following:

i the operation of rapid filters should avoid sudden surges of flow which may dislodge retained deposits; (paras 7.17–7.22, 10.2)

ii rapid filters should not be restarted after shutdown without backwashing; (paras 7.20, 10.2)

iii after cleaning, slow sand filters should not be brought back into use without an adequate "ripening period"; (paras 7.25–7.26)

iv by-passing of part of the water treatment process should be avoided. (Chapter 7, para 10.3)

14.20   Water companies should install monitors to make it possible to measure the turbidity on each rapid filter to assist early detection of conditions which may favour the breakthrough of oocysts into the treated water. (paras 7.22, 10.2)

14.21   Water companies should assess the value of coagulant aids to assist flocculation and retention of oocysts. (para 7.15)

14.22   Water companies should maintain borehole linings and seals to a high standard. (paras 7.4–7.5)

Developments in water treatment	When operated optimally and assuming no more than background levels of oocysts in raw water sources, current water treatment processes appear able to prevent contamination of water supplies by cryptosporidial oocysts. Nonetheless, current practices cannot guarantee the removal of all oocysts and since the infective dose of cryptosporidium for man may be a very small, this is a cause for concern.

Since the standard method of disinfecting treated water supplies by chlorination in ineffective against cryptosporidial oocysts, alternative disinfectants are required, particularly to treat recycled waste water from the water treatment process. There may also prove to be scope for changes at water treatment works to increase the removal of oocysts, for example by improvements to coagulant methods utilising the electrical and other surface properties of the oocysts, and by using different types of filters. |
| Recommendation | 14.23   Research is required into:

i the effect of ozone and other disinfectants, including chlorine dioxide and the use of ultraviolet light, on cryptosporidial oocysts and the potential for the use of these agents in water treatment, particularly in the treatment of recycled water from the water treatment process; (paras 7.27–7.34)

ii the electrical and other surface properties of the oocyst and the scope for applying the knowledge gained in water treatment processes; (para 7.14)

iii the use of different types of filters capable of trapping oocysts. (paras 7.17–7.19) |
| Disposal of contaminated sludge and process waste water | If a water treatment works exceptionally becomes contaminated with cryptosporidial oocysts, process waste water and sludge may contain very high numbers of oocysts. Eventually it is hoped that methods will be found to kill the oocysts and thereby remove any risk from recycling washwater or from returning large numbers of oocysts in sludge to land. In the short term, water companies must make arrangements for the disposal of sludge and washwater to minimise the risk of further contamination of water courses. |
| Recommendations | 14.24   Water companies should make arrangements with the appropriate authorities, including the National Rivers Authority, to dispose of sludge, which has become contaminated with oocysts, to designated sites where subsequent contamination of water courses is avoided. (para 7.28)

14.25   Water companies should establish with the National Rivers Authority contingency plans for the disposal of process waste water from the treatment process when it is contaminated with oocysts. (para 7.29) |
| Distribution system | The normal management of the distribution network should involve no hazard from cryptosporidial oocysts. Contamination may occur in an emergency when reduced water pressure may permit ground water, including possibly sewage leaked from sewers, to penetrate into the distribution system. Routine disinfection with chlorine following an emergency or during planned repair and replacement of mains, as set out in the existing Operational Guidelines*, cannot provide a safeguard against contamination with cryptosporidial oocysts although it is effective against other pathogens. |

* Operational Guidelines for the Protection of Drinking Water Supplies (WAA Sept. 1988.)

Recommendation	14.26 Water companies and the Drinking Water Inspectorate should keep under review the existing guidelines* for the repair and maintenance of distribution systems and should modify them whenever possible to take advantage of new methods of sampling and disinfection as these become available. (paras 7.35–7.36)
Service reservoirs	Most water distribution systems contain service reservoirs, some of which may be grass-covered and grazed by livestock.
Recommendation	14.27 In accordance with the current guidelines*, water companies should ensure that the grazing of livestock is not practised on grass-covered service reservoirs. (para 7.37)
Point of Use Devices	Point of use devices are sometimes used in an attempt to improve the quality of drinking water, whether from private or public supplies. Reliable data on the efficiency and safety of these devices are lacking.
Recommendations	14.28 Research should be undertaken:

14.28 Research should be undertaken:

i on the efficiency of point of use devices in removing contaminants, including cryptosporidial oocysts;

ii on the possible hazards that may be caused through the retention by point of use devices of harmful organisms or substances. (Chapter 8)

14.29 The Department of the Environment should promote the establishment of a testing protocol to set standards for point of use devices. (Chapter 8)

Monitoring for Cryptosporidial Oocysts
Monitoring strategy

The provisional method approved for the sampling, concentration and indentification of cryptosporidial oocysts is inefficient and unreliable, particularly at low levels. Furthermore it is not yet possible to distinguish the different species of cryptosporidium or to determine the viability of any oocysts detected. Given these shortcomings in the methodology and until more information is available from current research about the occurrence of cryptosporidium in water sources, the Group does not feel able to recommend that water companies should undertake routine monitoring of treated water for cryptosporidium. However, evidence from the documented outbreaks of cryptosporidiosis points to an increased risk of oocyst contamination following accidental agricultural pollution of source water or following a period of exceptionally heavy rainfall after a dry spell, especially when associated with recent spreading of slurry on agricultural land in the catchment area. The risks appear slightly higher in the spring and autumn. It also seems likely that water supplies are more susceptible to oocyst contamination when there has been a major change in water treatment process or, exceptionally, when a normal treatment process (such as a slow sand filter) has to be by-passed for operational reasons.

Recommendations

14.30 In association with local agricultural interests, the National Rivers Authority and health and local authorities, each water company should develop a strategy for monitoring treated water supplies which takes into account the importance of local environmental and agricultural factors in different catchment areas. (paras 10.4-10.6)

14.31 Each water company should regularly review its monitoring strategy. (para 10.6).

* Operational Guidelines for the Protection of Drinking Water Supplies (WAA Sept. 1988.)

14.32 In formulating a monitoring strategy, water companies should consider the desirability of monitoring treated water for cryptosporidial oocysts in the following circumstances:

i following exceptional contamination of water sources by agricultural pollution or sewage;

ii for a transitional period when a significant planned change in a water treatment process or distribution network takes place;

iii when, for exceptional operational reasons, the water treatment process is operating abnormally;

iv when turbidity readings or levels of indicator or other organisms deviate from the normal ranges;

v if an outbreak of cryptosporidiosis in the community is suspected as being linked to a water supply. (para 10.7)

Monitoring in an Outbreak

If a waterborne outbreak of cryptosporidiosis is suspected, water companies will need to establish an investigative programme of monitoring to determine whether oocysts are present at any stage in the water supply system.

Recommendation

14.33 If a waterborne outbreak of cryptosporidiosis is suspected, the water company should establish an investigative programme for monitoring for cryptosporidial oocysts as soon as possible and representative samples for examination should be taken from:

i the source waters;

ii the surrounding catchment areas and mud deposits in reservoirs, especially if there is evidence of the spreading of manure;

iii treatment works including backwash water sludge, filter beds and any recycled water;

iv pipelines and service reservoirs, especially if information on the geographical spread of the disease indicates an affected area smaller than the total area served by the water supply;

v points in the distribution network where contaminated water may still remain even after it has been flushed out of the rest of the system. (para 10.8)

Implementation

Although routine monitoring is not advocated at the present time, water companies need to be ready to implement a programme of monitoring should the need arise.

Recommendations

14.34 Water companies should have trained staff and the equipment available to sample water supplies for cryptosporidial oocysts and should make arrangements in advance so that these samples can be examined expeditiously when required. These arrangements must include provision for independent sampling and for cross-checking of the results of examination by independent laboratories with specialist experience. (paras 10.10, 12.32)

14.35 To ensure quality control, the Public Health Laboratory Service should promote the development of a national accreditation scheme for laboratories testing for cryptosporidium. (para 10.10)

Epidemiological studies

When an outbreak of cryptosporidiosis is recognised, it is clearly important that the source of infection is identified as soon as possible. Water may be suspected as a possible route of infection if epidemiological surveys reveal infection concentrated in particular localities served by a common water supply or if a significant number of primary cases is occurring among adults.

Recommendation

14.36 When an outbreak of cryptosporidiosis is recognised, the Director of Public Health should ensure that:

i medical laboratory services in the affected and surrounding areas consider the desirability of screening all stool samples for cryptosporidial oocysts; (para 10.11)

ii epidemiological investigation is undertaken at an early stage to indentify possible sources of disease and modes of transmission; (para 10.12)

iii where epidemiological survey establishes a link with pet animals, specimens are taken from these animals to ensure that they are not a source of infection; (para 10.13)

iv the Ministry of Agriculture Fisheries and Food Veterinary Investigation Centres are consulted to establish information on significant recent diarrhoeal disease in livestock on farms within the local water supply catchment or upstream of an abstraction point; (para 10.13)

v consideration is given to the establishment of case control studies. (para 10.14)

Investigation and Management of an Outbreak

Health authorities, local authorities and water companies already have policies and plans for the recognition and control of outbreaks of communicable disease, which should include arrangements to be made when water is suspected as a vehicle for the transmission of infection in the community. However, it is most important that close liaison is maintained routinely between health and local authorities and water companies to detect at a very early stage those situations in which the community may be at risk from infection. Should an outbreak occur, close cooperation at all times between these organisations is essential.

Recommendations
Plans

14.37 Health authorities, local authorities and water companies should review the adequacy of their existing emergency plans for dealing with a suspected waterborne outbreak of cryptosporidiosis and should together draw up an Outbreak Control Plan for the control of infection in the community, on the basis of the best practices outlined in Chapter 12. (Chapter 12)

14.38 Arrangments should be made to ensure that the plans are regularly tested and kept up-to-date and that any action recommended following an outbreak is carried out. (para 12.5)

14.39 Each of the plans should set out clearly:

i the statutory duties of the organisation and the responsibilities of named individuals; (paras 12.6–12.7)

ii the communication network to operate both routinely and on an emergency basis within the organisation and with other organisations such as the Ministry of Agriculture Fisheries and Food Veterinary Investigation Service and the National Rivers Authority. The chief officers involved should be the Director of Public Health, the Chief Environmental Health Officer and the water company's Technical Director or Director of Operational Services or equivalent; (paras 12.8–12.10)

iii the options available for the control of an outbreak and the action that would be required to implement them; (paras 12.17–12.30) iv guidelines on supplying information to the media and the public and the practical arrangements necessary to ensure speedy action. (paras 12.21–12.24)

Outbreak control team

14.40   The Outbreak Control Plan should provide for the establishment of an Outbreak Control Team which includes members from the health authority, local authority and water company, to be called into being by the Director of Public Health should he suspect an outbreak. (paras 12.11, 12.14)

14.41   Members of the Outbreak Control Team should be of such seniority and expertise that they are able to commit the organisations they represent to action. (paras 12.7, 12.13)

14.42   The terms of reference of the Outbreak Control Team should include the following:

i to review the evidence for an outbreak and the results of epidemiological and microbiological investigations;

ii to decide on control measures and to determine the necessary commitment of personnel and resources;

iii to make on-going arrangements for informing the public;

iv to decide when the outbreak has finished;

v after the outbreak, to prepare for submission to the Drinking Water Inspectorate and the Department of Health and to the health authorities, local authorities and water companies concerned, its report of the outbreak containing recommendations for further action. (para 12.15)

14.43   The Outbreak Control Team should meet frequently throughout the outbreak and should have full administrative and secretarial support. (para 12.16)

14.44   The Outbreak Control Team should decide on appropriate control measures, including whether to advise the public to boil all water used for drinking and culinary purposes. (paras 12.17–12.20)

14.45   Because of the complexities of issuing advice to boil water, the action required should be preplanned and periodically tested and evaluated by health authorities, local authorities and water companies. (para 12.24)

14.46   Information for the public and media during an outbreak should be controlled from one location to be agreed by the Outbeak Control Team. (paras 12.21–12.24)

Health authority plan

14.47   The health authority plan should specifically include:

i an enhanced surveillance system for the early detection of cases of cryptosporidiosis in the community, based on reports from laboratories;

ii arrangements to be made to alert general practitioners of a suspected outbreak, with the request that they inform the Consultant for Communicable Disease Control of all cases of diarrhoea and that they promote high standards of hygiene in the community, especially in the affected families to prevent secondary spread from person to person;

iii arrangements to inform and advise the staff of NHS hospitals and other NHS premises, private hospitals and nursing homes and the support teams for immunosuppressed persons in the community, such as those with AIDS and those on renal dialysis;

iv arrangements for additional medical and nursing staff to be made available and beds designated in the event that significant numbers of patients need to be hospitalised in a large community outbreak;

v a review of the implications for NHS hospitals and other health premises of advice to boil water. A survey will need to be carried out in advance to ensure that adequate supplies of boiled water or safe alternative supplies can be provided if necessary. (paras 12.25–12.26)

Local authority plan

14.48 The local authority plan should specifically include:

i arrangements to keep the authority informed about the quality of water supplies;

ii arrangements to inform and advise the public, the institutions including schools and residential homes for which it is responsible, the food and catering industry and other commercial organisations about an outbreak and on the action to be taken;

iii a review of the implications for the institutions for which it is responsible, the food and catering industry and other organisations of advice to boil water. (paras 12.27–12.29)

Water company plan

14.49 The water company plan should specifically include the action to be taken in the event of a suspected waterborne outbreak of cryptosporidiosis:

i to establish the boundaries of the water supply zone under suspicion;

ii to provide the Outbreak Control Team with up-to-date information (including maps) on water sources and distribution to the affected population;

iii to investigate the possibility of source pollution, for example, by incidents of pollution upstream of the raw water intake, liaising with the National Rivers Authority, the Ministry of Agriculture Fisheries and Food Veterinary Investigation Service, practising veterinary officers and farmers as appropriate, to establish what relevant farming practices have recently taken place and whether there has been an outbreak of cryptosporidiosis in livestock in the catchment area;

iv to establish whether any significant operational changes have taken place at the water treatment works, for example, by-passing of some element of treatment, or change in coagulant used;

v to establish by scrutinising records, whether there have been any unusual variations from normal operating conditions, for example:

a changes in raw water, for example, high turbidity, high colour, unusually high or low pH or changes in its microbiological quality;

b coagulation control lost or difficult;

c higher than usual turbidity of filtrate;

d filter runs of abnormal length;

e unusually high throughputs, or unusually rapid changes in throughput;

f changes in the microbiological quality of treated water;

g unusually high demands for chlorine;

vi to establish as soon as possible an investigative programme of monitoring for cryptosporidial oocysts;

vii to eliminate oocysts from water treatment processes, following the checklist in table 12.1;

71

viii to provide alternative supplies to any priority groups identified by the health authority and local authority where such action is agreed by the Outbreak Control Team to be necessary. (paras 12.30–12.34, table 12.1)

Future Research

Many of the topics identified by the Group as requiring research have already been included in the current national research programme. The programme will not provide answers to all the outstanding questions relating to cryptosporidium and further research will be required.

Recommendations

14.50   The Department of the Environment and water companies should promote further research into the development of a disinfectant capable of killing cryptosporidial oocysts, particularly into the use of ozone. (paras 13.17–13.19, 13.25)

14.51   The Department of Health should promote research into the development of a specific treatment for cryptosporidiosis. (para 13.25)

Part II – Paper I

Cryptosporidium – The Organism

Dr A E Wright

Former Director (retired)
Newcastle Regional Public Health Laboratory
Honorary Lecturer in Microbiology,
University of Newcastle upon Tyne

Introduction

Cryptosporidium is a small protozoan parasite found in man, in other mammals and also in birds, fish and reptiles. When first described at the turn of the century, the organism was thought to be nonpathogenic and indeed this view persisted into comparatively recent years. Tzipori[1], in a review, recorded only 15 reports of infection in animals prior to 1975. Since that date many scientific publications have appeared in the literature but most of the early papers described infection in animals especially calves, goats, lambs and pigs. The first description of infection in humans was reported as late as 1976 in a healthy $3\frac{1}{2}$ year old child [2] who lived on a farm. Subsequent human cases reported were confined to those who had close associations with animals or who were immunocompromised, more especially those suffering from the Acquired Immunodeficiency Syndrome (AIDS). Hence the infection was at first considered to be an opportunistic or zoonotic pathogen in those exposed to a heavy dosage or who had some abnormality in their immunological response. The recognition of the disease in humans in the form of a severe travellers' diarrhoea,[3] in town dwellers[1] and its transmission from person to person[4] was not consistent with this view[5]. Indeed it began to be suspected that the agent could be waterborne and confirmation was soon forthcoming when waterborne outbreaks of cryptosporidiosis occurred in a normal population in Texas[6], other areas of North America and in the UK (see Part II(VII)). Subsequently, [8,9] the oocysts of cryptosporidium were seen in raw drinking water and also in an outbreak[10] in Georgia USA when an estimated 13,000 people were infected. Further confirmation of spread by drinking water was obtained in the UK[11] when 27 patients in Ayrshire in Scotland were infected from a water supply in which the presence of oocysts was subsequently confirmed. A survey in the UK[12] by the Public Health Laboratory Service concluded that cryptosporidium is a cause of sporadic acute infection in children and in the 1–5 age group it is almost as common as campylobacter infection and three times as common as infection with shigella. Since 1983 when laboratory reports began to be received in the PHLS Communicable Disease Surveillance Centre to 1989 over 20,000 cases of cryptosporidial infection have been recorded. Most outbreaks[12,13] were reported in families and day nurseries (See Part II(V)).

Classification

Cryptosporidium is related to a number of other protozoa known as the coccidia and these can be found in man and a wide variety of other animals. It belongs to a suborder called the *Eimeriina* which includes, in addition to cryptosporidium, *Toxoplasma gondii, Isospora belli* and *Eimeria.* All these protozoa are well known to the medical and veterinary professions. Many of these related organisms may cause little illness in their hosts suggesting that they are well adapted to their environment and probably thus of great antiquity. Cryptosporidium, however, differs from the other members of the suborder in as much as it is able to complete its life cycle within a single host. In addition, it develops within the outer layer of the cells of the intestinal or sometimes the respiratory tract of its host but without penetrating the main body or cytoplasm of the host cell. Thus, although intra-cellular, it appears to lie on the surface of these cells in a pseudo-external location.

The cyst, measuring about 5 microns in diameter, is referred to as an oocyst and it is this which is excreted by the host and ingested by a new host in contaminated food or water or more commonly by the faecal-oral route.

There are now recorded numerous species of the genus *Cryptosporidium.* These include *C.muris, C.meleagridis* and *C.baileyi* but the only one of significance in human terms appears to be *C.parvum.* The existence of several species may present problems in identification when these are observed in environmental specimens.

When the oocyst is established in the gastrointestinal tract of a new host hatching or excystation begins. The oocyst releases four tiny motile bodies called sporozoites which invade epithelial cells to form a trophozoite (feeding stage) in which the organism buds internally to form a schizont or meront – a form of asexual reproduction. There are two such asexual stages producing two types of meront. A further stage in development results in the formation of male and female gametocytes which enables a sexual cycle to take place. This produces a zygote and finally an oocyst which develops internally (sporulates) to form four sporozoites. These oocysts are mainly thick-walled forms which are passed in the faeces[1,14,15] for the whole cycle to repeat itself. Some oocysts are thin-walled and difficult to find in the faeces but release sporozoites *in situ* in the intestine thus causing autoinfection. Although oocysts can be identified in the faeces by those experienced in microscopy, laboratory diagnosis has relied on their demonstration by staining methods. More recently,[17] monoclonal antibodies have been developed and this more specific identification will enable the observer to distinguish cysts from other parasites and morphologically similar bodies.

Animal reservoirs

Although infection with cryptosporidium is widespread in mammals, birds and reptiles it is the young who are most likely to develop symptomatic infection. Adult animals appear to carry and transmit the organism with little constitutional upset. This may in fact indicate a true infective stage as immunoglobulins G and M have been demonstrated in both animals and man without symptoms[18]. Historically, cryptosporidium species were thought to be host specific but cross-transmission studies now show that this is not so. Certainly oocysts from mammals are infective for other mammals and avian strains for avians. Transmission from birds to mammals does not, apparently, occur.

Cross-transmission experiments may be of considerable importance in the study of the epidemiology of the disease in man for we need to know for instance if contamination of water supplies by birds is of any significance. Such cross-transmission of infection has been confirmed between man, cattle, pigs, and cats, all of which are capable of contaminating their environment and thus water and food. There is however some evidence to suggest that there are some strain differences manifest by a limit to the number of times an isolate from one mammal can be passaged in another. In some instances only very young animals can be colonised and clinical illness does not result.

In addition to those animals already mentioned, deer, guinea pigs, mice, rats and sheep may all be included as forming an animal reservoir. An important reservoir in the UK must be calves in which diarrhoea, sometimes of considerable severity, occurs in those aged between one and four weeks. The average length of illness is seven days and the diarrhoea, dehydration and weakness may cause a significant morbidity and some mortality. Another possibly important animal source in the UK is lambs[19] in which a number of outbreaks have been recorded. It may be of particular significance in investigating the reservoir of infections for humans to note that lambs which recover from the primary infection may have a second bout of diarrhoea at a later date. Another factor of epidemiological importance is that the developmental cycle of this protozoan may be as short as 72 hours in the new-born lamb[20].

Although children in contact with pets may become infected with cryptosporidium, the organism has only occasionally been found to occur in dogs and cats. Horses are not thought to be a common source. Pets which may excrete the oocyst include monkeys, mice, rabbits and guinea pigs and probably more exotic species. There is no evidence at present available to link birds, reptiles or fish to human cryptosporidiosis.

Determinants of oocyst viability

The viability of oocysts declines during storage although preparations can be made for use in the laboratory which will allow study over several months provided they are kept cool and moist. Storage at 4°C in 2.5 per cent (wt/vol) aqueous potassium dichromate allows viability to be retained for 3–4 months although one author claims that at this temperature viability was retained for a year. No other details of storage were given[21]. Other authorities claim a loss of viability at low temperatures irrespective of the method of storage. Freezing, freeze-drying and heating above 60°C for 30 mins will kill oocysts. Viability is also lost by heating to 65°C for 5–10 mins, by bringing to the boil or by drying.

Oocysts will resist treatment with 60 per cent alcohol, a procedure often used to free them from other organisms prior to innoculation experiments. Iodophores, sodium hyprochlorite, benzylkonium chloride and aldehyde disinfectants do not affect the oocyst although this will depend upon the concentration and the length of time of exposure. The use of formalin-ether mixtures in laboratory concentration techniques is also ineffective in altering the viability of the oocyst.

Effective disinfectants include hydrogen peroxide (10 vol), ozone at high concentrations, chlorine dioxide (Alcide) and ammonia (5 per cent). Excystation of sporozoites from oocysts appears to be favoured by CO_2, body temperature, reducing conditions and the presence of pancreatic enzymes and bile salts[16].

It has also been observed that excystment of cryptosporidium will develop in an air gas phase and when stimulated by gentle warming and hypotonic stress. Bile salts can be replaced by a detergent.

Survival and multiplication outside the host

In common with the encysted stage of other organisms, the oocyst of cryptosporidium is extremely resistant to adverse circumstances. It is probable that the oocyst can survive for long periods after excretion in the faeces of animals and man. It is resistant to chlorine at the levels used in water treatment and may penetrate filters and thus survive methods used for the purification of water.

There do not appear to be any necessary developmental stages of the life cycle occurring outside the body but *in vitro* development has been achieved in cell cultures[16].

Association with other organisms

Although cryptosporidiosis is now recognised as a disease of animals and man in its own right, some infections have been associated with the presence of other pathogenic organisms. In animals rotavirus, coronavirus and enteropathogenic *Escherichia coli* have each, at one time or another, been found in association with the oocysts during outbreaks of diarrhoea. Neverthelelss, bacteria-free isolates of cryptosporidium fed to gnotobiotic piglets, calves and lambs will cause clinical disease.

In man, unless immunocompromised, there is little published evidence to associate cryptosporidiosis with viral or bacterial infections.[8,19.] Association has been reported[22] with *Giardia intestinalis (Giardia lamblia)* but as both these parasites could easily be acquired from the same source there is no reason at the moment, to consider any relationship. In southern India, on the other hand, there is reported to be such a high prevalence of cryptosporidium in the general population[23] due to poor living conditions that its presence in faeces in patients with diarrhoea, often associated with other known pathogens, is not necessarily indicative of a causal role. In other parts of the world cryptosporidium is clearly assoicated with clinical illness and not related to the presence of other organisms in the faeces[19,24,25,26]. In countries in which patients with AIDS have been studied extensively, *Candida albicans* has frequently been found in association with cryptosporidium and there are reports of association with other pathogens such as cytomegalovirus and *Isospora*[15].

References

1. Tzipori S Cryptosporidiosis in Animals and humans. Microbiological reviews 1983 **47** 84–96.
2. Nime FA, Burek J D, Page D L, Holsher M A and Yardley J H Acute entercolitis in a human being infected with the protozoan *Cryptosporidium.* Gastroenterology 1976 **70** 592–8.
3. Jokipii L, Pokjola S and Jokipii AMM *Cryptosporidium:* a frequent finding in patients with gastrointestinal symptoms. Lancet 1983 **2** 358–361.
4. Baxby D, Hart CA and Taylor C Human cryptosporidiosis: A possible case of hospital cross infection. British Medical Journal 1983 **287** 1760–61.
5. Casemore DP and Jackson F B Hypothesis: cryptosporidiosis in human beings is not primarily a zoonosis. Journal of Infection 1984 **9** 153–156.
6. D'Antonio RG, Winn RE, Taylor JP et al. A waterborne outbreak of cryptosporidiosis in normal hosts. Annals of Internal Medicine 1985 **103** 886–88.
7. Isaac-Renton JL, Fogel D, Stibbs HH and Ongerth JE *Giardia* and *Cryptosporidium* in drinking water. Lancet 1987 **1** 973–974.
8. Casemore DP, Jessop, EG, Douce D, Jackson FB, *Cryptosporidium* plus *campylobacter:* An outbreak in a semi-rural population, Journal of Hygiene 1986. **96:** 95–105.
9. Rush B A, Chapman P A, Ineson R W *Cryptosporidium* and drinking water. Lancet 1987 **2** 632–633.
10. Hayes E B, Matte T D, O'Brian T R *et al.* Contamination of a conventionally treated filtered public water supply by *Cryptosporidium* associated with a large community outbreak of cryptosporidiosis. New England Journal of Medicine 1989 **320** 1372–6.
11. Smith H V, Girdwood R W A, Patterson W J *et al.* Waterborne Outbreak of Cryptosporidiosis. Lancet 1988 **2** 1484.
12. Casemore D P, Palmer S. and Biffin A. Cryptosporidiosis PHLS Microbiology Digest 1987 **4** 1–8.
13. Anon. *Cryptosporidium* surveillance PHLS CDR 1987 **45.**
14. Fayer R and Ungar B L P *Cryptosporidium* spp. and Cryptosporidiosis. Microbiological Reviews 1986 **50** 458–485.
15. Soave R, and Armstrong D Cryptosporidiosis reviews of Infectious Diseases 1986 **7** 1012–1023.

16. Current W L *Cryptosporidium:* Its biology and potential for environmental transmission. CRC Critical Reviews in Environmental Control. 1986 **17** 21–51.

17. McLauchlin J, Casemore D P, Harrison T G, Gerron P J, Samuel D and Taylor A G Identification of *Cryptosporidium* oocysts by monoclonal antibody. Lancet 1987 **1** 51.

18. Casemore D P The antibody response to *Cryptosporidium:* developments of a serological test and its use in a study of immunologically normal persons. Journal of Infection 1987 **14** 125–134.

19. Casemore D P Epidemiological aspects of human cryptosporidiosis. Epidemiology and Infection 1990 **104** 1–28.

20. Angus K W Cryptosporidiosis in man, domestic animals and birds: a review. Journal Royal Society of Medicine 1983 **76** 62–70.

21. Naciri M, Yvoré P, and Levieux D (1984) Cryptosporidiose du Chevreau. Influence de la prise du colostrum. Essair de traitements. In: Colloque International sur les maladies de la chèvre, Institut National de la recherche Agronomique, Niort, France, 9–11 Oct, pp 465–471.

22. Jokipii AMM, Hemila M and Jokipii L. Prospective study of acquisition of *Cryptosporidium, Giardia lamblia* and gastrointestinal illness. Lancet 1985 **2** 487–489.

23. Mathan M M, Venkatesan S, George R, Mathew M and Mathan V I Cryptosporidium and diarrhoea in Southern Indian Children. Lancet 1985 **2** 1172–1175.

24. Corbett Feeney G. *Cryptosporidium* among children with acute diarrhoea in the West of Ireland. Journal of Infection 1987 **14** 79–84.

25. Smith G and van den Ende J Cryptosporidiosis among black children in hospital in South Africa. Journal of Infection 1986 **13** 25–30.

26. Taylor D N and, Echeverria P. When does *Cryptosporidium* cause diarrhoea. Letter Lancet 1986 **1** 320.

Part II – Paper II

Epidemiology of Cryptosporidiosis in Animals

Martin W Gregory BVSc DipIEMVT PhD CBiol MBiol MRCVS
Parasitology Department,
Central Veterinary Laboratory,
New Haw, Weybridge, Surrey KT15 3NB, UK

Summary

Cryptosporidium is ubiquitous: animals probably become infected before reaching adulthood, although very few show signs of disease. *C parvum* is regarded as the pathogenic species in all domestic mammals as well as man. It tends to be troublesome only when the conditions under which the animals are kept lead to heavy infections and/or lowered resistance. Cryptosporidiosis is most important in calves, but is an increasing problem in lambs. In other species the disease is rare and usually sporadic. Transmission is mainly by ingestion of oocysts derived from faeces. Oocysts are resistant to most chemical disinfectants. Disease occurs in animals less than 3 weeks old that receive a heavy infection when their resistance is low. Causes of lowered resistance include colostrum-deprivation and any stress, such as weaning, overcrowding, and concurrent infection. Such conditions are liable to occur under modern intensive management, which also leads to heavy environmental contamination. Thus the incidence of disease tends to reflect the conditions under which the animals live rather than the prevalence of the organism.

Contents

The parasites

Parasite species and host specificity

Cryptosporidium parvum appears to be the only species of clinical importance to domestic mammals and man.[22] Tyzzer's original description[97] was of *C muris*, which he found in the stomachs of mice. This species has since been found in the stomachs of cattle[7,112] and mountain gazelles.[78] Anderson[1] speculates that Tyzzer's mice got the infection from cattle in the first place.

Birds are infected by *C meleagridis* and *C baileyi*.[48] There is no evidence that these two species can infect mammals.[47,63] Levine[46] includes chickens among the hosts of *C parvum*, but Pavlásek failed to infect them.[67] Lindsay *et al* failed to infect mammals with cryptosporidia from chickens,[47] and O'Donoghue[63] failed with oocysts from quail and pheasants.

Cryptosporidium species from reptiles and fishes have been named *C crotali* and *C nasorum* respectively, but their relationships and host specificity have yet to be worked out. Unspecified cryptosporidia have been reported from 45 mammalian species, 5 birds, 18 reptiles, 1 amphibian and 2 fishes.[21] There is no evidence that cross-infection occurs between fishes, reptiles and mammals.

Pathogenicity of parasite species and strains

We know little about strain differences in pathogenicity. There is still disagreement as to whether *Cryptosporidium* is a serious pathogen at all. Fischer[27] found no difference in the *Cryptosporidium* oocyst output or weight gain of diarrhoeic and normal calves. Anderson[8] believes that *Cryptosporidium* is relatively harmless, and Fayer[24] found that it was associated with serious disease only in the presence of other organisms. Available data in piglets suggest that *Cryptosporidium* plays a secondary role in pathogenesis.[83] Overall, the evidence indicates that *Cryptosporidium parvum* is of low intrinsic pathogenicity, but can cause or exacerbate disease in animals whose resistance has been lowered (see host susceptibility, below).

Strain differences have been reported in pathogenicity of isolates from calves in different areas of the United States,[35] but morphological details were not given, so the two "strains" could have been those regarded by others as two species, *C parvum* and *C muris*.[8] *C muris* appears to do little harm to either mice or cattle.[7,8]

Prepatent and patent periods

The prepatent period varies between 2 and about 14 days.[111] It tends to be shorter in piglets, lambs, goats and calves (particularly if diarrhoea occurs), and longer in rodents. Naciri[58] found the prepatent period was shorter in goats than in lambs.

The patent period is usually 3–12 days in calves[1,93] but can extend to 20 days.[72] *C muris* (and possibly also *C parvum*) can be patent intermittently at a low level in adult cattle.

Site of infection

Anderson[4] reviewed the site of infection in the following species and classes of animals: calf, lamb, goat, deer, foal, cat, rat, mouse, guinea-pig, rabbit, macaque monkey, man, birds, reptiles and fishes. In mammals the small intestine was the most common site. Birds were infected mainly in the bursa fabricii and the respiratory tract.[4,41] Gardiner & Imes[27A] found it in the kidneys of a finch, and Pavlásek & Nikitin[62] found *Cryptosporidium* in the urinary system of heavily infected calves. One wonders whether more sites would be revealed if people looked in the right places. Experimentally, infection of the trachea and conjunctiva can be induced in piglets.[34]

Prevalence of the parasite

Cryptosporidium parvum appears to be ubiquitous. Animals (wild and domestic) probably never reach adulthood without becoming infected, unless they are kept in isolation.

Most environmental contamination is due to animals less than 3 weeks old. They may pass large numbers of oocysts whether they show clinical signs or not.[56] In adult animals *C parvum* is rarely detected.[75]

Serological testing of cattle, sheep, deer, horses, pigs, dogs, cats, chickens and man detected antibodies to *Cryptosporidium* in 80 to 100 per cent of samples.[103] All mice tested from an SPF colony were negative. The significance of these findings is not known, but they suggest that most animals have encountered the organism by the time they are adult.

Cattle

Heine & Boch[33] found *Cryptosporidium* in 14 per cent of healthy calves, 40 per cent of diarrhoeic calves, and 61 per cent of calves that had died of enteritis.

Anderson *et al*[3] attempted a random survey of twelve-day old calves. 44 per cent of 248 were positive. 56 per cent of the 73 herds were infected, and within the infected herds, 64 per cent were positive. 22–40 per cent of diarrhoeic calves discharged *Cryptosporidium* oocysts in their faeces. Ongerth & Stibbs[64] found *Cryptosporidium* in 51 per cent of calves between 7 and 21 days old.

Reynolds *et al*[81] found *Cryptosporidium* in 23 per cent of 465 calves with diarrhoea in 44 outbreaks in southern England, and in 8 per cent of healthy calves on the same premises. They found *Cryptosporidium* to be more prevalent in single and multiple-suckler beef herds than in dairy herds.

Chermette and Boufassa-Ouzrout[18] reviewed the epidemiology of this disease. Data on the prevalance of *Cryptosporidium* were fragmentary, but surveys of diarrhoeic calves in Australia, Belgium, Canada, Czechoslovakia, Denmark, France, Germany, Hungary, Italy, Romania, Spain, UK, USA and USSR gave figures ranging from 10 to 80 per cent. Healthy calves (mostly from affected herds) showed *Cryptosporidium* in 0 to 14 per cent. Stein *et al*[93] followed the course of naturally-infected calves.

Sheep and goats. Diarrhoeic lambs in France, Iran, UK and USA showed the organism in 7 to 43 per cent, and similar figures were found in goats.[18]

Pigs. Sanford[83] found *Cryptosporidium* in 5.3 per cent of pigs submitted for diagnosis.

Horses. *Cryptosporidium* was present in 13 of 82 healthy foals in France.[92] Other reports have shown a similar prevalence.[19]

Wild animals. Reports of infection in zoo and wild animals have been reviewed by Crawshaw and Mehren.[21] *Cryptosporidium* has been reported in a marsupial, 6 primates, 6 rodents, cottontail rabbits, 5 carnivores, 26 ruminants, 5 birds, 18 reptiles, 1 frog and 2 fishes.[21]

Birds. The organism has been found in chickens, turkeys, ducks, parrots, pheasants, peacocks[50] and quails,[95] but data on prevalence are lacking.[11,61]

Sources of infection, transmission

Route

The principal mode of transmission in mammals is by the ingestion of oocysts derived from faeces. Lambs can rapidly pick up the infection from their mothers' teats, after contamination by infected siblings.[2]

Infection probably also occurs by other routes, since oocysts have been found in sputum of man[22] and in urine of calves.[71] Evidence has been reported of human infection by inhalation of breath from an infected calf.[39] If airborne transmission can occur so easily from calf to man, it could also occur from calf to calf, and it probably occurs among birds. Experimentally, transmission via the conjunctiva and the trachea have been demonstrated.[34]

Infective dose

A dose/response relationship has been reported for baby mice,[18] but apparently it is difficult to establish such a relationship even in gnotobiotic animals.[20]

Sources

There is no evidence that cryptosporidia from reptiles or fishes can infect mammals. Although *C parvum* has been recorded in birds,[46] there is no evidence that infected birds pose a significant threat to mammals, or vice-versa.

Although *C parvum* can infect many mammalian species, and therefore in theory any can act as a source of infection for any other, it appears that in practice infections usually originate from the same host species.

In calves, the main source of infection is probably diarrhoeic calves 1-4 weeks old.[35] Heavy infections can lead to massive environmental contamination. The rate of infection appears to depend on the degree of environmental contamination.[16,55,56,69]

Morgan and colleagues studied the course of infection of *Cryptosporidium* and rotavirus in dairy calves, and found that *Cryptosporidium* tended to appear later and to spread more slowly than rotavirus.[55,56] This appears to apply to lambs as well,[9] and to goats.[106] An outbreak in goat kids started with one 5-day-old bottle-fed twin, after which there was a wave of infection among kids aged between 5 and 21 days.[106] Henriksen considers that since infection in adults is so rarely detected, it is unlikely to act as a source of infection for calves.[35]

Klesius *et al*[43] showed that *Cryptosporidium* isolated from wild mice *Mus musculus* were infective for mice and for calves. They did not attempt to distinguish between *C muris* and *C parvum*.

Host susceptibility

All newborn mammals appear to be susceptible to cryptosporidial infection, but normally they soon become resistant. Susceptibility to disease depends on age,[102,107] inoculating dose, and other factors such as acquired immunity,[108] and stress.

Age

Newborn animals tend to be highly susceptible to infection but relatively resistant to disease. As animals get older they become more and more resistant to infection with *Cryptosporidium parvum*.[102,107] To separate the effects of age *per se* from those of passive and active immunity, studies have been carried out using strict isolation. SPF **lambs** showed severe disease and death when inoculated at birth, and severe disease when inoculated at 5–20 days of age, but infection at 30 days caused no disease.[102] Gnotobiotic **piglets** showed severe enterocolitis following infection at 1 day of age, moderate diarrhoea when infected at 7 days of age, but only subclinical infection at 15 days of age.[107] The susceptibility of pigs reared under farm conditions was also found to depend on age.[104] Laboratory **mice** were susceptible to infection at birth, but their susceptibility decreased up to about 21 days, after which only transient infections could be induced.[86] Suckling **rabbits** are much more susceptible to disease than older rabbits.[73]

Immunity

Passive immunity

No clear-cut conclusions can yet be drawn concerning the role of passive immunity in cryptosporidiosis. There is evidence that colostrum reduces susceptibility in lambs,[9,100] but it is not always clear whether the difference is due to lack of colostrum or to the stress of artificial rearing.[100] There have been indications that mortality due to *Cryptosporidium* in lambs[9] was lower when ewes had been previously exposed to an infected lambing environment. Naciri and colleagues[57,58] showed that the offspring of goats inoculated during pregnancy and fed colostrum were protected to a considerable extent compared with offspring of non-inoculated goats fed colostrum and milk from non-inoculated goats or fed artificial milk. Fayer *et al*[25] showed that bovine colostrum protected mice against *Cryptosporidium*, but evidence of its effectiveness for calves appears to be lacking. Tzipori *et al*[110] found that hyperimmune bovine colostrum had curative activity for an immunodeficient child with cryptosporidiosis. Other workers found no protective effect of mouse colostrum for mice[53] or bovine colostrum for man.[84] Morgan and colleagues[55,56] found that the age of onset of infection with *Cryptosporidium* in calves was not affected by the amount of gamma globulin absorbed from the colostrum.[55,56]

Active immunity

Immunosuppression in animals is most commonly attributable to stress, which will be dealt with below. However, there are some infections that specifically depress immunity, and among these are infectious bursal disease and Marek's disease of chickens, both of which have been associated with cryptosporidiosis.[30,59,79,96] Cryptosporidiosis has also been seen in bursal atrophy of quails.[108] The high incidence of crypto sporidiosis in immunodeficient humans suggests that active immunity plays a part in the resistance of normal adults. This may apply to some animals (eg chickens[30,59,79,96] and horses[91]), but apparently it does not apply to all: mice lose their susceptibility to infection after the age of 3 weeks, and immunosuppression does not restore it.[86] The occurrence of cryptosporidiosis in immunodeficient foals[14,278,91] suggests that resistance in horses, as in man, is partly due to active immunity.

Stress

Concurrent infection

In most field outbreaks of cryptosporidiosis in animals, several enteropathogens are associated, and the pathogenic roles of each are hard to disentangle.[24,88,90] In fact the task is virtually impossible, because other organisms can be eliminated only in artificial conditions, which themselves can increase susceptibility. In some reports, *Cryptosporidium* appears to be the sole pathogen present,[60] but there could be others as yet unidentified.[90] In immunodeficient foals,[91] *Cryptosporidium* was accompanied by an adenovirus, and the relative pathogenicity of each was unclear. Cryptosporidiosis has been reported in an emaciated wild grey squirrel with cutaneous papillomata,[94] and avian cryptosporidiosis is often associated with other organisms.[31,96]

Morgan and colleagues[55,56] looked at the relationships between *Cryptosporidium* rotavirus, immune globulin absorption and diarrhoea in dairy calves. They found that of those infected with *Cryptosporidium* alone, 18 per cent were diarrhoeic; of those infected with rotavirus alone, 40 per cent were diarrhoeic; and of those that were infected with both, 75 per cent were diarrhoeic. An apparent association with *Mycobacterium johnei* infection in calves has been reported from the Veterinary Investigation Centre at Bangor (A Rees [1989] personal communication).

Snodgrass *et al*[89] used gnotobiotic lambs to eliminate all bacterial and viral pathogens, but they still got pathogenic effects. Tzipori *et al*[105] fed colostrum-deprived lambs artificially and found no clinical or histological difference between those inoculated with *Cryptosporidium* alone and those inoculated with *Cryptosporidium* and ETEC or rotavirus. Unlike some *Eimeria* infections, susceptibility of lambs and goats to *Cryptosporidium* appears not to be influenced by the absence of normal gut flora.[20]

Management

One would expect the disease to be more common among artificially-reared animals, than in naturally-reared animals, and this appears to be the case in lambs,[2,98,100] deer-calves[101] and goat-kids.[106] It may be difficult to distinguish between increase in susceptibility due to stress and that due to inadequate passive immunity.

Calves. Some workers have reported that in well-managed calves exposed to a contaminated environment, *Cryptosporidium* caused only mild diarrhoea with no inappetence.[8,13] On the other hand, Pavlásek *et al*[66,69] found no difference in the degree of diarrhoea due to cryptosporidiosis under different management methods. Indoor calves all suffered to the same extent whether they were in individual pens, or in groups, or left with their mothers. Leek and Fayer[45] found similar results. Tzipori *et al*[109] compared infections in calves under different conditions: (i) SPF colostrum-deprived; (ii) SPF colostrum-fed inoculated; (iii) suckled colostrum-fed infected by contact. The clinical differences were not great. One of the in-contact infected calves showed no clinical signs, suggesting that the severity of illness may be dose-related. Presumably the suckled calves were not subjected to stress other than daily faecal sampling, so the disease they showed could be attributed only to the heavy dose of oocysts given at one time, possibly in calves that had not encountered the organism before.

Lambs. Anderson[2] found that disease and patency were much less in suckling lambs than in lambs fed artificially. In non-inoculated contacts (that must have received a lower dose) they were even less.[2] Tzipori *et al*[100] described severe diarrhoea in 40 of 48 artificially-reared lambs, of which 16 died. Of a subsequent batch of lambs occupying the same premises, 100 that were suckled showed no disease, whereas 3 of 4 hand-reared orphans developed diarrhoea, and *Cryptosporidium* was demonstrated in two of them.

Weather

As with eimerian coccidiosis, susceptibility appears to be increased by cold wet weather, at least in lambs and red deer calves.[13]

Incidence of disease in animals

As data accumulate, a picture is building up of a ubiquitous organism whose intrinsic pathogenicity is low, but whose prevalence in diseased animals is high. *Cryptosporidium* can therefore be regarded as an opportunist. Other organisms are usually present to confuse the diagnosis. Because of this, it is difficult to separate figures for the incidence of disease from those for prevalence of the parasite.

In some mammalian species *Cryptosporidium* commonly causes disease (eg calves, lambs, goats); in others its effects are variable and its incidence sporadic (eg cats, horses, pigs, guinea-pigs, dogs).[111] In mice (and probably many other species) it is usually non-pathogenic. *Cryptosporidium* tends to be associated with enteritis in animals less than 3 weeks old. Disease is usually associated with concurrent infection or other predisposing causes such as stress or immunodeficiency. Disease attributable to *Cryptosporidium* alone is usually relatively mild[90, 99] but severe outbreaks with high mortality have been reported, even in naturally-reared animals,[9] and in these cases the infecting dose has presumably been very large.

The disease is of greatest economic importance in calves. Diagnoses in lambs are increasing, but in other species the occurrence is sporadic. Where pets are concerned, Angus believes that only cats are likely to pose a threat to their owners.[13]

Calves. Cryptosporidiosis is second to rotavirus as the most prevalent pathogen causing diarrhoea in calves.[1,111] It affects calves mainly in their second week of life. 827 outbreaks were diagnosed by Veterinary Investigation Centres in England and Wales in 1988. Seasonal peaks coincide with birth peaks in spring and autumn.[13] Mixed infections are extremely common. Severe disease with high mortality was seen in a series of cases in 1982.[82] The organism was identified in 26 per cent of 161 of diarrhoeic calves from 26 herds. Many of the calves were "hutch-reared", but otherwise the conditions were not stated. Enterotoxigenic *E coli* was often cultured in dead calves, and the part played by *Cryptosporidium* was not clear. As stated under prevalence, above, figures for the finding of *Cryptosporidium* in diarrhoeic calves vary between 10 per cent and 80 per cent.[3,18,81]

Lambs. The disease is not uncommon. 161 outbreaks were diagnosed by the Veterinary Investigation Service in 1988, which was almost double the figure for the previous year. Cryptosporidiosis is seen mostly in lambs aged 1–2 weeks, which appear mostly in the spring. Modern economic constraints are forcing farmers to go for earlier lambs, so they tend more and more to be born in the winter, in which case they must be kept indoors in crowded conditions that increase the risk of cryptosporidiosis.

Goats. *Cryptosporidium* was the most frequently identified cause of death in young goats in France.[114] It often occurs in association with other organisms,[61,76] but a case reported by Mason *et al*[51] revealed no bacterial or viral pathogens. The disease has been studied experimentally.[57,61]

Deer. Severe disease attributable to *Cryptosporidium* has been reported in artificially-reared[101] and in naturally-reared red-deer calves.[13,101]

Piglets. *Cryptosporidium* will cause diarrhoea if given to colostrum-deprived newborn piglets.[42,49] It caused disease in suckling piglets and in colostrum-fed artificially-reared piglets.[104] Older (weaned) piglets showed only subclinical infection.[104] Cryptosporidiosis has been reported in the field in association with *E coli*, but its significance is uncertain.[85] Sanford[83] found it in 5.3 per cent of piglets submitted for diagnosis; of these, 26 per cent had diarrhoea, most of which had other pathogens as well. There is thus little evidence that the disease is of clinical or economic significance in pigs.[13]

Horses. The disease has been diagnosed in immunodeficient[14,278,91] and normal foals[19,92] in combination with other pathogens.[13]

Cats. Clinical infection has been described in adults,[77] and young.[15] Cats are also subject to immune-depressing viruses (feline leukemia and an HIV-like virus)[13] so the possibility of *Cryptosporidium* must be borne in mind where diarrhoeic cats are concerned.

Dogs. The disease is apparently very rare.[13,75,113]

Mice. Infant mice can be infected with *C parvum*, but no disease results. Whatever the prevalence, the incidence of disease in mice is probably negligible.

Rabbits. There is evidence that *Cryptosporidium* can be troublesome under experimental conditions,[73] or when combined with other organisms (eg *Eimeria*).[13,73]

Guinea-pigs. Cryptosporidiosis has been described in laboratory guinea-pigs,[12,28] but is unlikely to be a problem in pets.[13]

Hamsters. Cases have been reported in association with proliferative enteritis.[23,65]

Zoo animals. Cryptosporidiosis is of most importance in newborn ruminants and reptiles.[21] *Cryptosporidium* was found in 28 per cent of zoo ruminants with diarrhoea.[26,36]

Birds. No data on incidence are available, but the disease is increasingly recognised, usually in association with intensive husbandry. It is unlikely to be a source of infection for mammals.[47]

Chickens. The bursa fabricius is commonly infected,[32,79,96] but disease is usually associated with respiratory infection, and can be severe.[32,64] Conjunctivitis has also been reported.[53]

Turkeys. The disease can affect the respiratory tract and the gut.[38,29]

Ducks. Experimental[47] and natural[96] infections have been described, (including conjunctivitis [Mason pers com]) but the incidence is unknown.

Canaries. Cryptosporidiosis has been reported in association with *Salmonella typhimurium* infection.[96]

Resistance of oocysts

Preservation

Sherwood et al[86] studied storage methods. Nine different cryopreservatives were used together with various regimes of cooling, freezing, thawing or freeze-drying. *Cryptosporidium* survived none of them. There was a progressive loss of infectivity in all media at 4°C.

No infectivity was detectable after 2 months storage in distilled water; the most stable preparation was in 2.5 per cent potassium dichromate, in which infectivity lasted for 4–6 months. There was complete loss of infectivity at 15–20°C within 2 weeks, and at 37°C within 5 days.

Henriksen,[35] on the other hand, found that oocysts stored in aqueous suspension at 4°C were fully infective for 2–6 months, and Naciri[57] found oocysts infective after one year's storage at 4°C, but she did not further specify the conditions.

Moon & Bemrick[52] stored oocysts successfully for up to 8 weeks in a final dilution of 1.7 per cent potassium dichromate at 20–25°C in a loosely covered glass jar to permit exchange of air.

Destruction

— by physical agents

Anderson[6] found that *Cryptosporidium*-laden calf faeces lost their infectivity for infant mice after 1–4 days of drying. Moist heat (45°C for 20 minutes) was also effective.[5] Tzipori states that oocysts were destroyed by freeze-drying, and by 30 minutes exposure to temperatures below 0° or above 65°C,[108] but he did not say what medium the oocysts were in. Coleman et al[19] suggested that dry weather could have explained a sudden drop in prevalence in horses in Louisiana in 1986.

I have found no data relating to the survival of *Cryptosporidium* oocysts in slurry, but Larsen and Henriksen[44] followed the progress of *Eimeria* oocysts in slurry at various temperatures. Inactivation was apparently achieved in 3 hours at 55°C, or 2 weeks at 35°C. After 30 days, 17 per cent of oocysts stored at 20°C were still viable, but those stored at 4°C were apparently still as healthy as at the start of the experiment. These data do not allow conclusions to be drawn regarding *Cryptosporidium* oocysts, but they suggest that infected slurry is likely to remain infective for some time.

— by chemical agents

Blewett[16] studied the efficacy of various disinfectants against *Cryptosporidium* oocysts. The criterion used for efficacy was a 90 per cent reduction of the excystation rate[80] following 30 minutes exposure to the disinfecting agent at 22°C. He also tried 35°C. Of 35 agents tried, only three had a satisfactory oocysticidal effect at 22°C: 10 volumes H_2O_2, Exspor (a proprietary product based on chlorine dioxide) and Oo-cide (a proprietary product based on ammonia). Of these, Exspor proved ineffective in the presence of 20 per cent serum, whereas the effect of H_2O_2 was slightly enhanced by the presence of the protein. The efficacy of these disinfectants in the field would be hard to assess rigorously, but the makers of Oo-cide (Antec International, Sudbury, Suffolk) claim that when premises were thoroughly cleaned beforehand, the use of Oo-cide led to improvements in the productivity of broilers.

Angus et al[10] tried 2 commercial aldehyde-based disinfectants (Tegodor, [Goldschmidt], and formula H [Hoechst]), both were ineffective. Pavlasek and Mares[68] found that sodium dichloroisocyanurate failed to kill *Cryptosporidium* oocysts in the laboratory or to control the spread of cryptosporidiosis in calves. Peeters et al[74] found that 2.27 mg ozone per litre killed 500,000 oocysts per ml water within 8 minutes, and 0.4 mg chlorine dioxide per litre significantly reduced infectivity.

Campbell et al[16A] subjected *Cryptosporidium* oocysts to 7 different disinfectants recommended by the Ministry of Agriculture for use in Veterinary Investigation Laboratories:

Cresylic acid	3%
Hypochlorite	2–5%
Formaldehyde	10%
Benzalkonium chloride	5%
Sodium hydroxide	0.02%
Iodophore	1–4%
Ammonia	5–10%

Only 10 per cent formaldehyde and 5–10 per cent ammonia were effective in killing *Cryptosporidium* oocysts after 18 hours exposure.

Pavlasek[70] tried a range of disinfectants (some of whose composition was not specified) against *Cryptosporidium* oocysts, and found no effect after 24 hours exposure:

Dikonit	3%
Formaldehyde	5%
Chloramine B	3%
Iodonal A	3%
Lastanox Q	0.2%
Mycolastanox	0.2%

Smith et al[87] found that free chlorine was not effective in killing *Cryptosporidium* oocysts at levels below 8000 mg/litre, for 24 hours, independent of pH or temperature.

References

1. Anderson B C (1981) Patterns of shedding cryptosporidial oocysts in Idaho calves. J am vet med Ass 178: 982–984.

2. Anderson B C (1982) Cryptosporidiosis in Idaho lambs: Natural and experimental infections. J am vet med Ass 181: 151–153.

3. Anderson BC, & Hall RF (1982) Cryptosporidial infection in Idaho dairy calves. J am vet med Ass 181: 484–485.

4. Anderson B C (1984) Location of cryptosporidia: review of the literature and experimental infections in calves. Am J vet Res 45: 1474–1477.

5. Anderson B C (1985) Moist heat inactivation of *Cryptosporidium* sp. Am J Pub Health 75: 1433–1434.

6. Anderson B C (1986) Effect of drying on the infectivity of cryptosporidia-laden calf faeces for 3- to 7-day-old mice. Am J vet Res 47: 2272–2273.

7. Anderson B C (1987) Abomasal cryptosporidiosis in cattle. Vet Pathol 24: 235–238.

8. Anderson B C (1988) *Cryptosporidium* spp. in cattle. In: Cryptosporidiosis. Proc 1st Int Workshop, Edinburgh 1988, Edited by KW Angus & D A Blewett, pp 55–63.

9. Angus K W, Appleyard WT, Menzies JD, Campbell I, & Sherwood D (1982) An outbreak of diarrhoea associated with cryptosporidiosis in naturally reared lambs. Vet Rec 110: 129–130.

10. Angus K W, Sherwood D, Hutchison G, & Campbell I (1982) Evaluation of the effect of two aldehyde-based disinfectants on the infectivity of faecal cryptosporidia for mice. Res vet Sci 33: 379–381.

11. Angus K W (1983) Crytosporidiosis in man, domestic animals and birds: a review. J roy Soc Med 76: 62–70.

12. Angus K W, Hutchison G. & Munro HMC (1985) Infectivity of a strain of Cryptosporidium found in the guinea-pig (*Cavia porcellus* for guinea-pig), mice and lambs. J comp Path 95: 151–165.

13. Angus K W (1988) Mammalian cryptosporidiosis: a veterinary perspective. In: Cryptosporidiosis. Proc 1st Int Workshop, Edinburgh 1988, Edited by K W Angus & D A Blewett, pp43–53.

14. Annual report (1982) Queensland Department of Primary Industries, Brisbane, Australia.

15. Bennett M, Baxby D, Blundell N, Gaskell C J, Hart C A, & Kelly D F (1985) Cryptosporidiosis in the domestic cat. Vet Rec 116: 73–74.

16. Blewett D A (1988) Disinfection and oocysts. In: Cryptosporidiosis. Proc 1st Int Workshop, Edinburgh 1988, Edited by K W Angus & D A Blewett, pp107–115.

16A. Campbell I, Tzipori S, Hutchison G, & Angus K W (1982) Effect of disinfectants on survival of *Cryptosporidium* oocysts. Vet Rec 111: 414–415.

17. Carlson B L, & Nielson S W (1982) Cryptosporidiosis in a raccoon. J amer vet med ass 181: 1405–1406.

18. Chermette R. & Boufassa-Ouzrout S (1988) Cryptosporidiosis: a cosmopolitan disease in animals and in man, 2nd edition. Office International des Epizooties, Paris.

19. Coleman S U, Klei T R, French D D, Chapman M R, & Corstvet R E (1989) Prevalence of *Cryptosporidium* sp in equids in Louisiana. Am J vet Res 50: 575–577.

20. Contrepois M, Gouet P, & Naciri M (1984) Cryptosporidiose expérimentale chez des checreaux et des agneaux axéniques. In: Colloque International sur les maladies de la chèvre, Institut National de la Recherche Agromonique, Niort, France, 9–11 Oct, pp 453–463.

21. Crawshaw G J & Mehren K G (1987) Cryptosporidiosis in zoo and wild animals. Proc 29th Int Symp Dis Zoo Anim, Cardiff, 1987. pp353-362.

22. Current W L (1988) The biology of *Cryptosporidium*. In: Parasitic infections, Edited by J H Leech, M A Sande, and R K Root. Churchill Livingstone, New York & London, pp109–132.

23. Davis A J, & Jenkins S J (1986) Cryptosporidiosis and proliferative ileitis in a hamster. Vet Pathol 23: 632–633.

24. Fayer R, Ernst J V, Miller R G & Leek R G (1985) Factors contributing to clinical illness in calves experimentally infected with a bovine isolate of *Crytosporidium*. Proc hel Soc Wash 52: 64–70.

25. Fayer R, Perryman L E, & Riggs M W (1989) Hyperimmune bovine colostrum neutralizes *Cryptosporidium* sporozoites and protects mice against oocyst challenge. J Parasitol 75: 151–153.

26. Fenwick B W (1983) Cryptosporidiosis in a neonatal gazella. J amer vet med Ass 183: 1331–1332.

27. Fischer O (1984) [Economic importance of coccidia of the genus *Cryptosporidium* in calf rearing] (In Czech; English summary). Vet Med Praha 29: 419–424.

27A. Gardiner C H, & Imes G D (1984) *Cryptosporidium* sp in the kidneys of a black-throated finch. J amer vet med Ass 185: 1401–1402.

27B. Gibson J A, Hill M W M, & Huber M J (1983) Cryptosporidiosis in Arabian foals with severe combined immunodeficiency. Aust vet J 60: 378–379.

28. Gibson S V, & Wagner J E (1986) Cryptosporidiosis in guinea-pigs: a retrospective study. J amer vet med Ass 189: 1033–1034.

29. Glisson J R, Brown T P, Brugh M, Page R K, Kleven S H, & Davis R B (1984) Sinusitis in turkeys associated with respiratory cryptosporidiosis. Avian Dis 28: 783–790.

30. Goodwin M A (1988) Small-intestinal cryptosporidiosis in a chicken. Avian Dis 32: 844–848.

31. Goodwin M A, Latimer K S, Brown J, Steffens W L, Martin P W, Resurreccion R S, Smeltzer M A, & Dickson T G (1988) Respiratory cryptosporidiosis in chickens. Poultry Sci 67: 1684–1693.

32. Gorham S L, Mallinson E T, Synder D B, & Odor E M (1987) Cryptosporidia in the bursa of Fabricius – a correlation with mortality rates in broiler chickens, Avia Pathol 16: 205–211.

33. Heine J, & Boch J (1981) Kryptosporidien-Infektionen bein Kalb. Nachweis, Vorkommen und experimentelle übertragung. Berl Münch Tierärztl Wschr 94: 289–292.

34. Heine J, Moon H W, Woodmansee Db, & Pohlenz JFL (1985) Experimental tracheal and conjunctival infections with *Cryptosporidium* sp. in pigs. VetParasitol 17: 17–25.

35. Henriksen S A (1988) Epidemiology of cryptosporidiosis in calves. In: Cryptosporidiosis. Proc 1st Int Workshop, Edinburgh 1988, Edited by K W Angus & D A Blewett, pp 79–83.

36. Heuschele W P, Oosterhuis J, Janssen D, Robinson P T, Ensley P K, Meier J E, Olson T, Anderson M P, & Benirschke K (1986) Cryptosporidial infections in captive wild animals. J. Wildl Dis 22: 493–496.

37. Hiepe T, Jungmann R, Plath P, & Schuster R (1985) Untersuchungen über Vorkommen, Nachweis und Krankheitsbild der Kryptosporidien-Infektion neugeborener Schaflämmer. Mh Vet-Med 40: 524–527.

38. Hoerr F J, Ranck F M, Hastings T F (1978) Respiratory cryptosporidiosis in turkeys. J. am vet med Ass 173: 1591–1593.

39. Højlyng N, Holten-Andersen W, & Jepsen S (1987) Cryptosporidiosis: a case of airborne transmission. Lancet ii: 271–272.

40. Hoover D M, Hoerr F J, Carlton W W, Hinsman E J, & Ferguson H W (1981) Enteric cryptosporidiosis in a naso tang (*Naso lituratus*, Bloch and Schneider). J. Fish dis 41: 425.

41. Itakura C, Goryo M, & Umemura T (1984) Cryptosporidial infection in chickens. Avian Pathol 13: 487–499.

42. Kennedy, G A, Kreitner G L, & Strafuss A C (1977) Cryptosporidiosis in three pigs. J am vet med Ass 170: 348–350.

43. Klesius P H, Haynes T B, & Malo L K (1986) Infectivity of *Cryptosporidium* sp isolated from wild mice for calves and mice. J am vet med Ass 189: 192–193.

44. Larsen A B & Henriksen S A (1989) Preliminary studies on the survival of oocysts of bovine *Eimeria* spp. in slurry incubated at different temperatures. Proc 5th International Coccidiosis Conference, Tours (France) 17–20 Oct 1989.

45. Leek R G, & Fayer R (1984) Prevalence of *Cryptosporidium* infections, and their relation to diarrhoea in calves on 12 dairy farms in Maryland. Proc hel soc Wash 51: 360–361.

46. Levine N D (1988) The Protozoan Phylum Apicompexa. CRC Press, Boca raton, Florida page 138.

47. Lindsay D S, Blagburn B L, & Sundermann C A (1986) Host specificity of *Cryptosporidium* sp. isolated from chickens. J Parasit 72: 565–568.

48. Lindsay D S, Blagburn B L, & Sundermann C A (1989) Morphometric comparison of the oocysts of *Cryptosporidium meleagridis* and *Cryptosporidium baileyi* from birds. Proc helminthol Soc Wash 56: 91–92.

49. Links I J (1982) Cryptosporidial infection of piglets. Aust vet J 58: 60–62.

50. Mason R W, & Hartley W J (1980) Respiratory cryptosporidiosis in a peacock chick. Avian dis 24: 771–776.

51. Mason R W, Hartley W J, & Tilt L (1981) Intestinal cryptosporidiosis in a kid goat. Aust vet J 57: 386–388.

52. Moon H W, & Bemrick W J (1981) Fecal transmission of calf cryptosporidia between calves and pigs. Vet Pathol 18: 248–255.

53. Moon H W, Woodmansee D B, Harp J A, Abel S, & Ungar B L P (1988) Lacteal immunity to enteric cryptosporidiosis in mice: immune dams do not protect their suckling pups. Inf Imm 56: 649–653.

54. Moore J A, Blagburn B L, & Lindsay D S (1988) Cryptosporidiosis in animals including humans. Compendium on Veterinary Continuing Education 10: 275–287.

55. Morgan J H, & Grady E A (1989) Longitudinal study of *Cryptosporidium* infection in dairy calves. Abstract of poster display, in Cryptosporidiosis, Proceedings of the First International Workshop, Edited by K W Angus & D A Blewett, Moredun Research Institute, Edinburgh, pp 119–120.

56. Morgan J H, Grady E A, & Pocock D H (1989) The epidemiology of enteric pathogens in dairy calves. Paper presented to the Association of Veterinary Teachers and Research Workers, Scarborough, p43.

57. Naciri M, Yvoré P, & Levieux D (1984) Cryptosporidiose du chevreau. Influence de la prise du colostrum. Essais de traitements. In: Colloque International sur les maladies de la chèvre, Institut National de la Recherche Agronomique, Niort, France, 9–11 Oct, pp465–471.

58. Naciri M (1987) Cryptosporidiose: nouveautés bibliographiques et observations personelles. Bulletin des Groupes Techniques Vétérinaires No 3: 39–42.

59. Naciri M, & Mazzella O (1988) Association cryptosporidiose et maladie de Marek chez des poulets nains. Rec Méd vét 164: 311–312.

60. Nagy B. Antal A, & Ratz F (1979) (Occurrence of bovine cryptosporidiosis in Hungary) (in Hungarian; English summary) Magy allat Lapja 34: 585–588.

61. Nagy B, Bozso M, Palfi V, Nagy G, & Sahiby M A (1984) Studies on cryptosporidial infection of goat kids. In: Colloque International sur les maladies de la chèvre. Institut National de la Recherche Agronomique, Niort, France, 9–11 Oct, pp443–451.

62. Navin T R, & Juranek D D (1984) Cryptosporidiosis: clinical, epidemiologic, and parasitologic review. Rev Inf Dis 6: 313–327.

63. O'Donoghue P J, Tham V L, de Saram W G, Paull K L, & McDermott S (1987) *Cryptosporidium* infections in birds and mammals and attempted cross transmission studies. Vet Parasitol 26: 1–11.

64. Ongerth J E, & Stibbs H H (1989) Prevalence of *Cryptosporidium* infection in dairy calves in western Washington. Am J vet Res 50: 1069–1070.

65. Orr J P (1988) *Cryptosporidium* infection associated with proliferative enteritis (wet tail) in Syrian hamsters. Can vet J 29: 843–844.

66. Pavlasek I (1982) (The occurrence of *Cryptosporidium* sp in emergency-slaughtered calves and the source of excretion of the protozoan oocysts in calves on two farms in the south Bohemian region) (In Czech; English summary). Vet Med Praha 27: 729–740.

67. Pavlasek I (1983) Experimental infection of cat and chicken with *Crystosporidium* sp oocysts isolated from a calf. Folia parasit (Praha) 30: 121–122.

68. Pavlasek I, & Mares J (1983) (The effect of single disinfection of a farm on the course of cryptosporidiosis infections in calves) (In Czech; English summary). Vet Med (Praha) 28: 499–455.

69. Pavlasek I, Zigmund B, Klima F (1983) (The influence of different housing methods of new born calves on the occurrence of *Cryptosporidium* sp.) (in Czech; English summary). Vet Med (Praha): 28: 31–36.

70. Pavlasek I (1984) (Effect of disinfectants in infectiousness of oocysts of *Cryptosporidium* sp) (in Czech; English summary). Cs Epidem 33: 97–101.

71. Pavlasek I, & Nikitin V F (1987) finding of coccidia of the genus *Cryptosporidium* in the organs of calf excretory system. Folio parasit 34: 197–198.

72. Peeters J E, Van Opdenbosch E, & Glorieux B (1982) Demonstration of cryptosporidia in calf faeces: a comparative study. Vlaams dierg Tijdschr 51: 513–523.

73. Peeters J E, Charlier G J, & Dussart P (1986) Pouvoir pathogène de *Cryptosporidium* sp. chez les lapereaux avant et après sevrage. Proc 4èmes Journées de la Recherche Cunicole. Paris, 10-11 Dec. Comm No 37.

74. Peeters J E, Arez Mazás E, Masschelein W J, Villacorta Martinez de Maturana I, & Debacker E (1989) Effect of disinfection of drinking water with ozone or chlorine dioxide on survival of *Cryptosporidium parvum* oocysts. Appl Env Microbiol 55: 1519–1522.

75. Pohjola-Steenroos S (1986) Diagnostic and epidemiological aspects of *Cryptosporidium* infection, a protozoan infection of increasing veterinary public health importance. Department of Food and Environmental Hygiene, College of Veterinary Medicine, Helsinki. (Dissertation, 97pp + reprinted publications).

76. Polack B, & Perrin G (1987) La cryptosporidiose du chevreau. Bull GTV (3): 45–46.

77. Poonacha K B, & Pippin C (1982) Intestinal cryptosporidiosis in a cat. Vet Pathol 19: 708–710.

78. Pospischil A, Stiglmair-Herb M T, von Hegel G, & Wiesner H (1987) Abomasal cryptosporidiosis in mountain gazelles. Vet Rec 121: 379–380.

79. Randall C J (1982) Cryptosporidiosis of the bursa od Fabricius and trachea in broilers. Avian Pathol 11: 95–102.

80. Reduker D W, & Speer C A (1985) Factors influencing excystation in *Cryptosporidium* oocysts from cattle. J. Parasit 71: 112–115.

81. Reynolds D J, Morgan J H, Chanter N, Jones P W, Bridger J C, Debney T G, & Bunch K J (1986) Microbiology of calf diarrhoea in southern Britain. Vet Rec 119: 34–39.

82. Sanford S E, & Josephson G K A (1982) Bovine cryptosporidiosis: clinical and pathological findings in forty-two scouring neonatal calves. Can vet J 23: 343–347.

83. Sanford S E (1987) Enteric cryptosporidial infection in pigs: 184 cases (1981–1985). J amer vet med Ass 190: 695–698.

84. Saxon A, & Weinstein W (1987) Oral administration of bovine colostrum anti-cryptosporidia antibody fails to alter the course of human cryptosporidiosis. J Parasitol 73: 413–415.

85. Schmidt U, & Neinhoff H (1982) Kryptosporidiose beim Schwein. Dtsch tierärztl Wschr 89: 437–439.

86. Sherwood, Angus K W, Snodgrass D R, & Tzipori S (1982) Experimental cryptosporidiosis in laboratory mice. Infec Immun 38: 471–475.

87. Smith H V, Smith A L, Girdwood R W A, & Carrington E G (1989). The effect of free chlorine on the viability of *Cryptosporidium* Spp oocysts. WRc, PO Box 16, Marlow, Bucks, SL7 2HD.

88. Snodgrass D R, Angus K W, Gray E W, Keir W A, & Clerihew L W (1980) Cryptosporidia associated with rotavirus and an *Escherichia coli* in an outbreak of calf scour. Vet Rec 106: 458–459.

89. Snodgrass D R, Angus K W, Gray E W (1984) Experimental cryptosporidiosis in germfree lambs. J. Comp Path 94: 141–152.

90. Snodgrass D R, Terzolo D, Sherwood D, Campbell I, Menzies J D, & Synge B A (1986) Aetiology of diarrhoea in young calves. Vet Rec 119: 31–34.

91. Snyder S P, England J J, & McChesney A E (1978) Cryptosporidiosis in immunodeficient Arabian foals. Vet Pathol 15: 12–17.

92. Soule C, Plateau E, Perret C, Chermette R, & Feton M M (1983) Observation de Cryptosporidies chez le poulain. Note préliminaire. Rec Méd Vét 159: 719–720.

93. Stein E, Boch J, Heine J, & Henkel G (1983) Der Verlauf natürlicher *Cryptosporidium*-Infektionen in vier Rinderzuchtbetrieben. Berl Münch Tierärztl Wschr 96: 222–225.

94. Sundberg J P, Hill D, & Ryan M J (1982) Cryptosporidiosis in a grey squirrel. J amer vet med Ass 181: 1420–1422.

95. Tham V L, Kniesberg S, & Dixon B R (1982) Cryptosporidiosis in quails. Avian Pathol 11: 619–626.

96. Tsai S S, Ho L F, Chang C F, & Chu R M (1983) Cryptosporidiosis in domestic birds. Chinese J Microbiol Immunol 16: 307–313.

97. Tyzzer E E (1907) A sporozoan found in the peptic glands of the common mouse. Proc Soc exp Biol Med 5: 12.

98. Tzipori S, Angus K W, Campbell I, & Gray E W (1980) *Cryptosporidium* evidence for a single-species genus. Infec Immun 30: 884–886.

99. Tzipori S, Campbell I, Sherwood D, & Snodgrass D R (1980 An outbreak of calf diarrhoea attributed to cryptosporidial infection. Vet rec 107: 579–580.

100. Tzipori S, Angus K W, Campbell I, & Clerihew L W (1981) Diarrhoea due to *Cryptosporidium* infection in artificially reared lambs. J clin Microbiol 14: 100–105.

101. Tzipori S, Angus K W, Campbell I, & Sherwood D (1981) Diarrhoea in young red deer associated with infection with *Cryptosporidium*. J inf Dis 144:170–175.

102. Tzipori S, Angus K W, Gray E W, Campbell I, & Allan F (1981) Diarrhoea in lambs experimentally infected with *Cryptosporidium* isolated from calves. Am J vet Res 42: 1400–1404.

103. Tzipori S, & Campbell I (1981) Prevalence of *Cryptosporidium* antibodies in 10 animal species. J clin Microbiol 14: 455–456.

104. Tzipori S, McCartney E, Lawson G H K, Rowland A C, & Campbell I (1981) Experimental infection of piglets with *Cryptosporidium*. Res vet Sci 31: 358–368.

105. Tzipori S, Sherwood D, Angus K W, Campbell I, & Gordon M (1981) Diarrhoea in lambs: experimental infections with enterotoxigenic *Eschericha coli, rotavirus* and *Cryptosporidium* sp. Infec Immun 33: 400–406.

106. Tzipori S, Larsen J, Smith M & Luefl R (1982) Diarrhoea in goat kids attributed to Cryptosporidium infection. Vet Rec 111: 35–36.

107. Tzipori S, Smith M, Makin T & Halpin C (1982) Entercolitis in piglets caused by *Cryptosporidium* sp. purified from calf faeces. vet Parasitol 11: 121–126.

108. Tzipori S (1983) Cryptosporidiosis in animals and humans. Microbiol Reviews 47: 84–96.

109. Tzipori S, Smith M, Halpin C, Angus K W, Sherwood D, & Campbell I (1983) Experimental cryptosporidiosis in calves: clinical manifestations and pathological findings. Vet Rec 112: 116–120.

110. Tzipori S, Roberton D, & Chapman C (1986) Remission of diarrhoea due to cryptosporidiosis in an immunodeficient child treated with hyperimmune bovine colostrum. Br med J 293: 1276–1277.

111. Tzipori S (1988) Cryptosporidiosis in perspective. In: Advances in Parasitology 27: 63–129, Edited by J R Baker & R Muller, Academic Press, London.

112. Upton S J, & Current W L (1985) The species of *Cryptosporidium* (Apicomplexa: Cryptosporidiidae) infecting mammals. J. Parasit 71: 625–629.

113. Wilson R B, Holscher M A, & Lyle S J (1983) Cryptosporidiosis in a pup. J amer vet med Ass 183: 1005–1006.

114. Yvoré P, Esnault A, Naciri M, Leclerc C, Bind J L, Contrepois M, Levieux D, & Laporte J (1984) Enquête épidémiologique sur les diarrhées néonatales des chevreaux dans les élevages de Touraine. In: Colloque International sur les maladies de la chèvre, Institut National de la Recherche Agronomique, Niort, France, Oct 9–11, pp437–443.

Part II – Paper III

Management of Livestock Manure

Mr S W Bailey, BSc (Hons.), MAgrSt
Pollution Scientist
Ministry of Agriculture, Fisheries and Food
Agricultural Development & Advisory Service
London
Note: This paper is not a statement of MAFF policy but a technical
      discussion of the subject.

Definitions

Manure refers to animal excreta in any form, with or without added bedding such as straw and with or without extraneous dilution water such as that from cleaning, leaking drinkers and rainfall.

Manures can be broadly divided into liquids or solids. The term slurry is used for liquids and semi-liquids. More specifically, slurry is a mixture of faeces, urine and water with a consistency that allows it to be pumped or discharged by gravity. It may contain bedding and waste feed, but only in quantities which still produce a liquid or semi-liquid consistency. In contrast, solid manures have a sufficiently high dry matter content to permit them to be stacked during storage. Usually this higher dry matter is a result of a high content of bedding material.

Comparative dry matter content of manure types:

Manure type		% DM
Dairy cow	Excreta	10
	Slurry	<15
Solid manure	Cattle farmyard manure	20–25 (straw bedding)
	Broiler litter	70 (wood shavings as bedding)

Management

For cattle, most manure is collected between the months of October and March. This is the period during which dairy and beef cattle are normally permanently housed. During the remainder of the year, most manure is returned to land during grazing. In contrast, nearly all pigs and poultry are permanently housed. Consequently manure requiring disposal is produced all year (see Tables III.1 and III.2).

In the vast majority of farm waste management systems the final end-point for manure which is collected during housing of the animals is disposal to land. Landspreading represents the main method of waste treatment and practically the sole method of recycling. There are isolated cases of farmers obtaining consent from the local Water Service Company or the National Rivers Authority to discharge certain very dilute effluents to the sewer or water courses. Similarly a very small number sell composted solid manure for horticultural use. However, both practices are rare.

The management system can be divided into three stages:

1. Collection
a. Solid manure

Some solid manures are scraped from pens on a regular basis (daily, weekly), with replacement fresh bedding (usually straw) then added to the pen. This is common in some piggeries. Usually the scraper is a simple tractor-mounted pusher. The manure is pushed to an outside stack for later landspreading. With broiler hens, (birds for the table) a large quantity of bedding (shavings) is added before the birds are housed, then cleaned out after the crop has left (about seven weeks). The manure is then dug out, usually by tractor with loading bucket and either landspread immediately or stacked, often on field margins, for later landspreading.

For housed cattle with a solid manure system (beef cattle and some dairy cattle) roofed-over yards are usually bedded each day with fresh straw or shavings without removing the existing manure so that manure is allowed to accumulate. Once the cattle have been returned to fields in spring, the manure is then dug out, either immediately with subsequent storage elsewhere before landspreading, or after being allowed to "mature" undisturbed in the roofed yard for several months.

Although battery hens (hens for egg production) are housed without bedding, the resulting manure is usually a solid rather than a liquid. The fresh excreta has a relatively high dry matter content (25 per cent). It is either allowed to fall to a pit below the cages which is cleaned perhaps once a year, or drops onto a conveyor, which takes it from the house, for temporary stacking or for direct landspreading when sufficient has accumulated. In either case, further air-drying in-house usually produces a solid manure.

b. Slurry

With slurry there is more opportunity for automated management because the manure can flow or be pumped. In a slurry-based dairy cow system, winter housing typically comprises a building, the floor of which has a central shallow channel or passageway bordered along each side by "cubicles" (metal rails) for each cow. Cattle lie in the cubicles, to which small amounts of bedding may be added, and excrete while walking or loafing in the passageway. The passageway is then scraped, at least twice daily, either by a tractor-mounted scraper or by automatic scrapers. This takes it to the slurry store, either directly or by gravity and pump via underground channels.

Some slurry-based pig systems use solid-floored pens with little or no bedding and with tractor-mounted scraping to the slurry store. Others use slatted-floor pens over under-floor collection channels or stores. The collection channels discharge by gravity to a store or reception pit outside the housing. Under-floor stores are either emptied directly for landspreading after a few days or weeks or, because of their small capacity, discharged to a larger store.

Table III.1 Approximate amounts of excreta produced by livestock

Type of livestock	Amount of excreta (faeces plus urine) (l/day)
1 dairy cow	45
1 beef bullock	27
1 pig—dry meal fed	4
1 pig—swill fed	14
1 dry sow	4.5
1 sow + litter to 3 weeks	15
1,000 laying hens	114
1,000 broilers (including litter)	45

2. Storage

The main purpose of manure storage is to permit landspreading of the manure at a time which is convenient with regard to the weather, the farm cropping pattern or the farmer's workload. The majority of farmers cannot rely on suitable opportunities for landspreading during at least a four month period between November and March. For most of this period the soil will be too wet to carry heavy spreading machinery and there is an increased risk of pollution from run-off. Also, if the manure is being spread on arable crops rather than grass then there are only certain stages of crop production when manure can be applied without damaging the crop. These are either when the soil is bare before sowing or possibly onto a growing crop during early growth. Therefore, although a few livestock farmers with free-draining soils have little manure storage capacity, the majority should have capacity for several months. Practically all manure stores, other than the in-house storage previously described, are not roofed.

a. Solid manure

Most solid manure is stored before landspreading for the additional reason of allowing some decomposition of the bedding material, which might otherwise interfere with crop growth. Purpose-built solid manure stores have a concrete base and at least two retaining walls. Ideally they should include an effluent collection system draining to an effluent tank, to collect liquid run-off from the stack. The manure stack is built to about 2 metres maximum height. Typically, the most recently added manure would remain in the stack for two or three months before landspreading (and hence the older manure would be around six months old), unless previously matured in-house in which case less storage time will be needed. Decomposition takes place during storage through composting, an aerobic microbial process in which temperatures in excess of 60°C will be reached in the centre of the stack.

In many cases, especially where manure has previously accumulated in-house, solid manure is stored in fields. Any liquid run-off from the stack seeps into the soil: good practice, as described later, recommends that such stacks are built away from potential pathways for water pollution (field under-drainage, ditches etc.).

b. Slurry

There are three main types of slurry store: earth-banked compounds, above-ground pre-fabricated tanks and weeping-wall stores (see Figure III.1).

Earth-banked compounds are common on farms with less permeable soils. These are compounds, usually up to two metres deep, excavated in soil in or near the farmstead. Normally these are filled by gravity from the collection system or by tractor-scraping off a ramp. Also common are pre-fabricated above-ground tanks. These are built on a reinforced concrete base, using enamelled steel or concrete panels for the tank. They are filled by pump from a below-ground slurry reception pit. Less common are weeping-wall stores for slurries containing a relatively high proportion of bedding. These have a concrete base and walls built from railway sleepers or concrete panels, but with purpose-made spaces between the panels. Rainfall and some liquid effluent drains through the walls to a collection channel and storage tank. The more solid fraction remains in the store.

The separation of liquid and solid fractions of slurry makes subsequent landspreading easier. In a weeping-wall store the liquid is more easily pumped, perhaps by irrigation and the more-solid store contents can be emptied by a tractor and loader entering the store. Slurry separation is also widely practised with pre-fabricated above-ground stores. Here a mechanical separator can be installed before the slurry enters the store. Such separators produce a stackable solid fraction, subsequently stored elsewhere as a solid and a more-easily pumped liquid fraction, which is stored in the pre-fabricated tank.

Typically the first slurry to enter the store will remain there for several months. However the most recent additions, just before stock are returned to the fields or the store is full, may have practically no residence time before landspreading. Slurry stores are essentially anaerobic. There may be attempts to agitate stores by stirrers or bubblers, to prevent crusting of the surface and sedimentation, both of which impede emptying. However, anaerobic conditions rapidly return after agitiation ceases.

c. Treatment

Active treatment of manure is practised by very few farmers. A small number enhance natural composting of solid manure, usually by regular turning of the stack for several weeks until a generally amorphous and odourless material is produced, which can be sold for horticultural use. A few farmers practise anaerobic digestion of slurry in specially designed digesters. Although the pollution potential (in particular the biochemical oxygen demand) is reduced by digestion, the digested slurry is still potentially polluting effluent and so is disposed of by landspreading. The incentives for adopting the process are either to reduce odour complaints or to utilise the methane produced. Aeration of slurry is also practised by a small number of farmers, using appropriate aerating equipment. Again the treated slurry is still landspread, the incentive being to reduce odour complaints.

Table III.2 Example of slurry volume requiring disposal

100-dairy cow herd, on slurry-based system:	
Volume of excreta from 180-day winter	810m³
Volume of slurry, including typical additional dilution	1,900 m³

3. Disposal
a. Methods

Solid manure is spread using equipment similar to the traditional muck-spreader. Modern spreaders typically hold about five tonnes of manure, which is flung out sideways or backwards from the travelling machine over distances of ten or twenty metres.

Slurry is surface-spread, by tanker or irrigation, or injected underground.

Table III.3 Typical application rates of fresh, undiluted cattle slurry to meet crop nutrient requirements*

Crop	Application rate (m³/ha)
Grass for first-cut silage	20
Main-crop potatoes	67
Winter wheat	20

*To satisfy demand for one, but not all, major plant nutrients, (N,P,K).

Tankers

Tankers typically hold about five cubic metres of slurry. In some, the slurry is emptied by an integral pump or other tractor-powered device. Others are filled by the creation of a vacuum in the tanker and discharged by pressure. However, vacuum tankers are more likely to cause odour nuisance.

The discharge pattern varies tremendously. Some tankers still use high trajectories to throw the slurry thirty metres or more over ground. Recently, though, there has been a steady increase in the use of low-trajectory spreaders, discharging a curtain of slurry only one or two metres above ground over distances of only a few metres. Again, the incentive is to reduce odour. In addition, new attachments for tankers are appearing, which release the slurry directly onto the ground through trailing flexible pipes or low-level booms up to 20 metres wide.

Irrigation

Slurry irrigation can be practised if the slurry is sufficiently dilute. If automated, it can release labour from tanker-spreading and can reduce soil and crop damage. Nevertheless, it is not widely practised: necessary investment in the associated equipment can be high and problems with equipment breakdown and odour complaints are common. Equipment which is used still tends to have a high trajectory of spread, though attempts have been made to produce self-propelled, low trajectory irrigators.

Irrigation is increasingly used for dirty yard water. This is dilute run-off produced by rainfall falling on yards over which stock have walked. It contains small quantities of manure and sometimes dairy cleaning water may be included. Low-rate irrigation is a popular means of disposal for this: after two or three days' settlement, the effluent is pumped out through static or self-propelled sprinklers. These irrigate over a small area at a very low application rate. In the right situation this allows the operation to continue even through much of the winter without causing pollution.

Injection

Sub-surface injection of slurry offers a reliable way of controlling odour during spreading. Tines penetrate the ground to a depth of between fifteen and twenty five centimetres. Slurry is pumped down a pipe at the back of the tine. When operated well, no slurry appears at the surface. However, injection has certain drawbacks, which prevent it being used widely in agriculture. The operation is slow; it is better suited to medium or light textured soil rather than the heavy clays of many dairying areas; it is unsuitable for very stoney soils; it cannot be used in growing cereal and similar arable crops and it will damage grass growth during the drier summer months.

b. Timing

The main spreading time for manure is during the spring and early summer. On dairy and cattle farms, this will mostly be from the time the cattle are returned to the fields. On grassland, the manure is commonly applied to fields which will be cut for silage, though it is also applied to grazing land if there is a sufficient time interval before grazing starts, (MAFF recommends at least three weeks). Spreading is likely to carry on into May or June, for example before second and subsequent cuts of silage. Most arable land used for manure disposal receives manure between crops, when the soil is bare. The manure is then incorporated into the soil by cultivation. This will either be between February and April for spring-sown crops such as potatoes, or in late summer and early autumn for autumn-sown crops such as winter cereals.

Solid manure cannot be spread on growing crops other than grass without causing crop damage. Slurry, especially more dilute or separated slurry can be spread on some growing crops such as cereals during early growth. There is increasing interest in doing this, so that slurry is spread on autumn-sown crops in the spring instead of early autumn: this has the advantage that the nitrogen in the slurry is better utilised by the crop. However, MAFF recommend that manure is never spread onto crops grown to be eaten raw by man.

Application rates used depend on ease of access to the land, the amount of land available for spreading and a general though usually approximate consideration of the crop requirements for the plant nutrients contained in the manure. Typically application rates of up to 50 cubic metres (slurry) or 50 tonnes (solid manure) per hectare are used per year, which often meets much of the crop's requirement for phosphate and potash (see Table III.3).

Water pollution

Manure is polluting if it enters surface or underground waters. Properties such as the high biochemical oxygen demand (BOD), ammonia content and nutrient-enriching potential can have very damaging effects on receiving waters.

Pollution can occur via several routes. Slurry stores can leak or burst. Through poor management they can overflow. The seepage from solid manure stores and the run-off from soiled yards (dirty yard water) might not be adequately collected and controlled, particularly in high rainfall areas. All these effluents can find their way to water courses, either directly or via drains. Following landspreading, direct run-off of liquid might reach water-courses, perhaps exacerbated by rainfall. Alternatively, manure may percolate through soil to field drainage systems, for example via cracks in dry soils and so pass to water courses.

Since 1985, MAFF and the Water Authorities, (now the NRA) have produced an annual joint report on water pollution from farm waste. This gives an analysis of reported farm pollution incidents from all sources (manure, silage effluent, oil spillage etc). The figures show that between 1985 and 1988 by far the greatest number of pollution incidents from farm waste involved slurry stores and dirty yard water, (on average 25 and 24 per cent of total incidents respectively). Pollution from land run-off of manure was relatively minor, at 9 per cent of reported incidents on average. In the much drier year of 1989, the total number of incidents fell. However, the number of incidents caused by run-off increased and consequently the proportion of total incidents from this source rose to 16 per cent. This reflects the problems of spreading manure on cracked soils over field drains in dry weather.

Legislation and Codes of Practice

The most important legislation with regard to manure management is the Water Act 1989. Under Section 107 of the Act, it is an offence for polluting matter to enter water, including ground water.

MAFF has produced a Code of Good Agricultural Practice, describing good practice to avoid water pollution. The Code includes recommendations on the storage, land application and disposal of fertilisers, manures and waste waters and pesticides. With regard to manures, it describes the care needed during storage and disposal. In particular it recommends keeping storage and landspreading operations away from water courses and boreholes. The dangers of spreading on frozen, waterlogged or cracked soil over field drains are highlighted. Further, it states that during landspreading, manure application rates should be matched to crop requirements for the nutrients contained in the manure and that the timing of application should take account of the crop's pattern of demand. Supporting documents to the Code give more specific technical advice on waste management and the associated pollution hazards. Under Section 31 of the Control of Pollution Act 1974, a farmer causing pollution was not guilty of an offence if the pollution was attributable to action in accordance with the Code of Good Agricultural Practice. Under the Water Act 1989 this special defence has been withdrawn.

In view of the high proportion of farm pollution incidents caused by slurry stores (and also silage effluent from silage stores), the DOE in consultation with MAFF is preparing regulations under the Water Act 1989. These will set minimum standards of construction for new slurry stores, silage stores and stores for agricultural fuel oil. It is proposed that the NRA, who will enforce these regulations, will also have the power to require existing structures to be brought up to the requirements of the regulations if there is a significant risk of pollution. It is hoped that these regulations will come into effect during the second half of 1990.

References

Water Pollution from Farm Waste 1989. A joint report by the National Rivers Authority and the Ministry of Agriculture Fisheries and Food. NRA, 30–34 Albert Embankment, London SE1 7TL. £3.00.

Code of Good Agricultural Practice (1985). Ministry of Agriculture Fisheries and Food and Welsh Office Agriculture Department. Obtainable from MAFF Publications, London SE99 7TP. Price free.

The Control of Pollution (Silage, Slurry and Agricultural Fuel Oil) Regulations 1990. Public consultation document on proposed regulations issued by the Department of the Environment, January 1990.

Part II – Paper IV

This article first appeared in Epidemiology and Infection, (1990), Vol 104, 1–28 and is reproduced by kind permission of the Editors.

Epidemiological Aspects of Human Cryptosporidiosis

D P Casemore
Public Health Laboratory Service, Rhyl

Introduction

The coccidian protozoan parasite *Cryptosporidium* has been described in many host species since its discovery in the early part of the century, but it remained obscure until the recognition by veterinary workers in the 1970s of its importance as a cause of scours in young livestock animals [1-4]. Subsequently, particularly as a result of collaborative studies involving both medical and veterinary workers, cryptosporidiosis was also recognized in man [1,4-7]. Many of the early reports of the infection in humans were in immunocompromised subjects, either immunodeficient subjects, particularly those suffering from the then newly emerging disease, AIDS, and in the immunosuppressed. Such early cases were often diagnosed histologically, sometimes as a chance finding. Diagnosis by means of detection of oocysts in animal faecal smears had been demonstrated by veterinary workers in the 1970s [1,3] and subsequently also in humans [5-8]. However, the presence of oocysts in faeces, and the significance of the infection, continued to be in doubt [9,10]. Some cases, particularly among the immunocompetent, appeared to have an association with animals, particularly cattle, but even when such a source was not apparent the infection was generally referred to as an emerging opportunist zoonosis [11,12]. At that time, little if anything was known of the epidemiology of the infection in the general population. The recognition of an apparently opportunist zoonosis occurring particularly in young calves and in AIDS patients who were primarily urban adult males seemed, however, to be epidemiologically inconsistent. A prospective study was therefore set up at the Rhyl Public Health Laboratory in early 1983 to look for the parasite in a mixed urban and rural population including representatives of all age groups [13]. Such preliminary prospective surveys, from north Wales and elsewhere, indicated the importance of the parasite as a cause of acute, sporadic gastroenteritis in otherwise healthy subjects, particularly children, in developed countries [14,15], in under-developed countries [16,17], and in travellers, most of whom were adults [18,19].

Increasing awareness of the parasite, and that it could be identified by means of detection of oocysts in faeces using variations of conventional microbiological staining methods [20-24], led the way to widespread investigation and reporting. *Cryptosporidium* is now widely recognized as a cause of acute, self-limiting, infective gastroenteritis in otherwise normal human subjects and of potentially fatal infection in the immunocompromised. However, examination of presumptive positive samples referred to the Rhyl Public Health Laboratory from various parts of the world indicate that some over-reporting undoubtedly occurs as a result of failure to discriminate between oocysts and the various oocyst-like bodies (fungal spores, etc.) which are not oocysts (see below). Conversely, dependence on microscopical detection of individual oocysts may result in some under-reporting. Few of the early reports included detailed descriptions of epidemiological field studies. The emergence of evidence of outbreaks indicated the need for control measures based on an understanding of the natural history of the infection using methods established for other gastrointestinal infections [25]. There was, therefore, clearly a need for more detailed epidemiological investigation of the infection, particularly in immunocompetent hosts [26]. Such studies were initiated in the UK, including north Wales.

In many laboratories worldwide, in both developed and developing countries, *Cryptosporidium* is now among the most commonly reported enteric pathogens. Varying patterns of incidence, by age, season, and geographical location, and of routes of transmission, have now emerged and have been reviewed [4,27–34]. Cryptosporidiosis continues to represent a serious threat to AIDS sufferers and others who are immunocompromised. Although there are some differences in the epidemiology of the infection between immunocompetent and immunocompromised subjects, e.g. in age distribution and in the severity and duration of symptoms, in general the epidemiology differs little except where indicated below.

BIOLOGY AND CLASSIFICATION

A knowledge of the biology of the parasite is essential to an understanding of the epidemiology of human cryptosporidiosis. Much of the earlier literature on *Cryptosporidium* describing its biology and classification is confused and contains inaccuracies in addition to areas of uncertainty. *Cryptosporidium* is a coccidian protozoan which, however, differs from other coccidia in several important respects. *Cryptosporidium* is so named because it appears to lack the sporocyst structure found in other coccidia. It is an obligate parasite with a complex life-cycle, which it completes without the need for development in a secondary host; ie it is monoxenous. [7,28–31] (Figs, IV 1, IV 2). Infection is initiated following ingestion of an environmentally resistant oocyst containing four, naked, motile sporozoites. Development is through several characteristic stages: excystment, merogeny (asexual), gamogony (sexual), zygote and oocyst formation, and sporulation. The fixed endogenous (tissue) stages have a pseudo-external location and are intracellular but extracytoplasmic. They are found primarily in the brush-border of the apical enterocytes of the small bowel but may develop on any epithelial surface and have been reported in a number of different organs and tissues. [32] The non-flagellate motile forms (zoites) are released into the lumen and are initially actively invasive. Once they have entered a cell they develop as a fixed (endogenous) stage within a parasitophorous vacuole thought to be formed from the host cell outer membrane. Recycling of asexual stages, and the presence of thin-walled oocysts which result in endogenous reinfection (autoinfection), permit very heavy infection to develop. [31,34] The infection is probably limited by a combination of humoral and cellular immune mechanisms. The oocyst stage does not require a period of external ripening. The various developmental stages have been elegantly illustrated by Current and his co-workers. [31,35,36]

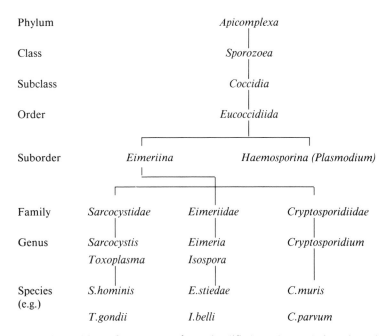

Phylum			*Apicomplexa*	
Class			*Sporozoea*	
Subclass			*Coccidia*	
Order			*Eucoccidiida*	
Suborder		*Eimeriina*		*Haemosporina (Plasmodium)*
Family	*Sarcocystidae*	*Eimeriidae*	*Cryptosporidiidae*	
Genus	*Sarcocystis*	*Eimeria*	*Cryptosporidium*	
	Toxoplasma	*Isospora*		
Species (e.g.)	*S.hominis*	*E.stiedae*	*C.muris*	
	T.gondii	*I.belli*	*C.parvum*	

Fig IV.1. Taxonomic position of *Cryptosporidium* simplified to show relationships with other medically important species. (Reproduced with permission from Casemore, Sands and Curry [7]).

Cryptosporidium is an ubiquitous parasite described in a large number of host species [28,31]. Early reports tended to assign species status to isolates from each newly reported host species in accordance with the practice for other coccidia which are generally both host and tissue-specific. Some of these identifications were based on inadequate information and were incorrect. Subsequently, evidence was adduced to suggest the possibility of a single species genus [4,37]. However, examination of the original findings of Tyzzer [38-40], disputed by some [4] but largely confirmed by others, reveal that *C.muris* and *C.parvum* are distinct species, both found in mice [7,31,34-36, 41-43]. *C.muris* appears to be restricted to the glands of the stomach. It has subsequently also been found to occur in cattle in which it is found in the abomasum and oocysts may be detected in the faeces [35,44]. Anderson in the USA [44], has reported finding the infection to be present in many herds of cattle, in which infection appears to be asymptomatic, but it has not yet been reported in the UK (K. Angus, personal communication). *C.parvum* was so described because of its smaller size. Tyzzer predicted that it might be capable of infecting more than one host species. The majority of infections in man and most livestock animals are probably with *C.parvum* [7,31,34,35]. There is insufficient data yet to confirm whether isolates can be sub-divided into host adapted strains or antigenic or other sub-types although there is some evidence to support this possibility (see below). Some antigenic variation appears to exist which may reflect the host species from which the isolate was derived [43,45,46]. Until more definitive information is available it is probably safer to refer to isolates from humans as *Cryptosporidium* species.

Cryptosporidia are known to occur in wild rodents which may act as a natural reservoir for livestock animals [41-43]. Although *in vivo* laboratory studies require the use of suckling mice, infection and excretion of oocysts appears to occur in adult wild mice. There are at least two avian species which, fortunately in public health terms, appear to be poorly transmissible, if at all, to man and other mammals [31,47-49]. Cryptosporidia have occasionally been reported in fish and reptiles but are poorly characterized and in some cases erroneously identified as such [31,34,49,50].

The biological and other features which determine the medical and epidemiological importance of the parasite are summarized in Table IV.1.

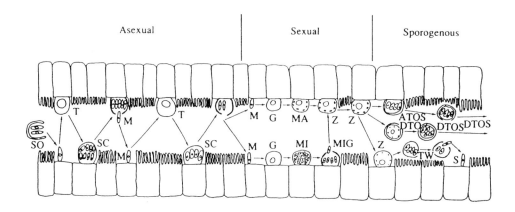

Figure IV.2 Diagrammatic representation
of the life cycle of *Cryptosporidium* sp.

Fig IV.2. Diagramatic representation of the life cycle of *Cryptosporidium* sp. Infection starts with ingestion of an oocyst containing four naked, motile, sporozoites (SO). Sporozoites (S) are released, attach to an epithelial cell and take up a pseudo-external position. They develop into a trophozoite (T) or uninucleate meront which, as it matures, undergoes schizogony (asexual multiple budding) to produce a schizont (SC). There are probably two asexual generations which undergo three and then two nuclear divisions, producing eight or four motile merozoites respectively (M). Merozoites of the first generation invade other cells to form new meronts. The second generation produce gamonts (G) of the sexual cycle. The latter may mature as either microgamonts (MI) which, or macrogametes (MA). Microgamonts produce 16 motile microgametes (MIG) which, on release, fertilize the macrogamete to produce a zygote (Z). The zygote may follow several sporogenous developmental routes: it may transform into a thick-walled oocyst in-situ (ATOS) which then sporulates before becoming detached from the host cell (DTOS), or be shed and subsequently sporulate (DTO); the zygote may develop into a thin-walled oocyst (TW) which releases its sporozoites while in-situ, thus spreading infection within the host. Microvilli have been omitted from infected cells for clarity. (Reproduced with permission from Casemore, Sands and Curry [7]).

Table IV.1 Biological/epidemiological characteristics of *Cryptosporidium parvum* associated with transmissibility to man

Lack of species specifity (host-species cross-transmissibility) (also lacks tissue specificity)
Ubiquitous (Man, food and companion animals—?not avian species)
Monoxenous (Full development in single host species)
Oocyst excreted fully sporulated (no external 'ripening' required)
Oocyst excreted in large numbers (?enhanced by autoinfective cycle)
Probably low infective dose-size (?< = 10–100 oocysts)
Oocysts environmentally resistant
Oocysts resistant to common disinfectants
Faecal-oral mode of infection (Plus? others—aerosol, vomit, etc.)
Person-to-person transmission (especially young children)

DISTRIBUTION OF HUMAN CRYPTOSPORIDIOSIS

Age and sex distribution

A variety of factors may bias laboratory study findings, particularly towards children. Specimens submitted to the laboratory are usually from selected populations and even when derived from general population groups are subject to a variety of ill-determined biases. Despite such biases, the use of laboratory based data is of value although care is needed in interpretation [25,51,52].

Early reports of *Cryptosporidiosis* in humans were often of infection in adults, reflecting the high proportion of immunocompromised subjects among such cases.[7] Attention was drawn in 1983 to sporadic infection in the community, especially in otherwise normal children[13-15]. Several subsequent studies have confirmed a peak incidence in children aged 1–5 years in most areas. A secondary peak in laboratory proven incidence may also be seen in adults aged 20–40 years and which may result from family contact with children, or occupational exposure[53,54]. Detailed examination of laboratory data from a national PHLS surveillance study[55] (Tables IV.2, IV.3) shows that approximately 60 per cent of positive findings are from children and 30 per cent from adults aged less than 45 years. Hence, the role of *Cryptosporidium* in diarrhoeal disease in young adults should not be under-estimated. *Cryptosporidiosis* in susceptible adults may be particularly unpleasant and may occasionally lead to severe disease and even death in some cases[32] (D. Casemore, unpublished observations). In our experience clinical infection is uncommon over the age of 40 although it occurs from time to time. Asymptomatic infection may be found in adults who are close contacts of cases. There is no evidence of increased incidence in the elderly. Infection in some Scandinavian countries appears to occur mainly in adults, most of whom acquire their infection abroad, especially Russia, or as a result of occupational exposure[18,54,56-58]. The reason for the preponderance of adult cases in Scandinavian countries and the relative infrequency of positive findings in children does not yet appear to have been adequately explained. Travellers would be predominantly adult: the low incidence in children may imply that autochthonous infection in Scandinavia is uncommon except in rural subjects in whom the infection is, apparently, often asymptomatic[58].

In the large 2-year PHLS UK survey[55] (Table IV.2) and locally in north Wales over more than 5 years,[43,53] infection was most common in the 1–5 years age group. These surveys included patients of all ages and examination of denominator data indicates that the peak is not the result of age sampling bias. Infection was less common in children aged under 1 year and occurred infrequently under 6 months of age. This pattern is similar to that reported by some others, in the UK,[59] the USA,[60] in rural Costa Rica,[61] Liberia,[62] Rwanda[17], Guinea-Bissau[63] and in Haiti[64]. However, in some other surveys in the UK,[15,65,66] in Eire,[67] and in some Third World countries,[68-70] infection has been found to occur commonly in children aged less than a year. The reasons for these differences are not yet clear but may relate to levels of maternal immunity and of exposure[43,45]. In rural settings in north Wales, clinical cryptosporidiosis in adults, and in infants aged under 6 months, is particularly uncommon and tends to be mild. Infection in rural infants seems to occur most frequently when they are becoming mobile, are teething, and are changing to a shared diet, including in some cases raw cows' milk. At this point, maternally acquired immunity will also be waning. This pattern of incidence thus probably reflects both the frequency of exposure and levels of immunity, including passively acquired immunity. Corbett-Feeney[67]

Table IV.2 Cryptosporidium-positive stools, age distribution symptomatic patients in PHLS (CDSC) UK Survey 1985–87*

Age (years)	GP samples (n)	Positive (%)	Hospital (n)	Positive (%)
< 1	2057	31 (1·5)	3537	24 (0·7)
1–5	4520	183 (4·0)	1972	59 (3·0)
5–15	2160	88 (4·0)	1306	28 (2·1)
15–25	3491	70 (2·0)	1778	19 (1·0)
25–35	4079	75 (1·8)	1011	13 (1·3)
35–45	3049	35 (1·1)	795	7 (0·9)
45–55	2904	14 (0·5)	707	2 (0·3)
55–65	2060	7 (0·3)	1634	1 (0·1)
> 65	2987	12 (0·4)	5971	14 (0·2)
NK	2721	23 (0·8)	1861	3 (0·2)
Total	30043	538 (1·8)	20572	170 (0·8)

*Adapted from Palmer and Biffin[55].

in Eire reported finding a protective effect in infants from breast feeding. This had previously been noted in some developing countries (see below). Though not studied critically, this would also appear to be the case in rural subjects in north Wales (D. Casemore, unpublished observation). There is, however, conflicting medical and veterinary evidence for the protective role of breast feeding and of colostral antibody in resistance to infection with Cryptosporidium[34,43,45]. Perinatal infection has been described and may lead to fetal distress or a failure to thrive[71,72]. Extra-intestinal infection has been demonstrated but there is no evidence of transplacental transmission[32].

The distribution of cases by sex appears to be generally unremarkable. However, experience with campylobacter infections shows that detailed attention to rates of infection may reveal differences in both age- and sex-specific distribution to those shown by analysis of simple incidence figures[52]. Such detailed analysis has yet to be reported for Cryptosporidium infection.

Frequency of occurrence

Most early reports of human cryptosporidiosis were of single sporadic cases, small clusters of cases, or of short clinical series. Population surveys began to be reported in 1983, from Australia,[14] Finland[18] and the UK,[13] and subsequently from numerous other centres[7,27-33]. Surveys were often of selected populations, usually based on specimens routinely submitted to the laboratory, and sometimes studied over short periods of time. Few studies were adequately controlled. Denominator figures were often not recorded other than as the total sample size. Other recognized potential pathogens were not always excluded. Accurate identification cannot be assumed in all studies (D. Casemore, unpublished data).

Table IV.3 Age-Group distribution of Cryptosporidiosis cases (PHLS National Survey)

Proportions of positives (excluding NKs)

Age group	Numbers examined (% of total n)	Positive (% + ve) (% of all + ves)
0–14	18792 (33)	769 (4·1) (62·4)
15–44	23993 (42·4)	398 (1·7) (32·3)
45–> 65	13770 (24·3)	65 (0·47) (5·3)

Adapted from Palmer and Biffin[55].

Laboratory-based surveys are subject to a variety of biases, as discussed above. From some of these studies therefore, it is difficult to gain an accurate picture of incidence rates, or of prevalence, or even to demonstrate unequivocally an aetiological role. They do, however, indicate the unbiquity of the parasite.

A few surveys have shown low prevalence in certain areas (<1 per cent) and the need for routine laboratory screening has been questioned [73-79]. Generalized recommendations discouraging screening, when based on localized and sometimes short-term, low-yield studies, should be viewed with caution. Even if such low figures are an accurate reflection of local prevalence, the simplicity and low cost of such screening, together with the clinical epidemiological, and other benefits obtained, suggest that the search for *Cryptosporidium* should now be undertaken by most laboratories, at least on selected specimens assessed over a sufficient period of time to allow for temporal variation [80-82].

Relative frequency of occurrence

In several studies, *Cryptosporidium* was found to occur as the third or fourth most commonly identified pathogen and at certain times was the most commonly detected of the agents looked for [17,23,30,55,59,65,67,69,80,83,84]. Such findings will tend to reflect the age of subjects sampled and seasonal variation in incidence of the different agents involved. Thus, in north Wales for example, although campylobacter is the most commonly identified enteric pathogen overall, and rotavirus in infants, during certain periods of the year *Cryptosporidium* is the most common finding in children. In the PHLS survey [55], *Cryptosporidium* occurred twice as often as salmonella and several times more commonly than shigella, in the 1-5 years age group over a 2-year study period.

Geographic distribution

Several reviews have tabulated the frequency of detection in a variety of survey populations in many countries worldwide [7,27-30,33]. Reported rates varied from less than 1 per cent to more than 30 per cent. Some of this variation may be attributed to genuine geographic variation, some to demographic or temporal factors. In some instances methodological factors may be important given the variation in sensitivity and specificity of the various methods used [24]. Composite tables of reported laboratory confirmed incidence generally yield average figures in developed countries of approximately 1-2 per cent positivity overall and about 4 per cent in children. As might be expected, reported rates are generally higher in Third World countries, especially in children.

Table IV.4 Outbreaks of cryptosporidiosis in livestock animals reported to veterinary data collection centre (VIDA)

Cattle	Jan.	Feb.	Mar.	Apr.	May.	June.	July.	Aug.	Sept.	Oct.	Nov.	Dec.	Total
1984	14	34	43	45	15	7	11	10	8	21	21	24	253
1985	41	48	94	67	50	17	10	12	14	21	34	37	445
1986	53	44	41	54	32	13	22	20	26	25	44	64	438
1987	72	79	94	120	53	49	22	16	58	57	83	102	805
Total	180	205	272	286	150	86	65	58	106	124	182	227	1941
Sheep													
1984	0	1	5	16	3	0	0	0	0	0	0	1	26
1985	1	3	4	29	9	3	0	0	0	1	0	1	51
1986	3	3	1	34	14	1	0	0	1	0	0	0	57
1987	4	5	18	37	22	1	1	0	0	0	0	0	88
Total	8	12	28	116	48	5	1	0	1	1	0	2	222

Data courtesy of Mr A. B. Davies (DVO, Bangor).

Temporal distribution and seasonality

Seasonal or temporal trends have been noted by a number of authors but these vary from country to country including; summer in Australia,[14] rainy season in Central America[61] and India,[85] spring[84] or late summer in north America,[60,86] and late summer in Germany[87]. Our own studies [43,53,88] and some others in the UK[55,59,65,66] (CDS/CDSC, unpublished reports) and in Eire,[67] indicate a peak of incidence in the spring and sometimes also in late autumn or early winter. These trends may indirectly reflect rainfall, farming events such as lambing and calving (Table IV.4), and practices such as slurry muck-spreading[53,88]. Paradoxically, more detailed study of data from the PHLS study,[55] failed to demonstrate clear seasonality nationally (S. R. Palmer, personal communication). Experience over the past 5 years suggests that outbreaks, or temporal clusters of apparently sporadic cases, occur in different parts of the UK, often at about the same time each year, but not recurring in the same locality year by year. Whether this relates to local herd immunity levels affecting either primary incidence or secondary person-to-person spread, or to other factors, is not yet known. Detailed sero-epidemiological studies might help in elucidating this[43,45].

RESERVOIRS AND ROUTES OF TRANSMISSION

Zoonotic and non-zoonotic infections

The natural history of cryptosporidiosis is complex and involves both zoonotic and 'urban' or non-zoonotic reservoirs and modes of transmission.

Zoonotic transmission. Current and his co-workers drew attention to the association of human infection with exposure to infected calves[5]. In recent reviews, more than 40 host species from which *Cryptosporidium* species had been isolated have been listed[28,31,49,89]. Cross-transmission has been demonstrated experimentally or naturally between a variety of host species[28,31,49,89]. There is, therefore, a potentially large zoonotic reservoir of infection. Most clinical infections in humans and livestock mammals, as stated above, are probably with a single species, *C. parvum,* which has spherical or slightly ovoid oocysts measuring some 4·5–5·0 μm[7,31,35,36,43]. Cryptosporidial oocysts morphologically identical to *C.muris,* and distinct from *C.parvum,* have been identified in cattle in the USA[35,44] but the epidemiological importance of this is not yet clear. The oocysts are more ellipsoidal and measure approximately 6 × 8 μm. The parasite appears, as with the original isolate discovered in mice by Tyzzer, to be restricted to the glands of the stomach (abomasum) and is not associated with symptoms other than poor weight gain in some cases[44] (K. W. Angus, personal communication). *C.muris* infection has not yet been reported in man. Large (⩾ 8 μm) spherical acid-fast objects sometimes found in human faeces, particularly in subjects from Asia and Africa, and thought by some to be cryptosporidia are probably fungal spores (D. Casemore, unpublished observation). The importance of measuring presumptive oocysts cannot be over-emphasized.

Livestock. Calves and lambs are commonly infected wth *Cryptosporidium* in the UK. Pigs are susceptible to infection but this does not appear to be common. Infection in foals may be more common than is currently recognized. Deer and goats are increasingly commonly kept as stock animals and may be severely affected by cryptosporidiosis[2,89]. Many human infections with *Cryptosporidium* are derived from livestock, particularly cattle, either directly, or indirectly. There is also evidence, at least in the UK, to implicate sheep in human infections[88,90,91]. The spring peak in incidence in humans in the UK closely parallels that

110

reported by the Central Veterinary Laboratories for lambs (Table IV.4). In an outbreak in north Wales an association was noted in two related cases with exposure to infected bottle-fed orphan lambs[88]. A case-control study was subsequently carried out during 1988 which confirmed a significant association between human cryptosporidiosis in north Wales during March and April and contact with sheep or lambs, particularly between children and bottle-fed lambs ($P = 0.00006$)[90]. Similar association has again been noted in the spring of 1989 (D. Casemore, unpublished data). In some cases studied, the recently increasing trend towards lambing in deep litter sheds close to the farm house had led to increased exposure of family members and visitors to infection. Exposure sometimes occurred as a result of educational visits to working farms during the lambing season, or away from farms when lambs were taken to urban schools and nurseries for education purposes. In several instances there was evidence of secondary spread within households or play-groups. Educational visits to farms and livestock markets may also lead to contact with other livestock such as calves which may also lead to cryptosporidiosis and to exposure to a variety of other infectious agents. There is, therefore, clearly a need for such zoonotic exposure to be controlled and for the importance of hygienic measures to be emphasised to those responsible. Guidelines to help limit hazards to children from this type of exposure have been circulated in the UK[92]. Zoonotic exposure of urban subjects also occurs when camping on farmland but, in such circumstances, exposure to more than one confounding risk factor (livestock animals, their excreta, raw milk and water, etc.) is common, often combined with lower standards of hygiene (D. Casemore, unpublished observations).

Although symptomatic infection in animals seems to be restricted generally to the very young, adult animals, especially deer, horses, pigs and sheep may excrete low numbers of oocysts[2,89] (K. W. Angus, personal communication). Such excretors may provide a reservoir for the young of their own species and for humans. A number of cases of human cryptosporidiosis have been investigated in north Wales for whom the only identified risk factor was recent attendance at riding stables or recent delivery of horse manure for garden fertilizer use in which small numbers of oocysts were identified (D. P. Casemore and P. Robinson, unpublished data).

Companion animals. Companion animals have been shown to be infected[28,31,34,54,89] and have been implicated in human disease from time to time. They include cats[93,94] and possibly dogs[86] (D. Casemore, unpublished observations). However, despite the frequency with which pets are present in households of infected patients, they do not seem to have been often implicated as a source of infection. With the possible exception of cats, companion animals probably do not represent a zoonotic reservoir for human cryptosporidiosis[2,34]. The finding of small numbers of oocysts in the stools of household pets need not imply that the animal is the source of human infection. In a recent episode investigated in north Wales, the family pet labrador dog was found to be excreting small number of oocysts. The dog had shown signs of mild gastrointestinal upset at the same time as the first affected family member but was not sampled until some time later. A similar isolated incident had previously been encountered with a cat. It is difficult to interpret the significance of such findings as it was not possible to exclude the possibility that the pet and the humans had been exposed to a common source of infection. Wild rodents in the home may potentially transmit infection to pets directly or by contamination of food.

Occupational zoonotic exposure. Human infection has been documented following occupational exposure to naturally and experimentally infected animals, including during the inoculation of infected material, especially by veterinary students[54,58,85,95–98]. A negative association has been noted in some instances between bovine and human cases, particularly with rural adults who are occupationally exposed[12,86]. Occupational exposure probably leads to repeated mild or asymptomatic infection and high levels of immunity. Repeated or recurrent infection has been noted occasionally in sporadic cases[99] (D. Casemore and P. Robinson, unpublished observations). In two cases in north Wales, the second episode was clinically milder than the first. In such cases, it is not yet possible to distinguish between continued low-level or intermittent excretion, recrudescent infection or reinfection.

Indirect zoonotic transmission. Occupationally exposed individuals may inadvertently carry infected material home with them to indirectly infect family members, especially toddlers. Such indirect transmission may have been the route for severe perinatal infection reported by Dale and co-workers[72]. In north Wales, indirect transmission was thought to have occurred on a number of occasions with toddler children of mechanical-digger operators living in urban areas, whose clothing and footwear had become contaminated with animal excreta while working on farms[43]. Rahman and his co-workers in Bangladesh emphasised the importance of person-to-person transmission among household contacts of calf handlers[85].

Food. The pattern of food-borne infection generally has been changing in recent years and an increasing variety of pathogens recognized[100]. Direct incrimination of food in the transmission of *Cryptosporidium* is hampered by the lack of the equivalent of bacteriological enrichment culture for recovery of small numbers of oocyts and for confirmation of viability. *In vitro* cultivation in tissue cultures and in fertile hens eggs is possible but does not result in amplification[31,34].

Based on epidemiological evidence, consumption of certain foods, especially sausages, offal and raw milk appear to be risk factors[53,55,59,83,88,101]. An unexpected finding of the study in north Wales[43,53,88] was the frequency with which sausages were admitted to have been consumed raw, either prior to cooking during meal preparation or even by using the contents as a pate. This practice is now known to occur elsewhere in the UK. The risks of bacterial milk-borne infection are well established[102]. The retail sale of raw milk continues to provide a vehicle or source of infection with a variety of agents, especially in rural areas. The epidemiological evidence adduced for the association of raw milk consumption with transmission of *Cryptosporidium* emphasizes further the need for pasteurization of all milk supplies. Clinical cryptosporidiosis associated with raw milk consumption in north Wales appears to occur most often in those who only occasionally consume it or have recently commenced doing so. Presumably those who regularly consume raw milk will maintain sufficient levels of immunity to prevent symptomatic infection. Whether infection from milk arises as a result of faecal contamination or from ascending infection of the teat duct is not yet known.

Environmental sources

Co-infection with *Giardia* has been noted in some cases, particularly in travellers (see below), suggesting the possibility of contaminated water or fruit and vegetables, as a source of infection as well as by person-to-person transmission[56,60,74,103–105]. Water-borne giardiasis has been reported from the UK[106]. Environmental sources of such infection have been

112

identified in the USA and may occur more commonly than is currently realised[107-109]. This may result from either human or animal pollution of the environment in the case of both these parasites.

Several studies have noted temporal or seasonal peaks in incidence of cryptosporidiosis (see above) which in some cases coincided with periods of maximal rainfall. The widespread practice, even in advanced countries, of disposal of both animal and human excreta to land, e.g. by muck and slurry spreading on pasture, may lead to infection directly, by aerosol spread, or indirectly by contamination of water courses and reservoir feeder streams. Surface waters polluted naturally or by these practices may lead to contamination of water supplies or of food crops during irrigation. *Giardia lamblia* may share a common mode of transmission via water or food polluted by sewage as noted above. Methods have been developed for the investigation of water (see below). Using such methods contaminated water has been identified including surface waters, and in a few instances potable supplies, in the UK[43,50,88,110-112] and in North America[105,107-109,113-117]. A number of cases or outbreaks have been investigated in which water was thought to have been the route of transmission. The epidemiological investigation of an outbreak in Texas in 1984, described by D'Antonio and others,[118] suggested contamination of the communal water supply with human sewage. Other cases in New Mexico, USA, also investigated epidemiologically, have been attributed to the water route[119,120] involving swimming in, or consumption of, surface water.

One confirmed waterborne outbreak in Carroltown, Georgia, USA, resulted in an estimated 13,000 cases[121,122]. This followed a partial failure of the water treatment system, particularly of flocculation, of river water abstracted for the municipal supply at a time of high demand although the water met all EPA quality standards. Although the river flowed through cattle pasture, evidence of infection was lacking in cattle on that land but there was evidence of pollution with sewage. Breakthrough may have resulted from unusually heavy challenge from a bolus of heavily polluted water at a time when the flocculant mixing mechanism was operating at less than optimal efficiency (J. Rose, personal communication). The finding of apparently satisfactory standards for the water may have resulted from sampling at an inappropriate point—at the point of distribution. For example, for turbidity levels, it is essential to check individual treatment plant sections (filter outputs) prior to mixing. In this episode, failure to adequately back-wash some filters almost certainly led to part of the supply having raised turbidity levels (> 1 nephelometric turbidity unit, NTU) although the final mixed supply had a satisfactory NTU value.

Several possible waterborne outbreaks have been investigated in England and Wales but most have not been confirmed[43,50,123,124] (D. Casemore, unpublished data). Most of these investigations, however, preceded the availability of the methods described below. Some outbreaks, at first thought to be waterborne, have shown epidemic curves suggestive of urban transmission when examined in detail[124]. Nonetheless, the initial cluster of cases may well have been of water-borne infection followed by person-to-person transmission. In a few sporadic cases investigated in north Wales, the only risk factor identified has been a breakdown in the local water supply during the preceding 1–2 weeks[53]. In an outbreak in the Sheffield area[50,112] cases showed a statistical association with consumption of potable water. Oocysts were demonstrated in surface waters in the catchment area and in cattle grazing on catchment land. An outbreak of cryptosporidiosis in Scotland[110,111] was confirmed both epidemiologically and microbiologically as water-borne. Contaminated surface water shown to contain oocysts gained access to the treated potable supply via a previously undetected land drain* and resulted in at least 27 confirmed cases, of whom 12 were admitted to hospital. Other outbreaks and clusters of cases have occurred more recently in different parts of the UK some of which may have been water-borne although proof is lacking in most cases.

Early in 1989, a very large outbreak of cryptosporidiosis occurred in the Oxford and Swindon areas of England supplied by Thames Water Authority[125,126]. This has been attributed to consumption of contaminated potable water supplies derived from a polluted reservoir. Samples were taken and examined using the methods developed in the USA, originally for *Gardia* and subsequently adapted by Rose and her co-workers[113,114,116]. Surface water, water-treatment filter backwash samples, and potable water were all shown to contain oocysts (J. Colbourne, personal communication). The total number of cases attributable to the water is difficult to estimate but 516 confirmed cases were identified in the affected area during the course of the outbreak between late December and late April (R. Mayon White, personal communication). The size of the outbreak and the public recognition of risk from treated water caused considerable media and political interest and concern. A number of issues were raised by the outbreak which have been addressed by a Government committee of enquiry and others[125-128]. These include, for example: the practical difficulties of the sampling methodology; the significance of changes in water-treatment practice including the change of flocculants used resulting from concern about the use of aluminium compounds; the problems arising from imposition of a water 'boiling order' including the practical difficulties this imposes upon hospitals and food industry users, and the relative risks of acquiring infection and of scalding injuries.

The safe disposal of sewage and the provision of safe water supplies have been pursued for more than a century[25,129-131]. For largely historical reasons, standards for evaluating the wholesomeness of potable supplies are based primarily on bacteriological parameters. The demonstration of transmission of *Cryptosporidium*, and *Giardia*, via potable water demonstrates that the safety of such supplies cannot be assumed. Neither can the standard bacteriological parameters be used to guarantee freedom from the risk of infection. The fiscal and political implications of this situation are considerable. Currently, only adequate physical methods of removal are likely to be effective. Although breakthrough of such treatment systems resulting from a heavy challenge may account for some episodes, some areas of the country receive water which is chemically treated but unfiltered. It is probable that, where filtration and/or flocculation are missing or defective, contamination of water supplies will occur which, with the known resistance of oocysts to chemical disinfection,[1,3,132-135] makes it likely that further outbreaks will be confirmed. The results of more recent disinfection studies are described below. Contamination of water supplies may in some cases be low-level and intermittent making monitoring difficult. Such contamination may account for some unexplained sporadic cases or small clusters of cases. The precise identity and the viability of oocysts found in water or other environmental samples cannot yet be reliably determined. Their significance is therefore likely to be uncertain although their presence should be taken as presumptive evidence for remedial action.

---

*This was subsequently identified as a redundant raw water collection pipe which records had incorrectly shown to have been disconnected.

An outbreak of more than 70 cases of cryptosporidiosis associated with a swimming pool has been reported in the UK[136]. Defects in pool filtration and of sewage disposal resulted in pollution of the pool water. The only controlling factors currently for *Cryptosporidium*, if faecal contamination of a pool occurs from someone excreting oocysts, are dilution and efficient filtration. However, it is probable that in well-managed pools this infection will not normally be a problem. In the event of an outbreak being suspected, the pool should be closed and flocculants used, with backwashing to waste, to increase filtration efficiency. Increasing the temperature of the water to $\geqslant 45°C$ may also be used to kill oocysts. The activity of other disinfection systems is currently under investigation (see below).

Raw surface waters and private untreated supplies may be consumed by susceptible individuals, especially those engaged in outdoor pursuits such as camping. This clearly carries a risk of acquiring enteric infection including cryptosporidiosis. Chemical treatment tablets may have little effect on the cysts of *Giardia* and *Cryptosporidium* but both are susceptible to heat treatment (see below).

Investigating environmental routes and reservoirs. The obligate parasitic nature and the ubiquity of *Cryptosporidium*, the variable but possible long incubation period, and the potential for subsequent person-to-person transmission, all make epidemiological investigation difficult. As with possible food-borne infection, the lack of an equivalent of bacterial enrichment culture is a constraint on investigation of environmental sources. Systems for the recovery and detection of oocysts from water have been developed, including Moore's swabs[43,88,124] and membrane[50,112] or cartridge filtration,[107–111,113–117,122,137] usually combined with centrifugation and or flotation. Cartridge filtration was extensively used and evaluated in the UK during the outbreaks in Scotland[110,111,137] and in Oxford and Swindon (J. Colbourne, personal communication). A tentative standard method has been produced in the UK, under the auspices of the Department of the Environment (DoE) Standing Committee of Analysts, based on the same methodology. The method can be made quantitative but gives no indication of either viability of oocysts or of their pathogenicity or virulence for man. The methods for recovery and identification of oocysts are time-consuming and labour-intensive and are unsuitable for routine public-health monitoring purposes on any scale.

Caution is needed in identifying objects found in water samples as oocysts of *Cryptosporidium*. Conventional tinctorial methods are of limited value because a variety of fungal spores and other objects resembling oocysts may be found in environmental samples, particularly by modified Ziehl-Neelsen and saffranin staining. These may be present in addition to genuine oocysts. Accurate size measurement is helpful, oocysts of *C.parvum* having a modal size, in stained preparations, of 4·5–5·0 μm[43]. The identity and significance of isolates from fish from reservoirs is uncertain as these have not yet been characterized. Detection and definitive identification of oocysts in clinical or environmental samples may be achieved by means of immunologically-based test such as immunofluorescence (IFAT) using either polyclonal [88,115,124,138] or by monoclonal antibody,[107–111,113,114,116,120,139–142] by ELISA[112] or by latex agglutination[54,143]. However, caution is needed as some antibodies, particularly monoclonals, may be too restrictive in the antigens which they will recognize. Others, particularly polyclonals, may detect group antigens present in cryptosporidia, from both mammalian and avian or other host species, which are of doubtful medical significance or cross-react with other objects such as yeasts. There appears to be incomplete concordance in the findings with the two monoclones currently available. Oocysts exposed to water treatment, especially to chlorine, may be both morphologically and antigenically altered [135] (D. Casemore, unpublished observation; J. Colbourne, personal communication). The monoclonal antibody described by McLauchlin and co-workers [141] has reacted with all human isolates so far tested in the author's laboratory, but reacts also, though less intensely, with *C. muris and C.baileyi*. It appears to work well with environmental samples, oocysts often showing a clearly defined suture or surface fold. Cross-reactivity has not been noted with a variety of fungal species tested including yeasts, and some *Mucor* spp. which produce acid-fast spores of approximately 5 μm (D. Casemore, unpublished observations). The monoclone used by American workers reacts specifically with *C.parvum* but not *C.baileyi* [140] or *C.muris*.

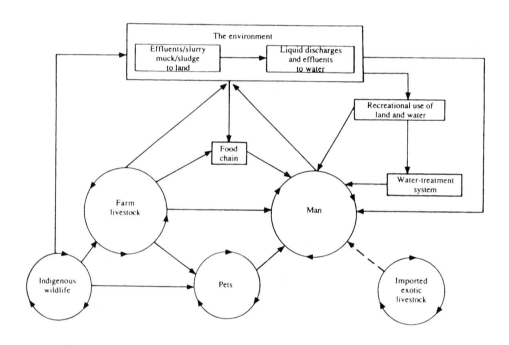

Figure IV.3 Reservoirs and routes of transmission of *Cryptosporidium*

There is a need to develop more sensitive but specific methods of detection which do not depend upon the labour-intensive and essentially subjective microscopical IFAT, particularly for screening out negative samples. These may be based upon ELISA, or gene-probe or polymerized chain reaction technology. There is also a need to be able to assess viability [135] and to identify and distinguish antigenic or iso-enzyme types. Little is currently known about the infectious dose-size (see below) and hence of the epidemiological significance of small numbers of oocysts.

The various potential reservoirs and routes of transmission are outlined in Fig. IV.3. Epidemiological investigation is often confounded by the presence of more than one of the risk factors indicated[88].

Urban or non-zoonotic transmission

Person-to-person transmission is now recognized to be common, thus confirming the hypothesis that cryptosporidiosis is not necessarily a zoonosis[12]. Infection is transmitted within families[53,88,144–148] in day-care centres,[53,144,145, 149–152] and elsewhere in an urban environment[53,59,153–159]. Opportunities for the spread of enteric infections in some Western urban day-care centres may rival those in some Third-World countries[103]. Both sporadic and day-care centre outbreak cases are often associated with confirmed secondary cases among families or of a history of recent diarrhoea among contacts who had not been investigated. Asymptomatic family contacts of confirmed cases are sometimes found to excrete oocysts in small numbers[53,88]. The existence of an asymptomatic carrier state, possibly involving the bile duct, has been reported[158] (see below). Clinically mild cases and asymptomatic excretors may provide a hidden reservoir of infection in the community. Evidence of either point-source or person-to-person transmission may be seen in family outbreaks[53]. Most urban infection probably occurs by the faecal-oral route, directly or via fomites. However, *Cryptosporidium* has been found in sputum and in vomit[32,88,159] and these may provide additional vehicles of transmission.

Nosocomial infection. Hospital cross infection, from patients to staff, has been documented and is further evidence of person-to-person transmission[155–157]. The reverse route, or patient-to-patient transmission, is clearly possible and is of considerable potential importance for immunocompromised patients. There is a risk of indirect transmission via endoscopes, etc[134, 160]. Given the known resistance of oocysts to disinfectants (see below), it is surprising that nosocomially acquired infection has not been documented more frequently.

Sexual transmission. Cryptosporidium may contribute to the so-called 'gay bowel syndrome' of sexually transmitted enteric infection[6,7,161]. However, continuing surveillance of infected practising homosexuals has failed to demonstrate an increased incidence of secondary cases in their partners (R. Soave, personal communication).

Travellers' diarrhoea. The infection has emerged as an important cause of travellers' diarrhoea[18,19,53–57,104,162–164]. Such cases often have mixed infections, especially with *Giardia*, suggesting a common epidemiology involving contaminated water or food. Increased exposure to livestock may be important in some areas. Direct and indirect person-to-person transmission will also be important given the generally poor hygienic conditions which prevail in many under-developed countries[165]. There is evidence to implicate flies in transmission in the Third World (C. Sterling, personal communication).

Travellers' diarrhoea is usually associated with travel to less-developed countries. However, urban subjects in the UK have sometimes been shown to have acquired infection when holidaying in more rural areas of the same country or in Western Europe. This often appears to be associated with consumption of raw (untreated) milk or water, or uncooked sausage, and with exposure to livestock [53,55] (CDSC, unpublished reports; D. Casemore, unpublished observations).

Indigenous (autochthonous) infection in the Third World

Cryptosporidium has been reported from many Third World countries where it may be associated with severe morbidity and sometimes mortality or with asymptomatic infection. The reported age-specific rates of infection differ in different areas of the world and the reason for this is not yet clear. Mata[61] found such differences in incidence to occur between urban and rural populations in Central America which he attributed to differences in breast feeding practices. An apparent protective effect from breast feeding was also noted in Haiti[64] and in Guatamala[68]. Hojlyng and his co-workers[62] in Liberia, reported a positive association with bottle feeding and with overcrowding in urban slums; Malla and co-workers[166] in India made positive links with bottle-feeding in rural children. Increased opportunity for exposure, in bottle-fed infants, and in children who are being weaned may be as important as the immunological properties of breast milk for the differing rates of infection[167]. The evidence for the role of humoral immunity in resistance to cryptosporidiosis is conflicting[43,45]. Transplacentally acquired passive immunity may be important and may explain the apparent low incidence of infection in infants under 6 months of age reported by some workers. Mathan and co-workers[70] in Southern India reported a high rate of asymptomatic infection in Southern Indian children and questioned the significance of the parasite. This differs from most other reports and the validity of the authors interpretation has been questioned[168]. However, such a pattern may reflect hyperendemicity with high levels of exposure and of antibody. There may be close association with livestock from an early age. Rahman and co-workers[85] emphasized the importance of person-to-person transmission among families of calf handlers, presumably introduced into the household from their animals, Carstensen and his co-workers[63] point out that the age-specific prevalence of cryptosporidiosis in their study was the reverse of that for most parasitic infections and suggest that early infection, probably by person-to-person transmission is followed by immunity to clinical infection. On the other hand, immunity impaired by malnutrition may delay clearing and hence prolong excretion. Cryptosporidiosis in the malnourished has been linked to severe persistent or chronic diarrhoea[169-171] which, in turn, may further increase the malnourishment. The severe diarrhoea sometimes associated with measles may be exacerbated by cryptosporidiosis in some cases[32].

Ethnic differences. Some reports have indicated differences in incidence in particular ethnic groups within the same study area, particularly of lower rates among muslims, which may reflect dietary differences, differing exposure to livestock animals, or to toiletting practices[59,62] (T. Rowbotham, personal communication).

Mixed enteric infections

Polymicrobial infections are commonly found in subjects in developing countries and are now more commonly being recognized in developed countries, especially in AIDS suffers. Although, in immunocompetent subjects, *Cryptosporidium* is most commonly found as the sole recognized enteric pathogen, a variety of agents have been reported in mixed infections. In developed countries, concurrent infection with such agents as *Giardia,*[53,60,104,105] *Campylobacter*[53,67,88] and *Shigella sonnei,*[153] may indicate a common epidemiology and dual transmission in some of those cases. Mixed infection with *Cryptosporidium* plus *Giardia* have been noted particularly with children in day-care centres and in travellers to Leningrad. However, such infections may not always be significantly associated[74,152] and may, particularly in under-developed countries, represent overlapping sequential infection or coincidental carriage of one agent detected as a result of acute infection with the other.

Incubation and excretion periods

The prepatent (incubation) period in naturally and experimentally infected animals has been shown to be usually 2–5 days, and the patent (excretion) period about 8–14 days, range < 7 to > 28 days[1,2,53,66,172-176]. Attempts have been made to define incubation and excretion periods

118

in man, both of which factors are epidemiologically important. Because of the ubiquity of the parasite and the diversity of potential sources and routes of transmission (see Fig. IV.3), it is usually not possible accurately to define the incubation period[177]. However, accidental laboratory infection [97] or other detailed exposure histories[18,66,95,97,104,146,174] suggest an incubation period of about 3 days to a week but longer in some cases. Some estimates are based on assumptions which may not be valid and ignore the existence of confounding factors. Periods of as little as 1 day have been suggested[174] but earlier exposure, or prior or co-infection with other agents having shorter incubation periods such as viruses, were not excluded[177]. The effect of infecting dose size is discussed below.

During the acute diarrhoeal phase, oocyst numbers may exceed $10^6/cm^3$ of stool. However, numbers of oocysts excreted during the course of the infection may fluctuate markedly and formed or semi-formed stools may be found to contain many oocysts while some fluid stools may contain few. The stools of some patients become oocyst-negative rapidly after cessation of their diarrhoea while others continue to excrete for a prolonged period, sometimes associated with the continuation of other symptoms. Accurate determination of the excretion period is limited by the availability of sequential specimens and by the sensitivity of oocyst detection sysems. Excretion in immunologically normal subjects, assessed by conventional tinctorial methods, usually seems to cease within 1–4 weeks of clinical resolution but may be longer in some cases[32,43,53,99, 174–176]. Use of a more sensitive IFAT method suggests that excretion may continue for longer[140,141,178]. The existence has been reported of 'atypical' oocysts not detectable by conventional staining methods[179–180]. Large numbers of oocysts may be detected in some stool samples when stained by IFAT, of which the majority can not be detected by other methods, even as unstained 'ghosts'[141] (D. Casemore, unpublished observation). The significance of these findings in relation to infectivity and control needs further elucidation.

Infection in immunocompromised subjects is sometimes mild or resolves unexpectedly[181,182] but the reason for this is not currently known. In some such cases anti-HIV treatment may permit sufficient immune response to return to induce control of the infection. This may parallel the situation reported in some leukaemic subjects[32]. Immunocompromised cases may harbour the parasite in the bile duct. Involvement of the bile duct has not yet been demonstrated in immunologically normal subjects[159]. One small study has adduced evidence for asymptomatic carriage by detection of oocysts in duodenal aspirates[158]. Endogenous stages were not found in biopsy sections but these may be easily overlooked[7]. The subjects did not have diarrhoea and oocysts were found in only a small proportion of their stool samples. Studies on more than 100 endoscopy fluids in north Wales have so far failed to confirm these findings (Casemore and Tynan, unpublished data). If the finding is confirmed, such cases may excrete oocysts at rates below the current threshold for detection but might, nonetheless, provide a reservoir of infection.

Infectivity and resistance Little is known of the infectious dose size but it is thought to be small[28,97,183]. Infectious dose sizes in single figures have been determined for some other protozoan cysts such as *Giardia* (D. Warhurst, personal communication). Experimental studies by Ernest and his co-workers[184] suggest that there may be a larger minimum infectious dose size and that the proportion of exposed subjects developing infection is a function of

119

the dose size. Conversely, a low infecting dose size may simply extend the incubation period or reduce the likelihood of symptomatic expression. The possibility of a small infecting dose size, together with the known resistence of oocysts,[1,3,4,31,132–135] emphasizes the potential for nosocomial and environmental transmission. Ten to 25 per cent commercial bleach may be used for bacterial decontamination of oocyst samples prior to animal inoculation without significantly reducing infectivity [31] although a reduction in *in vitro* excystation may occur. In studies using an *in vitro* excystation model, plus newborn mouse inoculation for confirmation,[133,134] some compounds tested showed an effect in preliminary screening but, as might be expected, were ineffective when retested in the presence of protein. Some showed more effect if used at temperatures above ambient. Of the common disinfectants and antiseptics assayed, only 10 vol. hydrogen peroxide was found to be rapidly effective at ambient temperature and was unaffected by the presence of protein. An agricultural proprietary product, Oo-cide (Antec International Ltd) was also found to be effective but this depends upon the action of ammonia with a biocide in a highly alkaline solution and is unsuitable for medical or domestic use. Its use in the treatment of a polluted swimming pool (see above) led to considerable damage to the activated sludge system of the receiving sewage works. Oocysts are susceptible to freezing, to heating above 45°C for 5–20 min, and to drying[133,173,185–187]. U.V. irradiation appeared to have some effect but less than that on bacteria or yeast cells similarly exposed (D. Blewett, S. E. Wright and D. Casemore, unpublished observations). Ozone at high concentrations (c 2·0 mg/l) has been reported to kill oocysts [188] but in other, preliminary, experiments exposure of oocysts at the time/temperature/concentration levels likely to be found in swimming-pool water treatment, excystation levels were not reduced (D. Casemore, unpublished observations). Laboratory scale studies by Upton and his co-workers show that pentaiodide resin may be capable of removing oocysts from water, probably by electrostatic forces [189] but the practical implications of this finding are uncertain. Thus, further studies are required to identify effective disinfectants suitable for domestic, hospital, and water-treatment purposes.

Seroepidemiology

Several attempts have been made to carry out serological studies using IFAT, ELISA, or laser densitometry[43,45,50,88,122,156,162,190-196]. The significance of the findings in these preliminary reports is unclear because of variations in methodology. Some studies have employed infected tissues containing endogenous stages as antigen while others have employed purified oocysts. Studies on oocysts have indicated that, as might be anticipated, they are antigenically complex but include some common antigens[46,140,194,195,197-199]. The effect which differences in antigen source or test system might have is not clear but it has been suggested that titres may be significantly higher using sporozoites or endogenous stages as antigen[4,45]. In some cases, titres were found to vary according to the host species from which the oocysts were derived suggesting the possibility of different antigenic types[43,45,46]. In some studies, persistent IgA and or IgM, and poor IgG responses were reported. There is some evidence of pre-existing immunity in asymptomatic close family contacts of cases consistent with immunity, presumably associated with previous exposure[43,45]. This seemed, in the north Wales study, to be associated mainly with the presence of IgG. As might be expected, seroprevalence rates tend to be much higher than the frequency of oocyst detection. In addition to giving some indication of prevalence in particular populations some of these studies have yielded information on the pattern of the immune response of value in the study of pathogenesis. Such studies may also provide alternative evidence of cases occurring in outbreaks[43,45,122]. Further studies are required to elicudate some of the questions raised.

Molecular epidemiology. Typing of epidemiologically important isolates of infective agents has usually depended on biotyping methods, based on both phenotypic and genotypic characteristics. The use of so-called 'molecular epidemiology' has proved of great value in the study of epidemiology, particularly of viruses[200]. Given the obligate parasitic nature of *Cryptosporidium*, the typing and sub-typing of isolates below species level must depend largely upon such molecular methods. Antigen and antibody analysis at the molecular level may yield epidemiologically useful information. Isoenzyme (zymodeme) profiling as used in the sub-typing of potentially pathogenic amoebae[201] may also be of value. The extraction and purification of nucleic acids and other molecular components has been achieved thus leading the way to the production of gene-probes and to other more sensitive means of detection and identification (D. Blewett and N. Gordon, personal communication).

CONCLUSION

Cryptosporidium sp. has emerged worldwide during the 1980s as an important cause of acute, often protracted but self-limited gastroenteritis in normal individuals while, in the immunocompromised, the infection may often prove chronic and life threatening. Infection in some cases extends beyond the gastrointestinal tract[32,159]. The importance of close collaboration between veterinary and medical workers for the control of zoonoses has been emphasised[202]. Much has been learned from such collaboration about *Cryptosporidium* and human cryptosporidiosis. Molecular methods for the study of epidemiology are already under way, particularly by veterinary workers who have contributed so much to the understanding of human cryptosporidiosis. The infection is transmitted by both zoonotic and urban routes. It occurs sporadically and in both family and community outbreaks and is more common in children and young adults. There is a variable geographic and temporal distribution of incidence. Given awareness of the infection, the diagnosis may be achieved simply and relatively inexpensively, thus alerting others to the risk of transmission. In times of great fiscal constraint it is tempting to ignore the search for a pathogen which in some geographical areas, and at certain times, may have a low prevalence. In the hospital setting, such patients represent a potential source of nosocomial infection. The severity of the infection, particularly in the Third World and in the ever increasing numbers of immunocompromised patients, makes awareness and control of the infection essential. In the UK, and elsewhere, cryptosporidiosis may be the most commonly detected enteric pathogen affecting AIDS patients[159, 203]. Control of human cryptosporidiosis can be achieved only by a thorough understanding of its natural history and epidemiology. Despite the advances made, much remains to be learned.

Acknowledgments

It is a pleasure to record my gratitude to the staff of the Rhyl PHL; to Dr S. R. Palmer, Communicable Disease Surveillance Centre, Welsh Unit; staff at the Moredun Institute, Edinburgh, and Mr A. Davies, DVO, Bangor for their help.

D. P. CASEMORE
Public Health Laboratory and Department of Microbiology,
Glan Clwyd Hospital,
Bodelwyddan,
Clwyd LL18 5UJ

References

1. Angus K W. Cryptosporidiosis in man, domestic animals and birds: a review. J Roy Soc Med 1983; **76**: 62–70.
2. Angus K W. Mammalian cryptosporidiosis: a veterinary perspective. In: Angus K W, Blewett D A, eds. Cryptosporidiosis. Proceedings of the First International Workshop. Edinburgh: Moredun Research Institute, 1988: 43–53.
3. Tzipori S. Cryptosporidiosis in animals and humans. Microbiol Rev. 1983; **47**: 84–96.
4. Tzipori S. Cryptosporidiosis in perspective. In: Baker J R, Muller R, eds. Advances in parasitology, vol. 27. London: Academic Press, 1988: 63–129.
5. Current W L, Reese N C, Ernst J V, et al. Human cryptosporidiosis in immunocompetent and immunodeficient persons. New Eng J Med 1983; **308**: 1252–7.
6. Pitlik S D, Fainstain V, Garza D, *et al.* Human cryptosporidiosis: Spectrum of disease. Arch Intern Med 1983; **143**: 2269–75.
7. Casemore D P, Sands R L, Curry A. Cryptosporidium species a 'new' human pathogen, J Clin Pathol 1985: **38**: 1321–36.
8. Tzipori S, Angus K W, Gray E W, Campbell I. Vomiting and diarrhoea associated with cryptosporidial infection. New Eng J Med 1980; **383**: 818.
9. Bird R G, Smith M D.Cryptosporidiosis in man: parasite life cycle and fine structural pathology. Pathology 1980; **132**: 217–33.
10. Ericsson C D, DuPont H L. Cryptosporidium and diarrhoea. Lancet 1983; ii: 914.
11. Schultz M G. Emerging zoonoses. New Eng J Med 1983; **308**: 1285–6.
12. Casemore D P, Jackson F B. Hypothesis: cryptosporidiosis in human beings is not primarily a zoonosis. J Infect 1984; **9**, 153–6.
13. Casemore D P, Jackson F B. Sporadic cryptosporidiosis in children. Lancet 1983; ii: 679.
14. Tzipori S, Smith M, Birch C, Barnes G, Bishop R. Cryptosporidiosis in hospital patients with gastroenteritis. Am J Trop Med Hyg 1983; **32**: 931–4.
15. Hart C A, Baxby D, Blendell N. Gastroenteritis due to Cryptosporidium: a prospective survey in a children's hospital. J Infect 1984; **9**: 264–70.
16. Hojlyng N, Molbak K, Jepsen S, Hansson A P. Cryptosporidiosis in Liberian children. Lancet 1984; i: 734.
17. Bogaerts J, Lepage P, Rouvroy D, Vandepitte J, *Cryptosporidium* spp., a frequent cause of diarrhoea in central Africa. J Clin Microbiol 1984; **20**: 874–6.
18. Jokipii L, Pohjola S, Jokipii A M M. Cryptosporidium: a frequent finding in patients with gastrointestinal symptoms. Lancet 1983; ii: 358–61.
19. Holten-Andersen W, Gerstoft J, Henriksen S A, Pedersen N S. Prevalence of Cryptosporidium among patients with acute enteric infection. J Infect 1984; **9**: 277–82.
20. Ma P, Soave R. Three-step stool examination for cryptosporidiosis in 10 homosexual men with protracted watery diarrhoea. J Infect Dis 1983; **147**: 824–8.
21. Garcia L S, Bruckner D A, Brewer T C, Shimizu R Y. Techniques for the recovery and identification of cryptosporidium oocysts from stool specimens. J Clin Microbiol 1983; **18**: 185–90.
22. Baxby D, Blundell N, Hart C A. The development and performance of a simple, sensitive method for the detection of *Cryptosporidium* oocysts in faeces. J Hyg 1984; **92**: 317–23.
23. Nichols G, Thom B T. Screening for cryptosporidium in stools. Lancet 1984; i: 735.
24. Casemore D P, Armstrong M, Sands R L. Laboratory diagnosis of cryptosporidiosis. J Clin Pathol 1985; **38**: 1337–41.
25. Galbraith N S. The application of epidemiological methods in the investigation and control of an acute episode of infection. In: Holland W W, Detels R, Knox G, eds. Oxford textbook of public health. Oxford: Oxford University Press, 1985; vol. 4; 3–21.
26. DuPont H L, Cryptosporidiosis and the healthy host. New Eng J Med 1985; **312**: 1319–20.
27. Soave R, Armstrong D. *Cryptosporidium* and cryptosporidiosis. Rev Infect Dis 1986; **8**: 1012–23.
28. Fayer R, Ungar L P. *Cryptosporidium* spp. and cryptosporidiosis. Microbiol Rev 1986; **50**, 458–83.
29. Ma P. Cryptosporidiosis and immune enteropathy: a review. In: Remington J S, Swartz M N, eds. Current clinical topics in infectious diseases. New York: McGraw Hill, 1987; 99–149.
30. Hart C A, Baxby D. Cryptosporidiosis in children. Pediatr Rev Commun 1987; **1**: 311–41.
31. Current W L. *Cryptosporidium*: its biology and potential for environmental transmission. CRC Crit Rev Envir Contr 1986; **17**: 21–51.
32. Casemore D P. Human cryptosporidiosis. In: Reeves D, Geddes A, eds. Recent advances in infection, No. 3. Edinburgh: Churhill Livingstone, 1988; 209–36.
33. Janoff E N, Reller L B. *Cryptosporidium* species, a protean protozoan. J Clin Microbiol 1987 **25**, 967–75.
34. Current W L. *Cryptosporidium* and cryptosporidiosis. In: Angus K W, Blewett D A, eds. Cryptosporidiosis. Proceedings of the First International Workshop: Moredun Research Institute, 1988: 1–17.
35. Upton S J, Current W L. The species of *Cryptosporidium* (Apicomplexa: Cryptosporidiidae) infecting mammals. Am Soc Parasitol 1985; **71**: 625–9.
36. Current W L, Reese N C. A comparison of endogenous development of three isolates of *Cryptosporidium* in suckling mice. J Protozool 1986; **33**, 98–108.
37. Tzipori S, Angus K W, Campbell I, Gray E W. *Cryptosporidium*: Evidence for a single-species genus. Infect Immun 1980; **30**: 884–6.
38. Tyzzer E E. A sporozoan in the peptic glands of the common mouse. Proc Soc Exp Biol Med 1907–08; **5**: 12–13.
39. Tyzzer E E. Extracellular coccidium, Cryptosporidium muris (Gen et sp nov) of the gastric glands of the common mouse. J Med Res 1910; **23**, 487–509.

40. Tyzzer E E. *Cryptosporidium parvum* (sp. nov.), a coccidium found in the small intestine of the common mouse. Archiv für Protistenkunde 1912; **26**, 394–412.

41. Anonymous. Health and parasites of a wild mouse population. Proc Zool Soc London 1931 (3): 607–878.

42. Klesius P H, Haynes T B, Malo L K. Infectivity of *Cryptosporidium* sp. isolated from wild mice for calves and mice. JAVMA 1986; **189**: 192–3.

43. Casemore D P. Gastroenteritis ina semi-rural population (The emergence of a 'new' pathogen, *Cryptosporidium*). PhD Thesis, 1987; School of Pharmacy, Liverpool.

44. Anderson B C. Cryptosporidium species in cattle. In: Angus K W, Blewett D A, eds. Cryptosporidiosis. Proceedings of the First International Workshop. Edinburgh, Moredun Institute, 1988: 55–63.

45. Casemore D P. The antibody response to Cryptosporidium: development of a serological test and its use in a study of immunologically normal persons. J Infect 1987; **14**: 125–34.

46. Nichols G, Dhanraj S, McLaughlin J. Characterization of oocyst surface antigens of *Cryptosporidium* spp. (Abstract). In: Angus K W, Blewett D A, eds. Cryptosporidiosis. Proceedings of the First International Workshop. Edinburgh: Moredun Research Institute, 1988: 121.

47. Current W L, Upton S J, Haynes T B. The life cycle of *Cryptosporidium baileyi* n.sp. (Apicomplexa, Cryptosporidiidae) infecting chickens. J Protozool 1986; **33**: 289–96.

48. Blagburn B L. Avian cryptosporidiosis. In: Angus K W, Blewett D A, eds. Cryptosporidiosis. Proceedings of the First International Workshop. Edinburgh: Moredun Research Institute, 1988: 27–42.

49. O'Donoghue P J. *Cryptosporidium* infections in man, birds and fish. Austr Vet J 1985; **62**, 253–8.

50. Rush B A, Chapman P A, Ineson R W. Cryptosporidium and drinking water. Lancet 1987; ii: 632–3.

51. Tillett H E, Thomas M E M. Monitoring infectious diseases using routine microbiology data I. Study of gastroenteritis in an urban area. J Hyg 1981; **86**: 49–69.

52. Skirrow M B. A demographic survey of campylobacter, salmonella ans shigella infections in England. Epidemiol Infect 1987; **99**: 647–57.

53. Casemore D P. Cryptosporidiosis. PHLS Microbiology Digest 1987; **4**: 1–5.

54. Pohjola-Stenroos S. Diagnostic and epidemiological aspects of Cryptosporidium infection, a protozoan infection of increasing veterinary public health importance. Academic dissertation,College of Veterinary Medicine, Helsinki, 1986.

55. Palmer S R, Biffin A. Cryptosporidiosis. PHLS Microbiology Digest 1987; **4**: 6–7.

56. Jokipii L, Pohjola S, Jokipii A M. Cryptosporidiosis associated with travelling and giardiasis. gastroenterol 1985; **89**, 838–42.

57. Atterholm I, Castor B, Norlin K. Cryptosporidiosis in southern Sweden. Scand J Infect Dis 1987; **19**, 231–4.

58. Pohjola S, Jokipii A M M, Jokipii L. Sporadic cryptosporidiosis in a rural population is asymptomatic and associated with contact to cattle. Acta Vet Scand 1986; **27**, 91–102.

59. Thomson M A, Benson J W T, Wright P A. Two year study of cryptosporidium infection Arch Dis Child 1987; **62**: 559–63.

60. Wolfson J S, Richter J M, Waldron M A, Weber D J, McCarthy D M, Hopkins C C. Cryptosporidiosis in immunocompetent patients. New Eng J Med 1985; **312**: 1278–82.

61. Mata L. *Cryptosporidium* and other protozoa in diarrheal disease in less developed countries. Ped Infect Dis (Suppl) 1986; **5**: S117–S129.

62. Hojlyng N, Molbak K, Jepsen S. *Cryptosporidium* spp., a frequent cause of diarrhoea in Liberian children. J Clin Microbiol 1986; **23**: 1109–13.

63. Carstensen H, Hansen H L, Kristiansen H O, Gomme G. The epidemiology of cryptosporidiosis and other intestinal parasitoses in children in southern Guinea-Bissau. Trans Roy Soc Trop Med Hyg 1987; **81**: 860–4.

64. Pape J W, Levine E, Beaulieu M E, Marshall F, Verdier R Johnston W D. Cryptosporidiosis in Haitian children. Am J Trop Med Hyg 1987; **36**: 333–7.

65. Baxby D, Hart C A. The incidence of cryptosporidiosis: a two-year prospective survey in a children's hospital. J Hyg 1986; **96**: 107–11.

66. Shepherd R C, Sinha G P, Reed C L, Russell F E. Cryptosporidiosis in the West of Scotland. Scot Med J 1989; **33**: 365–8.

67. Corbett-Feeney G. Cryptosporidium among children with acute diarrhoea in the west of Ireland. J Infect 1987; **14**, 79–84.

68. Cruz J R, Cano F, Caceres P, Chew F, Pareja G. Infection and diarrhoea caused by *Cryptosporidium* sp. among Guatemalan infants. J Clin Microbiol 1988; **26**, 88–91.

69. Smith G, van den Ende J. Cryptosporidiosis among black children in hospital in South Africa. J Infect 1986; **13**: 35–30.

70. Mathan M, Venkatesan S, George R, Mathew M, Mathan V I. Cryptosporidium and diarrhoea in southern Indian children. Lancet 1985; ii: 1172–5.

71. Lahdevirta J, Jokipii A M M, Sammalkorpi K, Jokipii L. Perinatal infection with cryptospopridium and failure to thrive. Lancet 1987; i: 48–9.

72. Dale B A S, Gordon G, Thomson R, Urquart R. Perinatal infection with cryptosporidium. Lancet 1987; i: 1042–3.

73. Hamoudi A C, Qualman S J, Marcon M J, *et al.* Do regional variations in prevalence of cryptosporidiosis occur? The central Ohio experience. Am J Public Health 1988; **78**: 273–5.

74. Skeels M R, Sokolow R, Hubbard C V, Foster L R. Screening for co-infection with *Cryptosporidium* and *Giardia* in Oregon public health clinics. Am J Public Health 1988: **78**: 270–3.

75. Kern W, Mayer S, Kreuzer P, Vanek E. Low prevalence of intestinal cryptosporidiosis among immunocompetent and immunocompromised patients with and without diarrhoea in southern Germany. Infection 1987; **15**: 440–2.

76. Marshall A R, Al-Jumaili I J, Fenwick G A, Bint A J, Record C O. Cryptosporidiosis in patients at a large teaching hospital. J Clin Microbiol 1987; **25**: 172–3.

77. Nachamkin I, Jones A, Hasyn H. Routine parasitological examination for *Cryptosporidium*. J Infect Dis 1986; **154**: 369–70.

78. Baron E J, Schenone C, Tanenbaum B. Comparison of three methods for detection of *Cryptosporidium* oocysts in a low-prevalence population. J Clin Microbiol 1989; **27**: 223–4.

79. Bissenden J G. Cryptosporidium and diarrhoea. Br Med J 1986; **293**: 287–8.

80. Waghorn D J, Hinkins R. Screening for cryptosporidial infection. J Clin Pathol 1986; **39**, 1363.

81. Tzipori S. Cryptosporidium and routine parasitological diagnosis. J Infect Dis 1987; **156**: 248.

82. Jackson F B, Casemore D P Cryptosporidium and diarrhoea. Br Med J 1986; **293**: 625–6.

83. Freidank H, Kist M. Cryptosporidia in immuocompetent patients with gastroenteritis. Europ J Clin Microbiol 1986; **6**: 56–9.

84. Holley H P, Dover C. *Cryptosporidium*: a common cause of parasitic diarrhoea in otherwise healthy individuals. J Infect Dis 1986; **153**: 365–8.

85. Rahman A S M H, Sanyal S C, Al-Mahmud K A, Sobhan A. *Cryptosporidium* diarrhoea in calves and their handlers in Bangladesh. Ind J Med Res 1985; **82**: 510–6.

86. Mann E D, Sekla L H, Nayer G P S, Koschik C. Infection with *Cryptosporidium* spp. in humans and cattle in Manitoba. Canad J Vet Res 1986; **50**: 174–8.

87. Nguyen X M. Cryptosporidial diarrhoea in children. Infection 1987; **15**: 444–6.

88. Casemore D P, Jessop E G, Douce D, Jackson F B. *Cryptosporidium* plus compylobacter: an outbreak in a semi-rural population. J Hyg 1986; **96**: 95–105.

89. Chermette R, Boufassa-Ouzrout S. Cryptosporidiosis: a cosmopolitan disease in animals and man, 2nd edition, Technical Series No. 5. Office International des Epizooties, Paris, 1988.

90. Casemore D P. Bottle-fed lambs as a source of human cryptosporidiosis. J Infect 1989; **19**: 101–4.

91. Casemore D P. Cryptosporidiosis: another source. Brit Med J 1989; **298**: 750–1.

92. Casemore D P. Educational farm visits and associated infection hazards. Communicable Disease Report 1989; 89/19: 3. PHLS Communicable Disease Surveillance centre, Public Health Laboratory Service, London.

93. Koch K L, Shankey V, Weinstein G S, *et al.* Cryptosporidiosis in a patient with hemophilia, common variable hypogammaglobulinemia, and the Acquired Immunodeficiency Syndrome. Ann Intern Med 1983; **99**: 337–40.

94. Lewis I J, Hart C A, Baxby D. Diarrhoea due to *Cryptosporidium* in acute lymphoblastic leukaemia. Arch Dis Child 1985; **60**: 60–2.

95. Pohjola S, Oksanen H, Jokipii L, Jokipii A M M. Outbreak of cryptosporidiosis among veterinary students. Scand J Infect Dis 1986; **18**: 173–8.

96. Hojlyng N, Holten-Andersen W, Jepsen S. Cryptosporidiosis: a case of airborne transmission. Lancet 1987; ii: 271–2.

97. Blagburn B L, Current W L. Accidental infection of a researcher with human *Cryptosporidium*. J Infect Dis 1983; **148**: 772–3.

98. Levine J F, Levy M G, Walker R L, Crittenden S. Cryptosporidiosis in veterinary students. J Am Vet Med Assoc 1988; **193**: 1413–4.

99. Baxby D, Hart C A, Blundell N. Shedding of oocysts by immunocompetent individuals with cryptosporidiosis. J Hyg 1985; **95**: 703–9.

100. Galbraith N S, Barrett N J, Sockett P N. The changing pattern of food-born disease in England and Wales. Publ Hlth 1987; **101**: 319–28.

101. Nichols G, Thom B T. Food poisoning caused by Cryptosporidium: a load of tripe. PHLS Communicable Disease Surveillance Centre, London, 1985; (unpublished report CDR 85/17: 3).

102. Barrett N J. Communicable disease associated with milk and dairy products in England and Wales: 1983–1984. J Infect 1986; **12**: 265–72.

103. Kraft J C. Giardia and giardiasis in childhood. Pediatr Infect Dis 1982; **1**: 196–211.

104. Jokipii A M M, Hemila M, Jokipii L. Prospective study of acquisition of Cryptosporidium, *Giardia lamblia*, and gastrointestinal illness. Lancet 1985; ii: 487–9.

105. Isaac-Renton J L, Fogel D, Stibbs H H, Ongerth J E. Giardia and Cryptosporidium in drinking water. Lancet 1987; i: 973–4.

106. Jephcott A E, Begg N T, Baker I A. Outbreak of giardiasis associated with mains water in the United Kingdom. Lancet 1986; i: 730–2.

107. Stetzenbach L D, Arrowood M J, Marshall M M, Sterling C R. Monoclonal antibody based immunofluorescent assay for *Giardia* and *Cryptosporidium* detection in water samples. Wat Sci Tech 1988; **20**: 193–8.

108. Rose J B, Darbin H, Gerba C P. Correlations of the protozoa *Cryptosporidium* and *Giardia*, with water quality variables in a watershed. Wat Sci Tech 1988; **20**: 271–6.

109. Rose J B, Kayed D, Madore M S, *et al.* Methods for the recovery of *Guiardia* and *Cryptosporidium* from environmental waters and their comparative occurrence. In: Wallis P M, Hammond B R, eds. Advances in *Giardia* research. Calgary: University of Calgary Press, 1988: 205–9.

110. Smith H V, Girdwood R W A, Patterson W J, *et al.* Waterborne outbreak of cryptosporidiosis. Lancet 1988; ii: 1484.

111. Smith H V, Patterson W J, Hardie R, *et al.* An outbreak of waterborne cryptosporidiosis caused by post-treatment contamination, Epidemiol Infect 1989. In press.

112. Chapman P A, Rush B A. The use of methods based on a monoclonal antibody to investigate the epidemiology of cryptosporidiosis. PHLS DMRQC Newsletter, Issue 2, 1987: 1–4. Public Health Laboratory Service, London.

113. Rose J B, Cifrino A, Madore M S, et al. Detection of *Cryptosporidium* from waste water and freshwater environments. Wat Sci Tech 1987; **18**: 233–9.

114. Madore M S, Rose J B, Gerba C P, Arrowood M J, Sterling C R. Occurrence of *Cryptosporidium* oocysts in sewage effluents and selected surface waters. J Parasitol 1987; **73**: 702–5.

115. Ongerth J E, Stibbs H H. Identification of *Cryptosporidium* oocysts in river water. Appl Env Microbiol 1987; **53**: 672–6.

116. Musial C E, Arrowood M J, Sterling C R, Gerba C P. Detection of *Cryptosporidium* in water by using polypropylene cartridge filters. Appl Env Microbiol 1987; **53L** 687–92.

117. Rose J B. Occurrence and significance of cryptosporidium in water. JAWWA 1988; **80**: 53–8.

118. D'Antonio R G, Winn R E, Taylor J P, *et al*. A waterborne outbreak of cryptosporidiosis in normal hosts. Ann Intern Med 1985; **103**: 886–8.

119. Anon. Cryptosporidiosis – New Mexico, 1986. Morbid Mortal Weekly Rep 1987; **39**: 561–3.

120. Gallaher M M, Herndon J L, Nims L J, Sterling C R, Grabowski D J, Hull H F. Cryptosporidiosis and surface water. AJPH 1989; **79**: 39–42.

121. Anon (Roundtable). Cryptosporidium. JAWWA 1988; **80**: 14–27.

122. Hayes E B, Matte T D, O'Brien T R, *et al*. Large community outbreak of cryptosporidiosis due to contamination of a filtered public water supply. New Eng J Med 1989; **320**: 1372–6.

123. Galbraith N S, Barrett N J, Stanwell-Smith R. Water and Disease after Croyden: A review of waterborne and water-associated disease in the UK 1937–86. J Inst Water Env Manag 1987; **1**: 7–21.

124. Brown E A E, Casemore D P, Gerken A, Greatorex I. Cryptosporidiosis in Great Yarmouth. Publ Hlth 1989; **103**: 3–9.

125. Dick T A. Report of enquiry into water supplies in Oxford and Swindon following an outbreak of cryptosporidiosis during February–March 1989. Thames Water, London, 1989.

126. Badenoch J. Progress report on the work of the DoE group of experts on cryptosporidium in water supplies. Department of the Environment, London, 1989.

127. Anon. Troubled waters. Lancet 1989; ii: 251–2.

128. Mayon-White R T, Frankenberg R A. 'Boil the water'. Lancet 1989; ii: 216.

129. Frankland P, Frankland Mrs P. Micro-organisms in water. Their significance, identification and removal. London: Longmans, 1894.

130. Anon. Mr Ridley's sewers. (Leading Article). Lancet 1988; ii: 1463–4.

131. Olson B H. The safety of our drinking water. Reason for concern but not alarm. New Eng J Med 1989; **320**: 1413–4.

132. Pavlasek I. Effect of disinfectants in infectiousness of oocysts of Cryptosporidium sp. Cs Epidem 1984; **33**: 97–101.

133. Blewett D A. Disinfection and oocysts. In: Angus K W, Blewett D A, eds. Cryptosporidiosis. Proceedings of the First International Workshop. Edinburgh: Moredun Research Institute, 1988: 107–15.

134. Casemore D P, Blewett D A, Wright S E. Cleaning and disinfection of equipment for flexible endoscopy. Gut 1989; **30**: 1156–7.

135. Smith H V, Smith A L, Girdwood R W A, Carrington E G. The effect of free chlorine on the viability of *Cryptosporidium* spp oocysts. WRc Publ PRU 2023-M. Medmenham, Bucks: Water Research Centre, 1988.

136. Galbraith N S. Cryptosporidiosis: another source. Br Med J 1989; **298**: 276–7.

137. Smith H V, Parker J F W, Girdwood R W A. A modified method for the detection of *Cryptosporidium* spp. oocysts in water-related samples. Communicable Disease, Scotland 1989; 89/15: 7–13.

138. Stibbs H H, Ongerth J E. Immunofluorescence detection of *Cryptosporidium* oocysts in fecal smears. J Clin Microbiol 1986; **24**: 517–21.

139. Sterling C R, Arrowood M J. Detection of *Cryptosporidium* sp. infections using a direct immunofluorescent assay. Pediatr Infect Dis 1986; **5**: (Suppl) S139–S142.

140. Arrowood M J, Sterling C R. Comparison of conventional staining methods and monoclonal antibody-based methods for *Cryptosporidium* oocyst detection. J Clin Microbiol 1989; **27**: 1490–5.

141. McLaughlin J, Casemore D P, Harrison T G, *et al*. Identification of cryptosporidium oocysts by monoclonal antibody. Lancet 1987; i: 51.

142. Garcia L S, Brewer T C, Bruckner D A. Fluorescence detection of *Cryptosporidium* oocysts in human fecal specimens by using monoclonal antibodies. J Clin Microbiol 1987; **25**: 119–21.

143. Pohjola S, Neuvonen E, Niskanen A, Rantama A. Rapid immunoassay for detection of cryptosporidium oocysts. Acta Vet Scand 1986; **27**: 71–9.

144. Heijbel H, Slaine K, Seigal B, et al. Outbreak of diarrhoea in a day-care centre with spread to household members: the role of *Cryptosporidium*. Pediatr Infect Dis J 1987; **6**: 532–5.

145. Hannah J, Riorden T. Case to case spread of cryptosporidiosis; Evidence from a day nursery outbreak. Publ Hlth 1988; **102**: 539–44.

146. Ribeiro C D, Palmer S R. Family outbreak of cryptosporidiosis. Brit Med J 1986; **292**: 377.

147. Isaacs D, Hunt G H, Phillips A D, *et al*. Cryptosporidiosis in immunocompetent children. J Clin Pathol 1985; **38**: 76–81.

148. Biggs B A, Megna R, Wickremesinghe S, Dwyer B. Human infection with *Cryptosporidium* spp.: results of a 24-month survey. Med J Austr 1987; **147**: 175–7.

149. Taylor J P, Perdue J N, Dingley D, *et al*. Cryptosporidiosis outbreak in a day-care centre. Am J Dis Child 1985; **139**:1023–5.

150. Combee C L, Collinge M L, Britt E M. Cryptosporidiosis in a hospital-associated day-care center. Pediatr Infect Dis 1986; **5**: 528–32.

151. Alpert G, Bell L M, Kirkpatrick C E. Outbreak of cryptosporidiosis in a day-care centre. Pediatr 1986; **77**: 152–7.

152. Melo Cristino J A G, Carvalho M I P, Salgado M J. An outbreak of cryptosporidiosis in a hospital day-care centre. Epidemiol Infect 1988; **101**: 355–9.

153. Nichols G. Cryptosporidiosis during an outbreak of *Shigella sonnei* dysentery. Communicable Diseases Surveillance Centre, London, 1986 (unpublished report, CDR 86/08: 3–4).

154. Hunt D A, Shannon R, Palmer S R, Jephcott A E. Cryptosporidiosis in an urban community. Br Med J 1984; **289**: 814–6.

155. Baxby D, Hart C A, Taylor C. Human cryptosporidiosis: a possible case of hospital cross infection. Br Med J 1983; **287**: 1760–1.

156. Koch K L, Phillips D J, Aber R C, Current W L. Cryptosporidiosis in hospital personnel. Ann Int Med 1985; **102**: 593–6.

157. Dryjanski J, Gold J W M, Ritchie M T, *et al*. Cryptosporidiosis. Case report in a health team worker. Am J Med 1986; **80**: 751–2.

158. Roberts W, Carr M F, Ma J, Ginsburgh A, Green P H R. Prevalence of cryptosporidium in patients undergoing endoscopy – evidence for an asymptomatic carrier state. Gastroenterol 1987; **92**: 1597.

159. Soave R. Clinical cryptosporidiosis in man. In: Angus K W, Blewett D A, eds. Cryptosporidiosis. Proceedings of the First International Workshop. Edinburgh: Moredun Research Institute, 1988: 19–26.

160. Anonymous. Cleaning and disinfection of equipment for gastrointestinal flexible endoscopy: interim recommendations of a working party of the British Society of Gastroenterology. Gut 1988; **29**: 1134–51.

161. Soave R, Danner R L, Honig C L, *et al*. Cryptosporidiosis in homosexual men. Ann Int Med 1984; **100**: 504–11.

162. Soave R, Ma P. Cryptosporidiosis. Traveler's diarrhoea in two families. Arch Int Med 1985; **145**: 70–2.

163. Ma P, Kauffman D L, Helmick C G, D'Souza A J, Havin T R. Cryptosporidiosis in tourists returning from the Caribbean. New Eng J Med 1985; **312**: 647–8.

164. Sterling C, Seegar K, Sinclair N A. *Cryptosporidium* as a causative agent of traveler's diarrhoea. J Inf Dis 1986; **153**: 380–1.

165. Ericsson C D, DuPont H L. Travelers' Diarrhoea: recent developments. In: Remington J S, Swartz M M, eds. Current clinical topics in infectious diseases. New York: McGraw Hill, 1985; 66–84.

166. Malla N, Sehgal R, Ganguly N K, Mahajan R C. Cryptosporidiosis in children in Chandrigarh. Ind J Med Res 1987; **86**: 722–5.

167. Cooke E M. *Escherichia coli* and man. Edinburgh: Churchill Livingstone, 1974.

168. Taylor D N, Echeverria P. When does cryptosporidium cause diarrhoea? Lancet 1986; i: 320.

169. Sallon S, Deckelbaum R J, Schmid I I, *et al*. *Cryptosporidium*, malnutrition, and chronic diarrhoea in children. Am J Dis Child 1988; **142**: 312–5.

170. MacFarlane D E, Horner-Bryce J. Cryptosporidiosis in well nourished and malnourished children. Acta Pediatr Scand 1987; **76**: 474–7.

171. Weitz J C, Tassara R, Mercado T M R, *et al*. Cryptosporidiosis in children of a nutritional care centre. Rev Chil Pediatr 1987; **58**: 50–3.

172. Blewett D A. Quantitative astudies in *Cryptosporidium* research. In: Angus K W, Blewett D A, eds. Cryptosporidiosis. Proceedings of the First International Workshop. Edinburgh: Moredun Research Institute, 1988: 85–95.

173. Henriksen S A. Epidemiology of cryptosporidiosis in calves. In: Angust K W, Blewett D A, eds. Cryptosporidiosis. Proceedings of the First International Workshop. Edinburgh: Moredun Research Institute, 1988: 79–83.

174. Jokipii L, Jokipii A M M. Timing of symptoms and oocyst excretion in human cryptosporidiosis. New Eng J Med 1986; **315**: 1643–7.

175. Stehr-Green J K, McCaig L, Remsen H M, Rains C S, Fox M, Juranek D D. Shedding of oocysts in immunocompetent individuals infected with *Cryptosporidium*. Am J Trop Med 1987; **36**: 338–42.

176. Shepherd R C, Reed C L, Sinha G P. Shedding of oocysts of *Cryptosporidium* in immunocompetent patients. J Clin Pathol 1988; **41**: 1104–6.

177. Casemore D P. Timing of symptoms and oocyst excretion in human cryptosporidiosis. New Eng J Med 1987; **317**: 168–9.

178. Garcia L S, Brewer T C, Bruckner D A. Incidence of *Cryptosporidium* in all patients submitting stool specimens for ova and parasite examination: Monoclonal antibody IFA method. Diagn Microbiol Infect Dis 1989; **11**: 25–7.

179. Baxby D, Blundell N, Hart C A. Excretion of atypical oocysts by patients with cryptosporidiosis. Lancet 1987; i: 974.

180. Baxby D, Blundell N. Recognition and laboratory characteristics of an atypical oocyst of *Cryptosporidium*. J Infect Dis 1988; **158**: 1038–45.

181. Zar F, Geiseler P G, Brown V A. Asymptomatic carriage of cryptosporidium in the stool of a patient with acquired immunodeficiency syndrome. J Infect Dis 1985; **151**: 195.

182. Scaglia M, Senaldi G, Di Perri G, Minoli L. Unusual low-grade cryptosporidial enteritis in AIDS: a case report. Infection 1986; **14**: 87–8.

183. Miller R A, Bronson M A, Morton W R. Determination of the infectious dose of *Cryptosporidium* and the influence of inoculum size on disease severity. A S M Abstracts of Annual Meeting 1986; p 49.

184. Ernest J A, Blagburn B L, Lindsay D S. Infection dynamics of *Cryptosporidium parvum* (Apicomplexa: Cryptosporidiidae) in neonatal mice (*Mus musculus*). J parasitol 1986; **72**: 796–8.

185. Sherwood D, Angus K W, Snodgrass D R, Tzipori S. Experimental cryptosporidiosis in laboratory mice. Infect Immun 1982; **38**: 471–5.

186. Anderson B C. Moist heat inactivation of *Cryptosporidium* sp. AJPH 1985; **75**: 1433–4.

187. Anderson B C. Effect of drying on the infectivity of cryptosporidia-laden calf faeces for 3- to 7-day-old mice. Am J Vet Res 1986; **47**: 2272–3.

188. Peeters J E, Mazas E A, Masschelein W J, de Maturana I V M, Debacker E. Effect of disinfection of drinking water with ozone or chlorine dioxide on survival of *Cryptosporidium parvum* oocysts. Appl Env Microbiol 1989; **55**: 1519–22.

189. Upton S J, Tilley M E, Marchin G L, Fina L R. Efficacy of a pentaiodide resin on *Cryptosporidium parvum* (Apicomplexa: Cryptosporidiidae) oocysts *in vitro*. J Parasitol 1988; **74**: 719–21.

190. Tzipori S, Campbell I. Prevalence of *Cryptosporidium* antibodies in 10 animal species. J Clin Microbiol 1981; **14**: 455–6.

191. Campbell P N, Current W L. Demonstration of serum antibodies to *Cryptosporidium* sp. in normal and immunodeficient humans with conformed infection. J Clin Microbiol 1983; **18**: 165–9.

192. Ungar B L P, Soave R, Fayer R, Nash T E. Enzyme immunoassay detection of immunoglobin M and G antibodies to *Cryptosporidium* in immunocompetent and immunocompromised persons. J Infect Dis 1986; **153**: 570–8.

193. Ungar B L P, Gilman R H, Lanata C F, Perez-Schael I. Seroepidemiology of *Cryptosporidium* infection in two Latin American populations. J Infect Dis 1988; **157**: 551–6.

194. Ungar B L P, Nash T E. Quantification of specific antibody response to *Cryptosporidium* antigens by laser densitometry. Infect Immun 1986; **53**: 124–8.

195. Hill B D. Immune responses in *Cryptosporidium* infections. In: Angus K W, Blewett D A, eds. Cryptosporidiosis. Proceedings of the First International Workshop. Edinburgh: Moredun Research Institute, 1988: 97–105.

196. Ungar B L P, Mulligan M, Nutman T B. Serologic evidence of *Cryptosporidium* infection in US volunteers before and during Peace Corps service in Africa. Arch Intern Med 1989; **149**: 894–7.

197. Luft B J, Payne D, Woodmansee D, Kim C W. Characterization of the *Cryptosporidium* antigens from sporulated oocysts of *Cryptosporidium parvum*. Infect Immun 1987; **55**: 2436–41.

198. Lazo A, Barriga O O, Redman D R, Bech-Nielsen S. Identification by transfer blot of antigens reactive in the enzyme-linked immunosorbent assay (ELISA) in rabbits immunized and a calf infected with *Cryptosporidium*. Vet Parasitol 1986; **21**: 151–63.

199. Mead J R, Arrowood M J, Current W L, Sterling C R. Field inversion gel electrophoretic separation of *Cryptosporidium* spp. chromosome-sized DNA. J Parasitol 1988; **74**: 366–9.

200. Oxford J S. Biochemical techniques for the genetic and phenotypic analysis of viruses: 'Molecular epidemiology'. J Hyg 1985; **94**: 1–7.

201. Anon. On three stages of amoebic research. Lancet 1986; ii: 1133–4.

202. Bell J C, Palmer S R. Control of zoonoses in Britain: past, present, and future. Br Med J 1983; **287**: 591–3.

203. Connolly G M, Dryden M S, Shanson D C, Gazzard B G. Cryptosporidial diarrhoea in AIDS and its treatment. Gut 1988; **29**: 593–7.

Part II – Paper V

How Common is Human Cryptosporidiosis?

Dr R E Joce MB BS MFCM DCH, Senior Registrar,
Dr C L R Bartlett MSc MB FFCM, Director
Communicable Disease Surveillance Centre of the Public Health
Laboratory Service

Introduction

Human infection with the coccidian parasite cryptosporidium was first reported in 1976 and has now been documented as a cause of gastrointestinal illness in both developed and developing countries[1]. There has recently been a marked increase in interest in cryptosporidiosis in the United Kingdom and this paper will attempt to put the available information on the frequency of human cryptosporidiosis into context against other commonly documented causes of gastointestinal illness.

Most gastrointestinal infections do not require medical intervention and not all that do result in a faecal sample being submitted in an attempt to identify the infective agent. Although it is important to know the total amount of illness that can be attributed to a particular infectious agent in the community, it is also one of the most difficult things to measure. This paper will first review epidemiological studies of the frequency of gastrointestinal illness in the community. This will be followed by a review of microbiological surveys of pathogens identified in faecal samples and reports on the frequency with which cryptosporidial infections are diagnosed by the laboratory. Finally, conclusions will be drawn from these studies on the frequency of human cryptosporidial infection, although it is not possible to determine the proportion of sporadic infections that are derived from water.

Community studies of acute gastrointestinal illness

One of the most extensive studies of acute enteric illness in a community was undertaken in residents of Tecumseh, Michigan, USA, who were studied over two periods, 1965 to 1971[2] and 1976 to 1981[3].

During the first period, households were recruited to the study for one year and telephoned weekly from the study centre when they were asked to report any acute illnesses, especially if there were respiratory or gastrointestinal symptons. To reduce seasonal biases only information from households that completed a full year of follow up was included in the final report. In all, 4,905 individuals were followed up. The definition of an enteric illness included diarrhoea, vomiting, upset stomach and nausea.

The overall incidence of enteric illness was 1.2 episodes per person year and in just over a quarter of the patients there were associated respiratory symptoms. About a tenth reported enteric symptoms in predominately respiratory illnesses which in turn were over twice as common as enteric illnesses. The incidence of enteric illness was highest in children under three years: 2.40 episodes per person year for males and 1.87 episodes per person year for females. The incidence fell between the ages of three and twenty years, rose slightly in those aged 20 to 29 years and fell steadily thereafter. Illness was reported most frequently in the winter (December, January and February; 37 per cent of reports) and least often in the three spring and three summer months (18 per cent and

17 per cent. respectively). Contact with a doctor was reported in 18.2 per cent of cases overall and in 29 per cent of cases in children under four years. No microbiological results were reported[2].

In the second study, after June 1978, stool samples were requested whenever an enteric illness was reported and were examined for bacterial and viral pathogens. In this study, households were kept under surveillance for as long as possible. On average, 1,138 people were under surveillance at the mid point of each year.

The definitions of illness were the same. The age distributions of enteric illness remained similar in both studies but the peak of illness occurred during the autumn rather than the winter.

A total of 480 faecal samples were taken when illnesses had been reported and all were examined for rotavirus which was identified in 18. Four hundred and twenty samples were also screened for bacterial pathogens which were found in only 14 (*Salmonella typhimurium 1, Shigella sonnei 1, Escherichia coli 9* (enterotoxigenic (ETEC) 5, enteropathogenic (EPEC)4), campylobacter 1, *Aeromonas hydrophila 2*)[3].

The small proportion of faecal samples from which a pathogen was identified is remarkable in comparison with other studies ((4), Table V.1). This may have reflected the reporting of non infectious enteric illness or enteric symptons associated with respiratory or other illnesses, a significant delay before sample collection (which is likely with a weekly telephone reporting system), non compliance with the study (a total of 480 samples over 3 years given the annual incidence of illness in the previous study seems low), unrecognised pathogens or laboratory techniques that were insufficiently sensitive to identify the organisms.

Another study investigated diarrhoea among families living in 3 locations in northern Canada: Winnipeg, Berens River and Eskimo Point[4]. Families were asked to report acute gastrointestinal or respiratory illnesses and agreed to regular three month follow up with stool, and serum samples. The average period of follow up ranged from 10 to 16 months. Only children in Winnipeg had faecal samples taken regularly during episodes of acute gastroenteritis. In these children, the number of episodes of acute gastrointestinal illness a year was 1.2 in neonates and children under one year and 0.83 for siblings. From a total of 166 children investigated microbiologically, 82 rotavirus infections were diagnosed. This study has a rather higher rate of isolation of bacterial pathogens than the Tecumseh study with 13 *E.Coli* (12 EPEC, 1 ETEC), one *Salmonella infantis* and five toxigenic *Aeromonas hydrophila* infections diagnosed out of 166 samples examined.

Community studies are complex and difficult to undertake and in an attempt to estimate the total amount of illness caused by salmonella infections, studies have been undertaken on the under-reporting of these infections in the USA and Canada. For salmonella infections, the number of cases occurring for each one reported has been estimated at between 30 and 40 (5.6). In any survey of gastrointestinal illness caused by a particular pathogen some knowledge of the proportions of asymptomatic and symptomatic infection, the proportion of symptomatic cases seeking medical advice and the likelihood of faecal samples being taken and positive results being appropriately notified is necessary. The data to make many of these estimates for cryptosporidiosis are lacking but a study of the incidence and aetiology of acute gastrointestinal illness in the community has been commissioned by the Department of Health following a recommendation in the Report of the Committee on the Microbiological Safety of Food (Richmond Report).

Table V.1 Studies of Acute Gastrointestinal Illness in the UK

Year(s) of Study duration	Selection Criteria	Number of patients or specimens studied	Sal-monella	Shigella	Pathogen Campylo-bacter	EPEC+	Other	Comment	Reference/Author
1957–1959 2 years	All GP patients with recent acute gastrointes-tinal illness who had not had antibiotics. 738 eligible patients, 84 per cent submitted sample	622 patients	3 (0.48)	115* (18.4)	not tested	7, only <2 yr olds tested		*Shigella sonnei outbreak early 1957 111/115 diagnosed then	Tuckman et al (7)
1977 Duration not stated	GP patients with diarrhoeal illness	196 patients	5 (2.5)	19 (6.7)	17 (8.7)		Giardia 13 (6.6)		Brunton et al (8)
June 1977 for 3 months	Patients with recent acute gastrointestinal illness who had samples submitted to laboratory	280 patients	12 (4.3)	11 (3.9)	39 (13.9)				Bruce et al (9)
1977–1978 9 months	All patients presenting to GP with acute gastro-enteritis including diarrhoea. Excluded if they had had antibiotics in the past four weeks	73 patients	2 (2.7)	1 (1.3)	11 (15.0)	nil	Viruses 14(19)		Rousseau 1983 (10)
1979–1981 3 years (Study a)	Approx. 1 in 2 patients presenting to GP with acute diarrhoea (3 or more stools in 24 hours) for at least 48 hours. 51 per cent eligible submitted sample	168 patients	6 (3.6)	1 (0.6)	34 (20.2)	Not reported			Kendall & Tanner 1982 (11)
1979–1981 3 years (Study b)	Samples submitted by other local GPs from patients with diarrhoea	3,250 patients	67 (2.1)	35 (1.1)	484 (14.9)	Not reported	Giardia 18(0.9)		Kendall & Tanner (11)
1983–1984 2 years	All faecal samples submitted to 5 PHLs from patients with gastrointestinal symptoms	33,857 specimens	1,151 (3.4)	271 (0.8)	1,862 (5.5)	Not reported			Skirrow (12)
Unknown 1 year	All faecal samples submitted to lab. (including some routine faecal samples)	3,784 patients	95 (2.5)	13 (0.34)	106 (2.8)		*Yersinia* spp. 132(3.5)		Greenwood 1987 (13)

+EPEC = enteropathogenic *E.coli*

Laboratory based prevalence studies from general practice

In a number of studies of the rate of isolation of pathogens from faecal samples from patients with a diarrhoeal illness submitted by general practitioners to laboratories, *Salmonella* spp. were found in two to four per cent, *Shigella* spp. in 0.3 to seven per cent and campylobacter in 8 to 20 per cent (Table V.1).

Studies of cryptosporidiosis

Studies have been undertaken to document the frequency with which cryptosporidiosis oocysts are identified in faecal samples from patients with acute gastroenteritis. In developed countries the reported range was 1–4 per cent and in developing countries up to 16 per cent[14] (Tables V.2.,V.3). Many of the studies were only on samples from children but when data from centres that examined samples from all age groups were reviewed by age, the frequency of infection was found to be higher in children, probably reflecting a lack of previous exposure to that infection[14].

In the UK, similar studies have been undertaken which report cryptosporidial oocysts in 1–6 per cent of specimens taken from patients with acute gastroenteritis (Table V.4). In addition, the Communicable Disease Surveillance Centre of the Public Health Laboratory Service routinely receives reports of all positive identifications on a voluntary basis from the 52 Public Health Laboratories and from hospital/district departments of microbiology. In Scotland, reporting by laboratories is to the Communicable Disease (Scotland) Unit (CD(S)U).

In England and Wales, laboratories only began to report the identification of cryptosporidial oocysts in 1983. The number of laboratories screening for cryptosporidial oocysts rose rapidly, encouraged by the PHLS surveillance study which began in 1985. The total numbers of reports were 61 in 1983, 876 in 1984, 1,874 in 1985, 3,560 in 1986, 3,277 in 1987, 2,750 in 1988 and 7,904 in 1989. The figure for 1989 shows an increase over previous years but increased public and medical awareness of cryptosporidiosis and changes in some laboratory policies on testing for cryptosporidial oocysts and in reporting methods may partly explain the rise.

In Scotland, laboratories first reported identification of cryptosporidial oocysts in 1984. The annual number of reports rose from 50 in 1984, to 265 in 1985, 414 in 1986, 493 in 1987, 545 in 1988 and 1,243 in 1989. The recommended laboratory testing policy had broadened in 1989 to incude all diarrhoeal samples and since January 1989, cryptosporidiosis has been a reportable infection; both these factors may have contributed to the increase in reports during 1989.

Sixteen PHLS laboratories in England and Wales undertook a two year study in which all faecal samples received from patients with presumed acute infectious diarrhoea were screened for cryptosporidial oocysts with the aim of estimating the proportion of acute infectious gastrointestinal illness caused by this organism.[15] All faecal samples were examined for salmonella, shigella and campylobacter by routine methods. A total of 62,421 patients were investigated via their GPs of whom 1,295 (2 per cent) were found to be excreting cryptosporidial oocysts. This rate varied from 0.5 per cent to 4 per cent by laboratory with the higher rates tending to be reported by laboratories serving a rural population. In addition 4,775 (8 per cent) of these patients were found to be excreting campylobacter, 2,050 (3 per cent) salmonella and 437 (0.7 per cent) shigella; virology was not undertaken routinely. Amongst children aged from 1–4 years, almost 5 per cent of them were found to be excreting cryptosporidial oocysts, making it the second commonest identification after campylobacter and in all other age groups it was the third or fourth commonest pathogen found (Table V.5).

In assessing the frequency of cryptosporidial infection, the particular importance of this study was that the salmonella, shigella or campylobacter rates were similar to those reported in other studies, so that an estimate that 2 per cent of faecal samples submitted from patients with diarrhoea will contain cryptosporidial oocysts seems reasonable. This will vary with age, with higher proportions in children.

Table V.2   The Frequency of Human Cryptosporidiosis Reported from Developed Countries (Excluding UK)

Town/Country	Number of patients tested	Proportion of those who were children	Number (%) positive for cryptosporidial oocysts	Reference
Victoria, Australia	884	Mostly	36 (4.1)	Tzipori *et al* (1983b)
Newfoundland, Canada	1,621	Over 50 per cent	19 (1.2)	Ratnam *et al* (1985)
British Columbia, Canada	7,300	Over 50 per cent	46 (0.6)	Montessori & Bischoff (1985)
Massachusetts, USA	1,703	Over 50 per cent	47 (2.8)	Wolfson *et al* (1985)
South Carolina, USA	582	Under 50 per cent	25 (4.3)	Holley and Dover (1985)
France	190	All	4 (2.1)	Arnaud-Battandier and Naciri (1985)
Finland	4,545	Under 50 per cent	119 (2.6) High proportion associated with recent travel	Jokipii *et al* (1985b)
Germany	1,501	33 per cent	9 (0.6)	Freidank *et al* (1987)[16]

Adapted from: Tzipori S. Cryptosporidiosis in Perspective. Advances in Parasitology 1988; vol 27: 63-129

Table V.3   The Frequency of Human Cryptosporidiosis Reported from Developing Countries

Town/Country	Number of patients tested	Proportion of those who were children	Number (%) positive for cryptosporidial oocysts	Reference
Bangkok, Thailand	410	All	13 (3.2)	Taylor and Echeverria (1986)
Dacca, Bangladesh	578	All	25 (4.3)	Shahid *et al* (1985)
Lahore, India	682	All	89 (13.1)	Mathan *et al* (1985)
Costa Rica	946	All	46 (4.9)	Mata (1986)
Brazil	117	All	9 (8)	Weikel *et al* (1985)
Liberia	278	All	22 (7.9)	Hojlyng *et al* (1984)
Ghana	474	All	61 (12.9)	Addy and Aikins-Bekoe (1986)
Rwanda	293	Mostly	23 (7.6)	Bogaerts *et al* (1986)
Haiti	702	All	116 (16.5)	Pape *et al* (1985)

Adapted from: Tzipori S. Cryptosporidiosis in Perspective. Advances in Parasitology 1988; vol 27: 63-129

Table V.4   Studies of Frequency of Cryptosporidial Oocyst Identification in the UK

Year/ duration of study	Selection Criteria	Number of patients or specimens studied	Pathogens identified: number (%)					References/ Author
			Crypto-sporidium	Sal-monella	Shigella	Campylo-bacter	Other	
May–August 1983 3 months	All first faecal samples submitted from patients with history of diarrhoea	500 patients	7 (1.4)	Not Listed				Casemore et al 1983[17]
1983–1984 3 months	Patients with diarrheoa who had faecal samples sent to laboratory	867 patients	43 (5.0)	37 (4.3)	7 (0.8)	49 (5.7)	Giardia 17 (2.0)	Hunt et al 1984[18]
June 1983– April 1984 10 months	All samples submitted to laboratory from patients with gastroenteritis	1,967 patients	27 (1.4)	36 (1.8)	0	31 (1.6)	Viruses approx. 50 per cent	Hart et al 1984[19]
1983–1984 15 months	All first faecal samples submitted from patients with history of diarrhoea (in first 3 months only samples from children under 16 years included)	2,573 patients	50 (1.9)	48 (1.9)	15 (0.6)	117 (4.5)	Giardia 25 EPEC 26 Rotavirus 84	Casemore et al 1983[20]
1984 6 months	All stool samples submitted to laboratory	2,174 specimens	24	48	13	70	Giardia 34 EPEC 20	Wright et al[21]
1984–1986 2 years	Children admitted to hospital with gastroenteritis	742 patients	46 (6.2)	23 (3.1)	34 (4.6)	46 (6.2)	Rotavirus 162[22]	Thomson et al 1987[22]

Table V.5   Positivity Rate for Cryptosporidium, Campylobacter, Salmonella, and Shigella by Age of Patient, as Assessed by PHLS Laboratories, England and Wales

Age (years)	<1	1–4	5–14	15–24	25–34	35–44	45–54	55–64	>65	Not known
Total No. Investigated:	4,090	9,880	4,822	8,235	9.048	6,710	4,492	3,846	5,432	5,866
No. (%) patients positive for:										
Cryptosporidium	79(1.9)	480(4.9)	210(4.4)	160(1.9)	155(1.7)	83(1.2)	32(0.7)	12(0.3)	21(0.4)	63(1.1)
Campylobacter	123(3.0)	551(5.6)	368(7.6)	905(11.0)	875(9.7)	672(10.0)	378(8.4)	311(8.1)	262(4.8)	330(5.6)
Salmonella	99(2.4)	221(2.2)	157(3.3)	358(4.3)	359(4.0)	280(4.2)	155(3.5)	119(3.1)	114(2.1)	188(3.2)
Shigella	14(0.3)	96(1.0)	100(2.1)	42(0.5)	62(0.7)	43(0.6)	26(0.6)	18(0.5)	8(0.1)	28(0.5)

Source: PHLS Study Group. Cryptosporidiosis in England and Wales: Prevalence and clinical epidemiological features.
     BR Med J 1990; 306:774–7 (corrected table).

Cryptosporidiosis and Human Immunodeficiency Virus Infection

Cryptosporidiosis has become recognised as an important cause of diarrhoea experienced by the immunosuppressed, especially those with human immunodeficiency virus (HIV) infection and AIDS, but also those with severe combined immune deficiency (SCID), congenital hypogammaglobulinaemia and those on chemotherapy. In addition, certain bacterial and viral infections (for example measles, chicken-pox) can temporarily disrupt the patient's immune system making them more susceptible to infection.

The Centers for Disease Control (CDC, USA) definition of AIDS includes HIV antibody positive patients with unexplained diarrhoea for more than a month or with diarrhoea caused by certain opportunist pathogens such as *Cryptosporidium* sp.[23]. From a sample of AIDS cases reported to CDSC and CD(S)U between March 1982, when reporting began, and August 1988, it is estimated that 7 per cent had had at least one episode of Cryptosporidiosis by the time of report. No information is available at CDSC about diseases contracted after the date of reporting. Altogether 222 (19 per cent) of the cases in the sample were reported as having had at least one spell of diarrhoea (Table V.6). In 69 of these 222 cases, cryptosporidium was considered to be the causative agent. In a further 16 cases a possible cause for the diarrhoea was recorded but the remaining 137 cases were either not tested or the test result was not reported. These estimates will certainly be much lower than the true prevalence rate because medical staff completing the forms often do not report diseases other than those needed to show that the case fulfills the CDC/WHO definition of AIDS. Cryptosporidiosis may not be mentioned if the patient already fulfills the definition because he or she had *Pneumocystis carinii* pneumonia or Kaposi's sarcoma.

Diarrhoea is commonly reported by patients with HIV infection. In one study, 179/1211 (16 per cent) of HIV antibody positive individuals (some of whom had AIDS) reported diarrhoea during a 15 month period[24]. Another study reported that 61/234 (26 per cent) of patients later diagnosed as having AIDS complained of diarrhoea at presentation[25] and up to 50 per cent of AIDS patients may complain of persistent looseness of their bowels[26].

In two published studies, HIV antibody positive patients with diarrhoea were extensively investigated, and at least one possible enteric pathogen was identified in 86/179 (48 per cent) of patients who did not all have AIDS[24], and 17/20 (85 per cent) of patients with AIDS[27]. Cryptosporidial oocysts were found in 9-15 per cent of AIDS patients with diarrhoea[25,27,28]; some patients had at least one other enteric pathogen identified at the same time. In some AIDS patients, the symptoms associated with cryptosporidiosis may diminish or disappear and then recur; it is uncertain whether this represents re-infection or recrudescence of the infection[1].

PART II(V)

Table V.6 Reported Occurrence of Cryptosporidiosis and/or Diarrhoea in Patients with AIDS

| Period of Report (Year/Month) | Number of Cases on Main File | Percentages (based on sample cases) | | | |
		Percentage of Cases in sample	Cases with Cryptosporidiosis (+/– Diarrhoea)	Cases with Diarrhoea (+/– Cryptosporidiosis)	Cases with Cryptosporidiosis or Diarrhoea
82/03-87/02	692	99	6	20	25
87/03	29	62	6	11	11
87/04	21	100	5	19	24
87/05-87/09	319	51	6	7	13
87/10-88/05	473	11	8	10	15
88/06-88/08	188	51	14	5	18
Total	**1,722**	**60***	**7***	**13***	**19***

Notes: *Weighted averages to adjust for variability in sampling ratio.

Source: Dr B Bannister and Mrs S E Whitmore, PHLS AIDS Centre at the Communicable Disease Surveillance Centre.

Conclusion

In summary, it is not known what proportion of gastroenteritis in the community is caused by Cryptosporidiosis although it appears that approximately 2 per cent of faecal samples submitted by GPs from patients with diarrhoea contain cryptosporidial oocysts. Following a recommendation in the Report of the Committee on the Microbiological Safety of Food (Richmond Report), the Department of Health has commissioned a study of the incidence and aetiology of acute gastrointestinal disease presenting to GPs in the community. This study is being planned and coordinated by the CDSC in collaboration with the Medical Research Council.

References

1. Casemore D P. Human Cryptosporidiosis. In: Recent Advances in Infection Eds. Reeves D S, Geddes A M. Churchill Livingstone, 1989.
2. Monto A S, Koopman J S. The Tecumseh Study. XI: Occurrence of Acute Enteric Illness in the Community. Am J Epidemiol 1980; 112 (3): 323–333.
3. Monto A S, Koopman J S, Longin I M, Isaacson R E. The Tecumseh study. XII: Enteric Agents in the Community, 1976–1981. J. Infect Dis 1983; 148(2): 284–291.
4. Gurwith M, Wenman W, Gurwith D et al. Diarrhoea among infants and young children in Canada: a longitudinal study in three Northern Communities. J Infect Dis 1983; 137(4): 685–691.
5. Chalker R B, Blaser M J. A review of human salmonellosis: III. Magnitude of salmonella infection in the United States. Rev Infect Dis 1988; 10 (1): 111–124.
6. Hauschild A H W, Bryan F L. Estimate of cases of food and waterborne illness in Canada and the United States. J Food Protection 1980; 43(6): 435–440.
7. Tuckman E, Chapple P A L, Franklin L M et al. Acute gastro-intestinal illness in General Practice. B M J, 1962; 1:135–141.
8. Telfer Brunton W A, Heggie D. Campylobacter-associated diarrhoea in Edinburgh. B M J, 1977; 2:956.
9. Bruce D, Zochowski W, Ferguson I R. Campylobacter enteritis. B M J 1977;2:1219.
10. Rousseau S A. Investigation of acute gastroenteritis in general practice – relevance of newer laboratory methods. J R, Coll Gen Pract 1983; 33: 514–516.
11. Kendell E J C, Tanner E I. Campylobacter enteritis in general practice. J Hyg Camb 1982; 8: 155–163.
12. Skirrow M A, demographic survey of campylobacter, salmonella and shigella infections in England. Epidemiol Infect 1987; 99: 647–657.
13. Greenwood M, Hooper W L. Human carriage of Yersinia spp. J Med Microbiol 1987; 23: 345–348.
14. Tzipori S. Cryptosporidiosis in Perspective. In: Advances in Parasitology vol 27. Eds Baker J R, and Muller R. Academic Press 1988.
15. PHLS Study Group. Cryptosporidiosis in England and Wales: prevalence and clinical and epidemiological features. B M J 1990; 330: 774–7.
16. Freidank H, Kist M. Cryptosporidia in Immunocompetent Patients with gastroenteritis. Eur J Clin Microbiol Infect Dis 1987; 1: 56–59.
17. Casemore D P, Jackson B. Sporadic Cryptosporidiosis in Children (letter). Lancet 1983; ii:679.
18. Hunt D A, Shannon R, Palmer S R, Jephcott A E. Cryptosporidiosis in an urban community. B M J, 1984; 289: 814–816.
19. Hart C A, Baxby D, Blundell N. Gastronenteritis due to cryptosporidium a prospective survey in a children's hospital. J Infect 1984; 9: 264–27.
20. Casemore D P, Armstrong M, Sands R L. Laboratory diagnosis of Cryptosporidiosis. J Clin Pathol 1985; 38: 1337–1341.
21. Wright P A, Harrison J M, Byrom I. Cryptosporidiosis (letter). B M J 1984; 289:1148.
22. Thomson M A, Benson J W T, Wright P A. Two year study of cryptosporidium infection. Arch Dis Child 1987; 62: 559–663.
23. Classification system for Human T-Lymphotrophic virus Type III/Lymphadenopathy Associated Virus infections. MMWR 1986; 35(20): 334–339.
24. Dryden M S, Shanson D C. The microbial causes of diarrhoea in patients infected with Human Immunodeficiency Virus. J Infect 1988; 17: 107–114.
25. Connolly G M, Dryden M S, Shanson D C et al. Cryptosporidial diarrhoea in AIDS and its treatment. Gut 1988; 29: 593–597.
26. Connolly G M, Shanson D C, Hawkins D A, et al. Non cryptosporidial diarrhoea in Human Immunodeficiency Virus (HIV) infected patients. Gut 1989; 30: 195–200.
27. Smith P D, Lane H C, Gill V J et al. Intestinal infection in patients with the Acquired Immunodeficiency Syndrome (AIDS). Ann Intern Med 1988; 108: 328–333.
28. Soave R, Danner R L, Honig C L et al. Cryptosporidiosis in homosexual men. Ann Intern Med 1984; 100: 504–511.

Part II – Paper VI

Clinical Features of Cryptosporidiosis

David A Warrell
Professor of Tropical Medicine and Infectious Diseases
University of Oxford

Summary

The first case of human cryptosporidiosis was described as recently as 1976. Since then it has been recognised as an important cause of self-limiting but unpleasant diarrhoeal disease in normal healthy individuals. However, in patients with weakened immune defences, such as those with AIDS, cryptosporidiosis is a common, distressing and life-threatening condition causing profuse intractable diarrhoea which may spread to other systems, notably the biliary system, and may lead to severe dehydration, malabsorption and wasting.

Cryptosporidiosis can now be diagnosed microscopically and serologically. It is indistinguishable clinically from giardiasis and isosporiasis and must be distinguished from other enteropathogens. There is currently no effective antimicrobial treatment for cryptosporidium species. Palliative treatment may be required in severe cases.

Introduction

Cryptosporidium was first described by Tyzzer (1907) in the peptic glands in the stomach of healthy laboratory mice and subsequently by the same author in the small intestine of rabbits and mice. Tyzzer had also described the oocyst stage in mouse faeces. Cryptosporidium was regarded as a harmless commensal until it was associated with diarrhoea in young turkeys (Slavin 1955). In the early 1970s it was put on the veterinary map after being associated with large outbreaks of diarrhoea in calves (Angus 1983). The first reported case of human cryptosporidiosis was diagnosed by rectal biopsy in an otherwise normal three year old girl in Tennessee (Nime *et al* 1976). The organism was for a while regarded as essentially an opportunistic pathogen, for five of the next seven human cases reported (between 1976 and 1981) were in immunocompromised patients (Soave & Armstrong 1986). During the next year 47 more cases were reported to the Centers for Disease Control USA, most of them in AIDS patients, and more than 500 more were described up to 1986. Human cryptosporidiosis in immunocompetent people has now been described in 26 countries with a prevalence of between 0.6 and 20 per cent in western countries and 4–20 per cent in developing countries (Soave & Johnson 1988). Among immunocompromised patients, it has a prevalence of 3 or 4 per cent of AIDS sufferers in the USA and prevalence of more than 50 per cent in these patients in Africa and Haiti (Soave & Johnson 1988).

People susceptible to cryptosporidiosis

Normal healthy people, especially children, can develop unpleasant gastrointestinal and "flu-like" symptoms as a result of infection with cryptosporidium and the illness is sometimes serious but not life-threatening. However, immunocompromised patients can develop severe, incurable and life-threatening diarrhoea and wasting. Such immunocompromised patients include those with AIDS, hypogamma-globulinaemia and severe combined immunodeficiency, those taking drugs such as cyclophosphamide and corticosteroid, and malnourished children in tropical countries where the infection may be associated with measles (De Mol *et al* 1984).

Among immunocompetent people, the group most likely to be infected with cryptosporidium are animal handlers, veterinarians, children in institutions and day care centres, household contacts of infected individuals, hospital personnel, travellers to tropical countries and other areas of high prevalence, and homosexual males. (Soave & Armstrong 1986).

Mode of infection

Infection may be acquired by contact with animals, by person to person spread or by drinking contaminated water. Rarely it may be acquired by ingesting milk or food contaminated with oocysts and possibly by sexual contact and aerosol. Zoonotic and faecal oral transmission are probably the most important.

Incubation period

In cases where the time of infection can be assessed (for example contact with an infected calf), the incubation period has ranged from two to 14 days.

Clinical features in immunocompetent patients

There is a sudden onset of gastrointestinal and sometimes systemic "flu-like" symptoms.

Diarrhoea is the commonest symptom (80–90 per cent). Patients may open their bowels between two and more than 20 times a day, producing stools which are usually described as "watery, greenish and very offensive" (with mucus in about 10 per cent) (Casemore 1987).

Abdominal pain, often severe, is experienced by about two-thirds of patients and is cramping (colicky) in nature. Vomiting and anorexia occur in about half of patients and abdominal distention, flatulence and significant weight loss (more than 10 per cent) may also occur.

Systemic "flu-like" symptoms occur in about 20–40 per cent of patients. They include malaise, headache, myalgia and feverishness. Gastrointestinal symptoms usually last about seven to 14 days, unusually five or six weeks, while persistent weakness, lethargy, mild abdominal pain and bowel looseness may persist for a month (Casemore 1987). However, oocyst excretion can continue for two to three weeks after the disappearance of symptoms which creates problems in the control of an outbreak (Soave & Armstrong 1986). Asymptomatic infections are uncommon.

The disease in immunocompetent people is not usually sufficiently severe to require hospital admission. In young children in the tropics, however, especially in those who are malnourished, the symptoms may be severe enough to cause dehydration, malabsorption and even death. These children should probably not be regarded as "immunocompetent".

Clinical features in immunocompromised patients

Immunocompromised patients usually develop symptoms of cryptosporidiosis insidiously. They develop very frequent watery diarrhoea—like cholera—opening their bowels six to 25 times per day and passing between one and 20 litres of stool per day. Associated symptoms include cramping, upper abdominal pain often associated with meals, profound weight loss (for example *averaging* 18 kilograms during a four to six month period in one series), weakness, malaise, anorexia and low grade fever (Whiteside *et al* 1984). Physical examination may reveal other features of HIV infection (for example, lymphadenopathy, oral candidiasis (thrush)), wasting, dehydration and diffuse abdominal tenderness.

Except in those patients in whom the suppression of the immune systems can be relieved by stopping immunosuppressant drugs, these distressing symptoms persist unabated until the patient dies from some other opportunistic infection or malignant disease (Soave & Armstrong 1986).

In immunocompromised patients, infection with cryptosporidium can involve the pharynx, oesophagus, stomach, duodenum, jejunum, ileum, appendix, colon, rectum, gall bladder, bile duct, pancreatic duct and the bronchial tree (in association with other pathogens such as cytomegalovirus (CMV) and *Pneumocystis carinii* (Ma *et al* 1984: Soave & Armstrong 1986: Cook 1987).

Cryptosporidial cholecystitis presents with right upper quadrant abdominal pain and persistent nausea and vomiting and is usually associated with severe diarrhoea. About 10 per cent of AIDS patients with cryptosporidiosis have biliary involvement (Soave & Johnson 1988).

Immunity to Cryptosporidium

IgM and IgG antibody responses have been detected using indirect immunofluorescence and ELISA in the sera of both immunocompetent and immunocompromised patients (Fayer & Ungar 1986: Campbell & Current 1983). These antibodies seem unlikely to be responsible for protection. Functional cellular and humoral immunity are probably needed to clear infection (Campbell & Current 1983). In immunucompetent people, infection usually results in protective immunity (Fayer & Ungar 1986) but at least one immunocompetent patient suffered from three episodes of cryptosporidiosis during a one year period (Campbell & Current 1983).

Laboratory investigations in patients with cryptosporidiosis diagnosis

Oocysts may be found in stool, duodenal or jejunal aspirate and biopsies of bowel mucosa. In experienced hands, the diagnosis will be made on the first stool specimen without a concentration method. Usually, the stool from patients with cryptosporidiosis does not contain blood, pus cells or Charcot-Leyden crystals. This may be helpful in distinguishing cryptosporidiosis from acute diarrhoeas caused by amoebiasis, bacillary dysentery and isosporiasis.

Serological tests are being developed. Both immunocompetent and immunocompromised patients develop IgG, IgM and IgA antibodies by about six to eight weeks after the start of infection. The levels of antibodies then decline. These antibodies can be detected by immunosorbent assay (ELISA).

It is important to realise that cryptosporidiosis may be associated with other bowel pathogens, both in presumed immunocompetent people in tropical countries (Mathan *et al* 1985: Taylor & Echeverria 1986) and in immunocompromised patients. In AIDS patients, common associated infections are with cytomegalovirus and *Isospora belli.*

Haematological and biochemical abnormalities. In immunocompetent patients, peripheral blood leucocytosis and serum electrolyte abnormalities are very unusual unless the patient become severely dehydrated.

Immunocompromised patients with profuse intractable diarrhoea may become severely dehydrated with associated disorders of electrolyte and acid base balance. In patients with cryptosporidial cholecystitis, serum alkaline phosphatase and gamma glutamyl transpeptidase levels are raised while transaminases and bilirubin may remain normal.

Radiography of the bowel shows prominent mucosal folds, thickening of the wall and abnormal motility, and in the biliary system, dilated biliary ducts, distal bowel duct stenosis with an irregular lumen and other changes reminiscent of primary sclerosing cholangitis (Soave & Johnson 1988).

Histological changes in the bowel mucosa indicate enterocyte damage with villous blunting, and inflammatory cell infiltration of the *lamina propria.* The histopathological features in the biliary tract also resemble primary sclerosing cholangitis (Cook 1987).

Differential diagnosis of cryptosporidiosis

In immunocompetent people, cryptosporidiosis will enter the differential diagnosis of any acute diarrhoeal illness associated with abdominal pain or other gastrointestinal symptoms with or without systemic "flu-like" symptoms. If the timing of exposure to infection is known, the incubation period of usually more than a week will help to distinguish cryptosporidiosis from viral, bacterial and bacterial-toxin diarrhoeas of short incubation period. It is important to remember cryptosporidiosis in patients with travellers' diarrhoea, in people who work with farm animals, in children from day care centres and institutions, and in medical personnel who may have acquired the infection from patients. In the immunocompetent patient, the commonest differential diagnosis will be from giardiasis. Compared with giardiasis, the duration of symptoms is longer, intense abdominal pain and cramps are commoner but bloating, anorexia and weakness are less common in cryptosporidiosis (Jokipii *et al* 1983).

In immunocompromised patients, especially in those with AIDS, isosporiasis is common and is clinically indistinguishable from cryptosporidiosis. This infection is diagnosed by finding the organisms in the stool, and is suggested by the presence of Charcot-Leyden crystals in the stool, and observing a response to treatment with trimethoprim and suplhamethoxazole, which has no effect in cryptosporidiosis. There are a number of other possible infective causes of diarrhoea in immunocompromised patients including cytomegalovirus, mycobacteria, and possible HIV itself. The use of incorrect staining may cause confusion: with Giemsa staining cryptosporidium may be confused with *Blastocystis hominis* and yeasts.

Treatment of cryptosporidiosis

In immunocompetent patients, the infection is self-limiting and, unless significant dehydration develops, treatment is unnecessary. However, in tropical countries at least, cryptosporidiosis in infants is associated with higher morbidity and even mortality (Wittenberg *et al* 1989).

In immunocompetent Costa Rican children, 100 mg/kg/day of spiramycin in two divided doses for 10 days reduced the duration of diarrhoea and the excretion of cryptosporidial oocysts (Saez-Llorens *et al* 1989). In immunocompromised patients, cryptosporidiosis causes great misery and morbidity and contributes to an early fatal outcome. Over 40 antimicrobial agents have been tested against cryptosporidium in animals and humans but few appear to have any effect (Tzipori 1983). Limited and transient effects have been reported in patients treated with spiramycin (a macrolide antibiotic), alpha difluoromethylornithine (DFMO) (but it is probably too toxic to be used), hyperimmune bovine colostrum, cow's milk globulin IgA-enriched cow's milk and bovine transfer factor (Centers for Disease Control 1984; Wittenberg *et al* 1989; Soave & Johnson 1988). Diclazuril, originally used as prophylaxis for coccidiosis in chickens has been tried in AIDS patients in Zaire, New York and London. Some efficacy was shown but the results were inconclusive and a double blind study is planned. At present, it seems that there is no effective anticryptosporidial treatment.

Immunocompromised patients with severe diarrhoea and malabsorption are treated palliatively. They should avoid excess milk as lactose intolerance may develop. Parenteral feeding, with fluid, electrolyte and nutrient replacement, is helpful. Antiperistaltic agents may increase abdominal pain and bloating. None has any particular advantage. Temporary relief of biliary obstruction has been obtained by endoscopic papillotomy (Soave & Johnson 1988).

Clinical features of cryptosporidiosis References

Angus K W, J Roy Soc Med **76** 62–70, 1983

Cambell P N & Current W L. J Clin Microbiol **18** (1) 165–9 1983

Casemore D, PHLS Microbiology Digest **4** (1) 1–6, 1987

Centers for Disease Control. M M W R March 9, 117–9 1984

Cook G C. Quarterly Journal of Medicine **65** 967–83, 1987

De Mol P *et al* Lancet July 7 1984

Fayer R G, Ungar B L T. Microbiological Reviews **50** 458–483, 1986

Jokipii L *et al* Lancet **ii** 358–360. 1983

Ma P, Villanueva T G, Kaufman D, Gillooley J F. J A M A **252** (10) 1298–1301, 1984

Mathan M M *et al* Lancet **ii** 1172–5, 1985

Nime F A *et al* Gastroenterology **70** 592–598. 1976

Saez-Llorens X *et al* Ped. Infect Dies. 1989. **8** 136–140

Slavin D J Comparative Pathology **65** 262–266. 1955

Soave R & Armstong W D. Reviews Infect Dis **8** (6) 1012–1023 1986

Soave R & Johnson W D. J Infect Dis **157** (2) 225–229, 1988

Taylor D N & Echeverria P. Lancet 8 February 1986

Tyzzer E E Proc Soc Experimental Biol Med **5** 12–13 1907

Tzipori S Microbiological Reviews **47** (1) 84–96, 1983

Whiteside M E *et al* American J Trop Med Hyg **33** (6) 1065–1072 1984

Wittenberg D F *et al* Infect Dis **159** (1) 131–2. 1989.

Part II – Paper VII

Waterborne Cryptosporidiosis

This article first appeared in *Parasitology Today, vol. 6, no. 1, 1990* and is reproduced by kind permission of the Editor.

H V Smith and J B Rose

Huw Smith is at the Scottish Parasite Diagnostic Laboratory, Stobhill General Hospital, Glasgow G21 3UW, UK and Joan Rose is at the Department of Environmental and Occupational Health, College of Public Health, University of South Florida, Tampa, FL, USA.

Awareness of the importance of Cryptosporidium *as a gastrointestinal parasite of developed countries not only stems from its prevalence in AIDS patients but also from its recent recognition as a possible contaminant of drinking water supplies. The importance of* Cryptosporidium *to public health has recently been revealed by a series of major epidemics of diarrhoeal disease in the USA and UK. In this review, Huw Smith and Joan Rose document what is known of the causes of some of these outbreaks and explain why this parasite can escape the battery of treatment processes normally used for drinking water supplies in these countries.*

The coccidians *Cryptosporidium* spp are intracellular protozoan parasites of the grastrointestinal and respiratory tracts of numerous animals, and at present four species are known, ie. *C. parvum* and *C. muris,* which infect mammals, and *C. baileyi* and *C. meleagridis,* which infect birds[1]. *C. parvum* is the major species responsible for clinical disease in man and domestic animals[1]. In the 1980s, cryptosporidiosis was recognized as a common cause of acute self-limiting gastroenteritis in immunocompetent people. At present, there is no effective treatment even though infection in the immunocompetent has been described in 26 countries, with a prevalence of 0·6–20 per cent reported in western countries and 4–20 per cent in developing countries[2]. In the immunocompromised, such as those with AIDS, crypotosporidiosis can become a life-threatening condition causing profuse intractable diarrhoea with severe dehydration, malabsorption and wasting, and sometimes the parasites spread to other organs[3]. Among AIDS patients, cryptosporidiosis has a prevalence of 3–4 per cent in the USA and >50 per cent in Africa and Haiti[1].

Cryptosporidium completes it life cycle (Fig. VII.1) within a single host and transmission is via an environmentally robust oocyst excreted in the faeces of the infected host. Person-to-person transmission occurs[4], but oocysts from humans are also infective for numerous mammals, including cattle and sheep[5]. Infected calves and lambs can excrete up to 10^{10} oocysts daily for up to 14 days[6], and both domestic and feral animals may be reservoirs of human infection[7]. The broad host range, together with the high output of oocysts, ensures a high level of contamination in the environment, and favours waterborne transmission. Infected humans, domestic animals and wildlife may all contribute to the pool of oocysts in a watershed through wastewater discharges and runoff (see Box 1).

Waterborne transmission of cryptosporidiosis was first suggested because of its association with traveller's diarrhoea, and with *Giardia* infections[8], which are well-documented causes of waterborne diarrhoea, particularly in the USA[9]. Similarly it has been suggested that people who drink untreated surface waters are more at risk of contracting cryptosporidiosis[10]. Since 1982, five confirmed and three suspected waterborne outbreaks have been documented[11,12]. Other waterborne diarrhoeal outbreaks, in which no aetiological agent was detected, may also have been caused by *Cryptosporidium*.

C. parvum oocysts are 4–6 μm in diameter, and are very resistant: they can survive for over 12 months in Hanks' balanced salt solution at 4°C, although viability may be reduced by 70 per cent (D A Blewett, pers. commun.). Of great practical importance is their insensitivity to the chlorination regimes normally used for water treatment: in *in vitro* excystation tests up to 16,000 mg/l free chlorine where necessary to reduce viability to zero[13].

Consequently, in chlorinated drinking water bacterial indicator systems, used to assess microbial water quality, are inadequate for testing parasitological water quality[13], and at present, there is no simple, routine test that can be used to measure the presence of oocysts in water.

Recovery and detection

As oocysts tend to occur in low numbers in water, a system that allows their efficient recovery from large volumes is required. Currently for drinking water, 500–1000 l are processed through a cartridge filter of 1 μm nominal pore size[14–16], and to release the oocysts, the filter matrix is cut, teased apart and eluted with up to 4 l of 0·1 per cent Tween 80 in distilled water. The resulting suspension is centrifuged and the pellet clarified by a flotation technique using a sucrose solution (1·18 sp. gr.) on which the oocysts float. Oocysts extracted in this way can be visualized by stains originally developed for the detection of oocysts in faecal samples, the most effective being fluorescently labelled monoclonal antibodies (mAbs) specific for the oocyst wall[15,17].

Table VII.1. Reactivity of commercially available monoclonal antibody (mAb) kits with *Cryptosporidium* spp oocysts

Cryptosporidium spp	Reactivity of oocysts with mAbs	
	Meridian[a]	Northumbria[b]
C. parvum[c]	+	+
C. baileyi[c]	−	+
C. muris[c]	−	+
C. meleagridis	+	NT

[a] Meridian Diagnostics Inc., Cincinnati, OH 45244, USA. [b] Northumbria Biologicals Ltd, Cramlington, Northumberland, NE23 9HL, UK. [c] Preparations tested after 3·7 per cent formaldehyde, water and 2·5 per cent $K_2Cr_2O_7$ treatment.
NT, not tested.

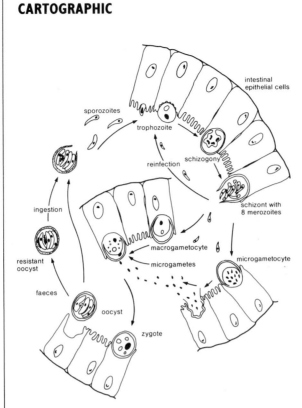

CARTOGRAPHIC

Fig. VII 1. Life cycle of Cryptosporidium *sp.*
The infectious stage is the sporulated oocyst. When the oocyst is ingested it releases sporozoites in the small intestine. Each sporozoite can infect a columnar epithelial cell, becoming embedded at the base of the microvilli, and start the asexual cycle. The parasite differentiates into the intracellular trophozoite. This transforms into the schizont, which produces eight merozoites. The merozoites leave the host cell and can infect other cells to repeat the asexual cycle. Alternatively, a merozite can differentiate into either a micro- or macrogametocyte. Microgametocytes produce microgametes which burst out of their host cell and fertilize a macrogametocyte — still within its host cell. The xygote is called an oocyst, and this secretes an impervious outer wall, before entering the lumen of the small intestine. On reaching the external environment, the oocyst sporulates and becomes infective.

Figure VII.1 Life cycle of *Cryptosporidium* sp.

Limitations of recovery and detection methods

The occurrence of *Cryptosporidium* in water is greatly underestimated due to limitations in methods of recovery and detection of oocysts. Up to 85 per cent of oocysts can be retained within a filter, and filter processing and sample clarification can result in >90 per cent of these being lost[14,18]. Recovery and identification are also influenced by the presence of algae and suspended solids; however, the addition of detergents prior to sucrose flotation enhances recovery[14]. Overall recovery efficiencies range from 9 per cent in river water[19] to 59 per cent in tap water[20]. Both fluorescent polyclonal antibodies[19] and fluorescent mAbs[17,21–23] have greatly enhanced the ability to detect oocysts, but some are plagued by specificity problems[17,24] (see Table VII.1) and at present, none is specific for *C. parvum*. Undoubtedly, specific high-affinity mAbs will be produced; however, for use with water samples they will have to react with environmentally robust epitopes. Moreover, the standardization of filtration, concentration and identification procedures is imperative for the correct interpretation of results (see Box 2).

The limitations of our current technologies not only mean that *Cryptosporidium* contamination will continue to be underestimated, but also that confusion will arise from the detection of non-mammalian 'species'[25] that may have no significance to human health. Until we can determine the viability of oocysts, we must assume that each oocyst detected in drinking water is infectious.

Occurrence of *Cryptosporidium*

Wastewater may contain varying numbers of oocysts depending on the size of the community as well as the rate of infection within it, and up to 13,700 oocysts/l have been reported in raw sewage[26] (Table VII.2).

The work of Madore *et al.*[26] suggested that agricultural sources of water pollution (eg. run-off from dairies and grazing lands) may be of as much concern as wastewater from human sources. In three separate surveys of surface waters, where agricultural sources could be distinguished from human sewage discharges[19,26], the concentrations of oocysts were found to be 1.5–1.9-fold greater in waters polluted by agricultural run-off.

Box 1. Factors that Favour Waterborne Cryptosporidiosis

- Lack of species specifity
- Close association between human and animal hosts
- Low infective dose
- Monoxenous development, with autoinfective cycle
- Large numbers of oocysts excreted
- Fully sporulated oocysts excreted
- Oocysts are environmentally robust and chlorine insensitive
- Small size of oocysts

Box 2. Detection of *Cryptosporidium* spp Oocysts in Water-related Samples

Four criteria are recommended for the identification of *Cryptosporidium* oocysts in environmental samples by fluorescent antibodies.
(1) Characteristic fluorescence specifically around the oocysts wall.
(2) Shape (spherical)
(3) Size (4–6 µm diameter).
(4) Characteristic folding in the oocyst wall. The folding in the wall may occur in 60 per cent of a well-preserved control sample but be less apparent in water samples.

When no oocysts are seen in the sample concentrate, the interpretation of these negative results becomes difficult and several considerations need to be taken into account.
(1) The number of samples collected.
(2) The site of collection with the identification of point and non-point sources of pollution.
(3) The manner in which the sample was collected. It has been noted that long-term filtration at slower flow rates will increase the potential of a positive sample.
(4) The volume collected.
(5) Water quality influencing recovery efficiencies.
(6) The equivalent volume examined.

Cryptosporidium oocysts have been detected in a wide range of water sources, both raw and treated, by various disinfection and filtration methods (Table VII.2). Contamination from these sources may contribute to either an endemic level of disease or an increased level of herd immunity in the exposed population. Few surveys have been undertaken in the UK, and these have concentrated on the occurrence of oocysts in raw and final waters (H. Smith, unpublished; Table VII.2).

Waterborne outbreaks

The first identified waterborne outbreak of *Cryptosporidium* in human populations in the USA occurred in Texas[27], following the presumed contamination of an artesian well by sewage; however, no oocysts were detected in the chlorinated well water supply. The rate of diarrhoea was 12-fold greater than that of the neighbouring communities, and oocysts were detected in 47 of 79 individuals with diarrhoea. Although the disinfection method for the artesian well was adequate to control coliform bacteria, it was apparently insufficient to inactivate *Cryptosporidium* oocysts.

The second outbreak in the USA occurred in Carrollton, Georgia, in January 1987[28,29]. The prevalence of illness was significantly greater in patients using the city's drinking water, despite comprehensive treatment, compared with a population using untreated well water. *Cryptosporidium* oocysts were identified in 39 per cent of the stool specimens, and no other pathogen was detected. In this major outbreak the overall attack rate was 40 per cent, with an estimated 13,000 individuals affected. Seven of the nine water samples collected were positive for *Cryptosporidium* oocysts, and concentrations averaged 0.63 oocysts/l within the

144

distribution system, with the highest level (2.2/l) being detected in a 24 h sample taken after filtration. The source of contamination was not identified and no unusually high levels of oocysts were detected in samples at the intake to the drinking water treatment plant. Likewise, investigations at the treatment plant revealed no violations for coliforms or turbidity levels and cholorine concentrations had been maintained at 0.5 mg/l within the distribution system. However, there were some operational irregularities which may have caused the release of oocysts into the distribution system[30,31].

A possible, but unconfirmed, waterborne outbreak occurred in Sheffield, UK, between April and October 1986[12]. Of 104 patients with cryptosporidiosis, 81 per cent had drunk water supplied from the same reservoir complex, an association that was found to be statistically significant compared with people whose water came from other sources. Furthermore, oocysts were detected in faecal samples from cattle on farms adjoining the reservoir area, in surface waters from the reservoir and feeder streams, and also from brown trout caught from the reservoir[32].

The first confirmed UK outbreak occurred in Ayrshire in April 1988[33], when between 2- and 5-fold the expected rate of diarrhoeal disease occurred in two towns supplied by the same source of treated water. Twenty-seven patients who consumed the water were diagnosed as *Cryptosporidium*-positive, and oocysts were found in two of the seven treated water samples as well as within the treatment works, but not in the raw water entering, or treated water leaving the works. Post-treatment contamination was suspected and a tank along the transmission pipeline was discovered to contain 0.04 oocysts/l A broken fire-clay pipe was found that ran into this tank, and it is likely that oocysts were introduced via run-off from the surrounding catchment area during heavy rainfall and thus into the chlorinated water supply for distribution. Cattle slurry and dung had been sprayed on land in the vicinity of the broken pipe before the outbreak, and oocysts (32/g) were found in soil and grass adjacent to the pipe.

Table VII.2 Occurrence of *Cryptosporidium* spp oocysts in water-related samples

Type of sample	No. of samples	Oocysts/l	Location
WASTEWATER			
(1) Raw sewage	15	4—5180	USA
(2) Activated sludge effluent	25	4—1297	USA
	9	3.3—8.51	UK
(3) Waste stabilization ponds	22	1×10^3—2×10^4	East Africa
SURFACE WATER			
(1) Receiving agricultural or	150	0.58—1.20	USA
wastewater discharges	42	0.006—2.5	UK
(2) Pristine	20	0.02—0.08	USA
DRINKING WATER			
(1) No association with outbreak	36	0.04—0.26	USA
	65	0.006—0.26	UK
(2) Association with outbreak	20	0.46—2.2	USA
	7	0.04—4.8	UK
COOLING TOWERS	10	154	UK
RECREATIONAL WATER	28	0.66—500	UK

The second outbreak in the UK occurred in a swimming pool in Yorkshire between August and October 1988 and affected at least 62 people[34]. The pool water was found to contain 500 oocysts/l. These large numbers of oocysts were assumed to originate from raw sewage that had contaminated the pool via broken drainage connections from the public toilet in the swimming pool complex.

A third outbreak occurred in the Oxfordshire/Swindon area in February and March 1989. Although the number of cases of cryptosporidiosis had been on the increase since the end of January, the outbreak only became apparent in mid-February following the recognition that most of the patients resided within the distribution system of one particular reservoir and treatment works. Up to 5,000 people may have been affected. Oocysts were detected in the treatment works, although no obvious fault in water treatment was detected.[35]

Significance of oocysts in water

Finding oocysts in water may not necessarily mean that the population exposed to it is at risk, and low oocyst levels (0.003 — 0.3/l) can be found in samples from numerous treated waters. The detection of oocysts in treated waters implies that either the numbers of oocysts in the raw water are sufficiently high to overcome the removal capacity of the treatment plant or that the integrity of the post-treatment distribution system, especially the underground pipework, is unsatisfactory. The significance of oocysts in water, their possible seasonal peaks in numbers and the likelihood of contamination events must be balanced against the economics and technical feasibility of treating water to remove oocysts. Contaminated waters are normally assessed for the prevalence of oocysts following a suspected outbreak but recorded levels may bear little relationship to those that caused infection. Continuous sampling throughout the year is necessary to determine whether there are any seasonal peaks in the occurrence of waterborne oocysts and whether they have any relationship to outbreaks of cryptosporidiosis.

Clumping of oocysts can occur in water, and water treatment may increase or reduce this effect. If clumping occurs before filtration, oocysts should be more easily filtered out of water; however, if clumping occurs after filtration, a higher risk of contracting clinical disease may ensue because of the likelihood of ingesting larger numbers of oocysts. An analysis is needed of the biophysical and biochemical mechanisms effective at the oocyst surface that influence clumping.

Currently there is no procedure available to test the viability of small numbers of oocysts, and thus each oocyst detected has to be regarded as potentially infective. A viability assay for small numbers of oocysts will be necessary to determine the likely risk of infection from a contaminated water source.

In humans, the risk from contracting waterborne infection is likely to vary between individuals since they consume varying quantities of cold drinking water, and vary in susceptibility to infectious agents. A certain proportion of those infected will be asymptomatic (about 1.7 per cent; D. A. Warrell, pers. commun.), and some degree of immunity will exist. The infective dose to humans is not known, although as in *Giardia intestinalis*, it is likely to be low: 100 *Cryptosporidium* oocysts produced patent infections in 22 per cent of mice tested,[35] whereas 10 oocysts initiated patent infections in two out of two primates.[36] In addition, illness patterns may vary according to the infective dose, and the virulence of the parasite strain involved. At present there is little information available on such parameters.

The impact of livestock as a source for human disease in water catchment areas must be assessed, and considerable attention should be given to current agricultural practices. The most significant gap in our knowledge is the lack of information on oocyst survival in the environment and on the removal and inactivation of oocysts by water treatment processes.

Although the Texas and Ayrshire outbreaks were presumably caused by post-treatment contamination, the Carrollton and Oxfordshire/Swindon outbreaks occurred in water treatment works that met the accepted standards of water quality. These outbreaks show how oocysts can gain access into a drinking water system by a variety of routes, and they demonstrate the need for research into the origin, fate and survival of oocysts in the environment. Such research is pertinent not only because of the large number of people potentially at risk from a contaminated supply of drinking water, but also because of the large numbers of immunocompromised patients now present in both developed and underdeveloped countries.

References

1. Current, W L (1988) *Am Soc Microbiol News* **54**: 605–611.

2. Soave, R and Johnson, W D (1988) *J Infect Dis* **157**: 225–229.

3. Soave, R and Armstrong, D (1986) *Rev Infect Dis* **8**: 1012–1023.

4. Current, W L *et al* (1983) *New Engl J Med* **308**: 1252–1257.

5. Fayer, R and Ungar, B L P (1986) *Microbiol Rev* **50**: 458–483.

6. Blewett, D A (1989) in *Cryptosporidiosis. Proceedings of the First International Workshop* (Angus, K W and Blewett, D A, eds) pp85–95, The Animal Diseases Research Association.

7. Centres for Disease Control (1982) *Morbid Mortal Wkly Rep* **31**: 252–254.

8. Jokipii, L, Polijola, S and Jokipii, A (1985) *Gastroenterology* **89**: 838–842.

9. Craun, G F (1988) *J Am Water Works Assoc* **80**: 40–52.

10. Gallaher, M M *et al* (1989) *Am J Public Health* **79**: 39–42.

11. Galbraith N S, Barrett N J and Stanwell-Smith R (1987) *J Inst Water Env Manage* **1**: 7–21.

12. Rush, B A, Chapman, P A and Ineson, R W (1987) *Lancet* **2**: 632–633.

13. Smith, H V *et al* (1988) *WRC Publication PRU 2023-M* Water Research Centre.

14. Musial, C E *et al* (1987) *Appl Env Microbiol* **53**: 687–692.

15. Rose, J B (1988) *J Am Water Works Assoc* **80**: 53–58.

16. Smith, H V *et al* (1989) *Commun Dis Scotland Wkly Rep* **89/15**: 7–13.

17. Smith, H V *et al Parasitology* (in press).

18. Rose, J B *et al* (1988) in *Advances in Giardia Research* (Wallis P and Hammond P, eds) pp205–209, University of Calgary Press.

19. Ongerth, J E and Stibbs H H (1987) *Appl Env Microbiol* **53**: 672–676.

20. Rose, J B *et al* (1986) *Water Sci Technol* **18**: 233–239.

21. Sterling, C R and Arrowood, M J (1986) *Pediatr Infect Dis* **5**: 5139–5142.

22. Garcia, L S *et al* (1987) *J Clin Microbiol* **25**: 119–121.

23. McLauchlin, J *et al* (1987) *Lancet* **1**: 51.

24. Darlington M V and Blagburn B L (1988) in *Proceedings of the Annual Meeting of the Southeastern Society of Parasitologists* (Patton, S, ed) Abstr No 34 Southeastern Society of Parasitologists, Tennessee.

25. Blagburn, B L (1989) in *Cryptosporidiosis. Proceedings of the First International Workshop* (Angus K W and Blewett D A, eds) pp27–42, The Animal Diseases Research Association.

26. Madore, M S *et al* (1987) *J Parasitol* **73**: 702–705.

27. D'Antonio, R G *et al* (1985) *Ann Int Med* **103**: 886–888.

28. Hayes, E B *et al* (1989) *New Engl J Med* **320**: 1372–1376.

29. Rose J B (1989) in *Advances in Drinking Water Microbiology Research* (McFeters G A, ed) pp290–317 Springer-Verlag.

30. Mason, L (1988) in *Water Quality Technology Conference* pp 889–898, American Water Works Association.

31. Logsdon, G S (1987) *J Am Water Works Assoc* **79**: 82–92.

32. Rush, B A and Chapman, P A (1989) in *Cryptosporidiosis. Proceedings of the First International Workshop* (Angus, K W and Blewett D A, eds) p124, The Animal Diseases Research Association.

33. Smith, H V *et al* (1988) *Lancet* **2**: 1484.

34. Galbraith, N S (1989) *Br Med J* **298**: 276–277.

35. Anon (1989) *Lancet* **2**: 251–252 [cites report by T A Dick].

36. Ernest, J A *et al* (1987) *J Parasitol* **75**: 796–798.

37. Miller R A, Brondson M A and Morton W R (1986) in *Abstracts of the Annual Meeting of the American Society of Microbiologists* p49, American Society of Microbiology.

Footnote to paper. Prepared by Dr H V Smith following first publication of paper.

The taxonomic classification of 'species' within the genus *Cryptosporidium* is in a transitional state, at present.

The discovery of *Cryptosporidium* spp. in 31 different hosts, worldwide, led to the naming of 20 'species' within the genus *Cryptosporidium*, based on the incorrect assumption that the parasite was host specific. This lack of host specificity of such 'species' infecting mammals led Tzipori *et al* (1980) to consider *Cryptosporidium* as a single species genus. Levine (1984) consolidated the 20 named 'species' into 4 species, one each for those infecting mammals (*C. muris*), birds (*C. meleagridis*), reptiles (*C. crotali*) and fish (*C. nasorum*). This classification is now regarded as being incorrect because at least two valid species infect mammals (*C. muris* and *C. parvum*) and at least two valid species infect birds (*C. meleagridis* and *C. baileyi*) (Current, 1989). In addition, *C. crotali* is now considered to be a member of another genus (*Sarcocystis*), but another species (*C. serpentis*) infects reptiles (Upton *et al*, 1989), and according to these authors, at least four more species may exist in reptiles.

Current, W L (1989). *In:* New Strategies in Parasitology (ed. McAdam, K P W J). Chapter 14, pp257–273. Churchill Livingstone, London.

Levine, N D (1984) *Journal of Protozoology* **31**: 94–98.

Tzipori, S, Angus, K W, Campbell, I, and Gray, E W, (1980) *Infection and Immunity* **30**: 884 886.

Upton, S J, McAllister, C T, Freed, P S, and Barnard, S M, (1989). *Journal of Wildlife Disease* **25**: 20–30.

Part II – Paper VIII

Cryptosporidium and Water Supplies: Treatment Processes and Oocyst Removal

Professor Ken Ives
Department of Civil Engineering
University College, London

Section

Introduction

There are now sufficient reported cases of waterborne cryptosporidiosis to enable a review to be taken of water quality and treatment, with respect to the presence of *Cryptosporidium* oocysts in water supplies.

Although there may be a widespread, but low level, presence of oocysts in the water environment, it seems that a significant health hazard from waterborne *Cryptosporidium* oocysts only arises when a local high concentration appears in the raw water source. This may be localised in place and in time, and if sufficient numbers of oocysts penetrate the drinking water treatment processes an outbreak of cryptosporidiosis is possible.

Catchment control may reduce the risk of this occurring, but ultimately the threat in the water must be removed by water treatment. The use of multiple barriers in the treatment processes is common practice, so that although no single process is currently able to remove oocysts entirely, the sequence of unit processes, operated in an integrated manner, may reduce the numbers of oocysts to a level of very low hazard.

This review examines the processes of plain sedimentation, microstraining, flocculation, rapid filtration, slow filtration and disinfection, to report what is known, and to consider what is possible for the elimination of oocysts. It further considers the implications of waste water and sludge disposal, and concludes with some comments on the management of distribution systems to reduce hazards arising from the presence of oocysts.

1 Overview of Treatment Processes

1.1   Water treatment is an integrated operation, although it proceeds through a series of unit processes. Generally, the objectives remain the same: to provide safe drinking water as defined by the relevant regulations.

1.2   The quality of the raw water is the major determinant of the treatment processes, but there is more than one solution to purifying the water. Typical sequences from surface water sources are as follows:

Example 1	Example 2	Example 3	Example 4
River	River	River	Lake
Flocculation	Reservoir	Reservoir	Microstraining
Sedimentation	Flocculation	Primary	Chlorination
Rapid Filtration	Flotation	Filtration	
Activated Carbon	Rapid Filtration	Slow Sand	
Chlorination	Chlorination	Filtration	
		Chlorination	

1.3   Due to the fact that no two raw water qualities are identical, these unit processes may be grouped in many other ways, and balances are considered among the processes to share the removal load. For example, in Example 2, the flocculation/flotation steps may be by-passed when the reservoir water quality is very good, although some flocculants may be added directly to the rapid filter inlets. Variations in the chemical dosing of aluminium or ferric salts, or the addition of polyelectrolytes, may meet changes in the raw water quality.

1.4   The ubiquitous use of chlorine as a final disinfectant enables all of these process sequences to meet the bacteriological standards required for drinking water. The arrival of cryptosporidial oocysts transforms the situation. Oocysts are resistant to chlorine at any dose which is practical in water treatment (see section 10). Therefore, until an alternative disinfectant, effective against oocysts, is proven and available, there must be a more careful consideration of the other treatment processes. This not only includes their capabilities for removing oocysts from the water, but also requires the treatment, handling and disposal of waste water from filter washing and clarifier desludging.

The principal contaminants to be removed from water are:

turbidity
colour
precipitates
algae and zooplankton
natural organic molecules, including taste and odour
synthetic organic molecules
intestinal and pathogenic bacteria

To this we must now add:

pathogenic parasites (including cryptosporidial oocysts)

The processes normally available for water treatment comprise:

flocculation with subsequent clarification
adsorption
filtration, including microstraining
disinfection
sludge treatment (dewatering, incineration)

1.5   No water, unless prepared specially in the laboratory, is totally clear of small particles (less than 10 microns). It may appear clear to the naked eye, or by turbidimetric nephelometry, (less than 0·1 NTU), but thousands of particles/ml may be detected by more sophisticated techniques. Certainly, bacterial and algal cells (0·5–5 microns) are present in drinking water that is meeting regulatory standards. Therefore, the penetration of oocysts (4–5 microns) through drinking water treatment processes is possible if the incoming numbers are high enough.

2 Ground Water

2.1 Ground water, derived from wells and boreholes, is regarded as hygienically safe due to the protection provided by the long passage of water from rain on an outcrop to the water abstraction point. Nevertheless, ground water for public supply is normally disinfected with chlorine as a safeguard against chance contamination.

2.2 Wells and boreholes are protected from intrusion of contaminants from the surface if there is an impermeable layer over the water bearing aquifer. Without that protective aquiclude, it is possible, particularly with fissured rocks, for surface contaminants to enter the ground water. These may arise from leaking sewers, septic tanks, cesspits and slurry tanks, as well as the land surface.

2.3 Therefore, there is a small risk that if the surface is used for maintaining livestock, which have cryptosporidiosis, or cryptosporidial oocysts are in local sewage or slurries then the ground water may become contaminated. If so, routine chlorination is no protection against the oocysts passing into the water supply. Direct contamination down a well is most unlikely with properly maintained wellheads, pumps and pipework.

3 Catchment Control

3.1 The grazing of livestock, particularly cattle and sheep, is so widespread in agricultural areas, that it would be impossible to prevent their access to catchments of rivers and lakes, which may be used for water supply. The diffuse contamination from livestock dung containing oocysts must remain a small risk on watersheds. But point sources, as could arise with slurry tanks, and their discharges, are much more significant as these could contaminate a stream or river with an exceptionally high spike input of oocysts. This was surmised as the origin of the 1989 Swindon/Oxfordshire outbreak of cryptosporidiosis (Colbourne, 1989).

3.2 Other sources arising on the catchment may be from domestic sewage discharges which may contain oocysts if there is cryptosporidiosis in the community. This creates problems of control, as there is no certainty that sewage treatment processes will remove oocysts to any extent. Also the monitoring of oocysts in such dirty waste water would prove to be difficult.

3.3 Although the control of agricultural slurry discharges may be possible, other contamination by oocysts of a catchment does not seem possible to control. Therefore, the responsibility must pass to the water treatment works.

4 Reservoir Storage

4.1   The retention of water in reservoirs for several weeks generally improves its quality due to sedimentation of some of the suspended matter, and die-off of intestinal bacteria due to the unfavourable environment, and predation by zooplankton. The deterioration of water quality due to algal growth depends on its trophic state, and can be limited by removal of phosphorus. Also induced circulation by hydraulic or pneumatic means may suppress some plankton growth.

4.2   None of this is likely materially to affect oocysts if they are present in the water, except that their small settling velocity will easily be disturbed by natural currents caused by wind or convection, and more so by induced currents from hydraulic jets or pneumatic bubbling.

4.3   Stokes' Law define the terminal settling velocity of a sphere under gravity as

$$v_t = \frac{g}{18} \frac{(p_s - p)}{\mu} d^2$$

where v_t = terminal settling velocity (m/s)

  g = gravitational acceleration (9.81 m/s^2)

  p_s = density of oocysts (1050 kg/m^3)

  p = density of water (998 kg/m^3 at 20°C)

  μ = viscosity of water (1.01 × 10^{-3} kg/m s at 20°C)

  d = oocyst diameter (4 × 10^{-6}m)

This gives v_t approximately equal to 0.5 × 10^{-6} m/s or 0.5 μm/s. If the reservoir is 20m deep, and no currents disturb the quiescent settling of an oocyst, it will take 20/(0.5 × 10^{-6}) seconds = 463 days to settle to the bottom. As this is well over a year, sedimentation will play a minor role in oocyst removal in reservoirs.

4.4   Aggregates of oocysts if they exist, may settle faster due to their larger "diameters", but this is partially offset by the aggregate (cluster of spherical oocysts) containing water space which reduces effective density (p_s). Even a 10 oocyst aggregate, containing about 50 per cent water space, will only settle at 1.6 μm/s, and would take 145 days quiescently to settle through 20 m. If oocysts are attached to other solid particles of larger size and density, then they may settle out, according to the settling velocity of the solid particle.

4.5   The above calculations are based on the favourable condition of summer water temperature (20°C). In winter, with water temperatures near 0°C, the viscosity rises to 1.79 × 10^{-3} kg/m s, and an inversely slower rate of settling, down to less than 0.3 μm/s.

4.6   It may be of interest to compare cryptosporidial oocysts with giardia cysts with respect to settling. Assuming a mean "diameter" of giardia cysts at 14 microns, they will settle at 20°C at (14/4)^2 times the oocyst velocity, being about 5.5 μm/s, and would take 38 days to settle through a depth of 20 m. Assuming undisturbed settling, a retention period of about 6 weeks, could lead to removal of giardia cysts from reservoir water. But as calculated above, it does not follow that cryptosporidial oocysts will be removed under the same conditions.

4.7 It is possible that some oocysts may be removed by predation by protozoa or invertebrate plankton, but there is little evidence of this happening or of the survival of oocysts in free water bodies.

5 Microstraining

5.1 The apertures of microstrainers are described by the size of the sphere that will just pass through the micromesh openings. Due to the geometry of the twill-type weave of the fine stainless steel or plastic wires, the openings have a twisted triangular shape. Microstrainers used in water treatment usually have apertures of 35 μm opening (Mark 1) or 25 μm opening (Mark 0). Clearly, neither of these can be expected to retain 4 μm oocysts, when the micromesh is clean. This is when the mesh on the microstrainer drum first enters the water after being cleaned by high pressure water jets. As the drum continues to rotate, immersed in water, the head difference (maximum 150 mm) drives water through the micromesh, which strains out particles, frequently algae. These retained algae themselves form a straining layer on the micromesh, so that they retain particles much smaller than the original mesh apertures.

5.2 So it is possible that some oocysts may be retained during the rotation cycle of a drum microstrainer. This is not a reliable removal process, depending as it does on the presence of other particles, such as algae, in the water to improve the straining.

5.3 Unlike filters containing sand, or other granular media, there is no "defence in depth" with microstrainers. Any oocysts which pass through a microstrainer will require removal in a subsequent process unit. If microstraining is followed only by chlorination, the removal of oocysts will be small or negligible. However, where microstraining is followed by slow sand filtration, it is the latter which must provide the effective barrier.

5.4 Microstraining produces a washwater (about 3 per cent of the throughput) which is a concentrate of the particles which have been strained out. This washwater requires attention and handling as discussed in section 9.

6 Flocculation

Self-flocculation

6.1 Small particles in water will aggregate into clumps (flocs) providing there are no physico-chemical barriers to their contact. The most common barrier is that due to electrostatic repulsion, caused by small voltages of like sign (electrokinetic or zeta potential). If these potentials are small (typically less than about -15 mV) and if the water contains sufficient ions in solution, the electrostatic repulsion is of small magnitude and range.

6.2 This appears to be the case for oocysts; the few measurements of zeta-potential which have been reported, are smaller than -10 mV. The range in many surface waters, is substantially less that 1 micron and so in colloid chemical terms oocysts are destabilised. Other surface chemical effects may prevent final contact and aggregation, or conversely may provide linkages (e.g. Ca^{++} ion) which may bridge between oocyst surfaces. Final adhesion may be provided by van der Waals' forces, or hydrogen bonding. However, the basic physico-chemical parameters of aggregation still require elucidation by controlled research.

6.3 Even if the oocysts are completely destabilised, offering no resistance to contact, adhesion and aggregation, the particles must experience relative motion in order that they may collide. Because of their large size (4 μm) on the colloidal scale, there will be little relative motion by Brownian motion (perikinesis), as this can only provide sufficient movement for particles significantly less than 1 micron diameter, in water.

6.4 Consequently, relative motion must be created by physical means (usually hydrodynamically, with stirrers, labyrinths, baffled channels, etc.). This is velocity gradient flocculation (orthokinesis), which is engineered in tanks, channels or pipes. The rate of flocculation (contact per unit time) is directly proportional to the velocity gradient, proportional to the sqaure of the number concentration of particles, and proportional to the cube of the particle diameter. Even in water highly contaminated with oocysts their number concentration is small in kinetic terms and their size (4 μm) very small. Consequently, orthokinetic flocculation of oocyst suspensions requires very high velocity gradients, even if they are destabilised. Aggregation without additional chemicals is likely to be a slow and uncertain process.

Floc precipitate enmeshment

6.5 The use of aluminium and ferric salts, which hydrolyse and form hydroxide precipitates in water, brings about some additional mechanisms in flocculation.

6.6 The hydroxides are not simply $Al(OH)_3$ or $Fe(OH)_3$, but a series of partially hydrolysed oxides, such as $Al_2(OH)_5^+$ or $Al(OH)^{++}$, with residual positive charges. These provide some positive potentials in the weakly polymerising hydroxides, which attractively interact with the negative potentials of particles in the water, including oocysts. The result is oocysts surrounded by an increasing flocculent mass and which behave as if they were hydroxide floc particles, due to the coating of hydroxide. This process has been demonstrated microphotographically for algae (Ives, 1957) which may be similar. In addition, the oocysts may become enmeshed by flocculent hydroxide masses being swept through the water by hydraulic velocity gradients (orthokinetic flocculation) and by differential settling. This process is sometimes referred to as "sweep floc".

6.7   The precipitation of aluminium and ferric hydroxides is best at certain pH values, temperatures, chemical doses and chemistry (particularly alkalinity) of the water. In cold water, the precipitation-flocculation of aluminium hydroxide may be improved by using partially polymerised polyaluminium chloride (PAC) instead of aluminium sulphate (alum). The alternative use of ferric salts (sulphate or chloride) is principally determined by the water chemistry. The ferric hydroxides are fundamentally more dense than aluminium hydroxide (due to the greater atomic weight of Fe(56) compared with Al(27)). However, the density of a floc is highly dependent also on the amount of contained water (its self-porosity).

6.8   Therefore, there are no reasons to suppose that aluminium flocculation is any different from ferric flocculation, given appropriate chemical and hydraulic conditions for the removal of oocysts.

6.9   If the floc masses, containing embedded oocysts, are subject to hydrodynamic shear (shear stress is proportional to viscosity and velocity gradient), they may break-up. This can occur at the tips of stirrer blades, or at weirs or orifices, and during flow through pipes and pumps. Although such break-up will form small flocs, less readily settled or filtered, it seems unlikely that naked oocysts would be released. If oocysts escape from flocs, it is probable that they will remain coated with hydroxides and continue to act like small hydroxide flocs. Nevertheless, such floc shear which is undesirable and should be avoided, may lead to oocysts escaping from clarification and rapid filtration processes.

Polymers

6.10   Synthetic or natural polymers may be added to water treatment processes, either at the flocculation stage (coagulant aids) or just prior to rapid filtration (filter aids). These polymers may be polyelectrolytes, with anionic or cationic properties, with the degree of ionisation and coiling usually pH dependent.

6.11   In water treatment, polymers are usually added to strengthen weak hydroxide flocs against shear. The resultant flocs can be large (several mm) and tenacious, with rapid settling velocities. In filters the flocs are readily retained, but cause a rapid clogging and consequent rise in head loss.

6.12   Mainly anionic polymers are used as coagulant aids, but in highly concentrated suspensions cationic polymers may be used alone to bridge between negatively charged particles, to aggregate them. The negative potential on oocysts seems a suitable target for cationic polymers, but the concentrations (even of millions per litre) are not conducive to rapid collection of polymers on the oocyst surfaces and consequent aggregation (particle concentrations of the order of 10^{12} per litre are necessary for satisfactory kinetics). Some enhancement of the removal of oocysts by rapid filtration may be possible with the use of polyelectrolytes, but research is required to study this.

159

Clarification tanks

6.13 The tanks in which flocculation and clarification processes take place may be basically horizontal flow (linear or radial), vertical flow (including floc blanket clarifiers), lamella separators, solids contact (floc recycle) or combinations of these. All types work satisfactorily in appropriate conditions, and there are no reasons to believe that any particular design is more or less suitable for the flocculation and removal of oocysts.

6.14 The fundamental process requirements are good mixing of the coagulant chemicals with the inflowing water, uniform inflow, controlled orthokinetic (velocity gradient) flocculation, floc separation to produce clarified water, and uniform removal of the clarified water.

6.15 The separation process is by settling in most cases. The most significant alternative is the dissolved air flotation process which is applied to light flocs, eg removing algae, or colour. This process involves the release of pressurised air from solution in water to form minute bubbles. These attach to suspension particles, which are then floated to the surface and removed as a frothy scum.

6.16 As aluminium or ferric salts are continuously dosed into the clarifiers, the flocculent precipitates which are formed, together with the retained particulate impurities, have to be removed. This is usually achieved intermittently as a settled concentrated sludge, although some tank designs have a continuous, more dilute, floc suspension withdrawal. In the case of flotation tanks, the sludge is derived from the skimming, on an intermittent cycle, of a froth from the surface.

6.17 These sludges, amount to 1–3 per cent of the total flow, containing concentrations of the impurities, including oocysts if present. They are often combined with filter washwater, which is settled in separate tanks (lagoons) so that sludge concentrate can be treated and disposed of, with the supernatant water available for recycling through the water treatment works, or discharged to drain or river.

Summary and conclusions

6.18 The flocculation process involving aluminium or ferric salts should be effective in retaining oocysts, as well as other particles of comparable size. No differences are to be expected between the use of aluminium sulphate, polyaluminium chloride, ferric sulphate and ferric chloride, if properly applied.

6.19 Polymers used as coagulant aids may enhance the strength and retention of flocs, but not especially oocysts. Polymers used as filter aids may improve rapid filtration of oocysts, but this requires research to elucidate. Direct polyelectrolyte flocculation of oocysts is unlikely to be effective, due to poor kinetics.

6.20 Any clarifier which separates flocs satisfactorily should effectively remove oocysts with the flocs. Sludges from clarifiers require special consideration with respect to supernatant water recycling.

7 Rapid Filtration

Depth filtration characteristics

7.1 Particles in suspension entering a deep bed of granular material, such as sand, are in a random network of interconnected pores, in which the flow is laminar. The pores range in size from about 0.2 to 1.0 times the local grain sieve size, ie from about 100 μm to 500 μm for 0.5 mm grains (B.S. 30 sieve). Laminar flow in such pores is ordered (streamlines do not cross) but not uniform, as the flow passes through constrictions and expansions of the interconnected pores. Local velocities are zero at the grain boundaries and maximum in the centres of pores. Water shear stress (viscosity × velocity gradient) is maximum at the grain boundary and minimum at the pore centre.

7.2 In such a flow and pore structure, oocyst particles of about 4 μm will not be trapped significantly by straining, nor is it likely even if they are embedded in residual flocs, up to about 30 μm in size. (See Figure VIII. 1).

7.3 Mechanisms other than straining account for the transport of such small particles, across the streamlines to reach grain surfaces where they attach. Such transport mechanisms are attributed to forces arising from gravity, Brownian motion (diffusion) and hydrodynamic effects. The size of particles is also independently significant, as larger particles will touch the grain surfaces sooner (the interception mechanism).

7.4 Individual oocysts are too large for significant Brownian motion; this is observed only with colloidal particles well below 1 μm in diameter. Also, gravity effects (settling) following Stokes' Law (see Section 4.3) are extremely small compared with the mean flow velocity in the pores. Oocyst settling velocity in water at $20^\circ C = 0.5$ μm/s. Mean pore velocity at filtration rate of 5 m/h = 3500 μm/s.

7.5 If the oocysts are flocculated into aggregates of cells, the calculation of Stokes' Law (which is only valid for spheres) is less precise. Making the assumption that a multi-spherical aggregate has twice the effective volume (because 50 per cent of the aggregate is space between the spheres), the mean diameter varies as the cube-root of the effective volume. Hence for 2-particle aggregates, effective volume $= 2 \times 2 \times \frac{\pi}{6} \times 4^3$ μm^3; that is, 4 times the volume of a single sphere. Consequently the effective mean diameter of this 2-particle aggregate is $= 4^{1/3} \times 4$ μm $= 6.5$ μm; the aggregate will only be half the relative density, as half of the volume will be space filled with water. Stokes' Law gives the settling velocity as 0.6 μm/s, which is little increase over the 0.5 μm/s for a single oocyst. Even for a 10-oocyst aggregate, the settling velocity is only 1.6 μm/s, which is still negligible compared with the mean pore velocity of 3500 μm/s. Whether aggregates of this size are possible, and if so whether they would survive the water shear stress in the pores, is unknown.

7.6 The third principal transport mechanism is hydrodynamic and is minimal if the particles are spherical. Asymmetric particles, such as discs (observe for example a coin released to fall in water) rotate and oscillate due to out-of-balance forces, leading to an apparent drifting motion through water. The hydrodynamic motion of symmetric particles, such as oocyst spheres is only perturbed by the velocity gradient in the pore flow, which cause very small rotations, and insignificant translations, of the spherical particles. Some enhanced hydrodynamic effects would be expected of doublets, triplets and higher aggregates due to their lack of symmetry.

7.7 In consequence the transport of oocysts, even if aggregated, to the grain surfaces is likely to be very small. This concurs with well-established data and theory in deep bed filtration that a minimum in filtration efficiency occurs for particles which are close to 1 µm in size (Yao, 1971). (See Figure VIII.2.)

7.8 These transport mechanisms are temperature dependent, and the foregoing calculations represent a favourable case at 20°C. As water temperatures fall, the viscosity rises, so that at 0°C it is 1·8 times the 20°C value. There is a proportional fall in Stokes' settling velocity, but shear stresses rise proportionately, so aggregates and attachments are more likely to be disrupted.

7.9 Attachment of particles after transport to the grain surface, depends on physico-chemical interactions. Since the grain surfaces are electronegative in water (about − 20mV), and oocysts are also electronegative (typically less than − 10mV, see Section 6), no mutual electrostatic attraction is possible. But such low electronegative potentials, also create negligible electrostatic repulsion, particularly in waters containing significant quantities of dissolved salts, such as most lowland rivers. Attraction would be due to London-van der Waals' forces of electronic origin; in addition specific ion bridging would be possible, such as Ca^{++}.

7.10 The addition of polymers, as filter aids, may be advantageous, particularly cationic or non-ionic polymers which may provide molecular bridges to link oocysts together, or oocysts to grain surfaces.

7.11 It should be appreciated that surface-chemical forces are of extremely small range, typically less than 0.1 µm in water. Consequently they are only effective on virtual contact, and the surface roughness of filter grains is of larger physical significance.

7.12 The foregoing discussion indicates that little success is likely with deep bed filtration of oocysts, even if aggregated. Consequently prior flocculation into an aluminium or ferric hydroxide floc is vital as such flocs are more readily filtered, principally due to their larger size. This conclusion is supported by the retrospective examination of the Carrollton incident, where flocculation was ineffective due to the removal of flocculation-impellers from the clarifiers, for maintenance purposes (Logsdon *et al*, 1988). It also follows that pre-filtration before slow sand filtration, which is normally used without any chemical addition, will not significantly reduce oocyst numbers, particularly as such primary filters use coarser-sized grains.

7.13 Although no detailed data of oocyst filtration are available, an estimate of sand filter efficiency may be made assuming that uncellular algae of *Chlorella vulgaris* are surrogates for *Cryptosporidium parvum* oocysts. These algae are spherical, approximately 6 µm diameter, with a density of 1100 kg/m^3 and a surface (zeta) potential of about − 7 mV.

Experimental data (Ives, 1962) based on filtration of chlorella though 0.7 mm geometric mean size sand at 5 m/h at 25°C gave an initial filter coefficient value of 0.042 cm^{-1}.

7.14 The filter coefficient (λ) is the proportional number of particles removed per unit depth of filter.

$$\lambda = \frac{\text{no. of particles removed in a layer of filter}}{\text{no. of particles entering the layer} \times \text{thickness of layer}}.$$

This represents a logarithmic decline in the number of particles:

$$\frac{N}{No} = \exp(-\lambda L)$$

or $2.303 \log \left(\dfrac{N}{No}\right) = -\lambda L$ where L = depth of the filter.

7.15 The logarithmic decline in particle suspension numbers with depth is a manifestation of the concept of "defence in depth" in granular media filtration. Each grain represents a probability of capture of a particle. For a 1m deep filter, containing 1mm grains, there are 1000 opportunities for particle capture. Nevertheless, the logarithmic decline means that zero is never reached, and a small number of particles are invariably present in the filtrate of a deep bed filter.

7.16 This logarithmic law is valid at the commencement of filtration when the filter grains are clean. Filtration improves with time during the filter run, until the pores become so loaded with deposited particles, that the filtrate quality deteriorates due to "breakthrough". Filters have to be backwashed before this breakthrough occurs.

7.17 Applying the above equations to the chlorella/sand data, for 2 log removal, N/No = 0.01, $\lambda = 0.042$ cm^{-1}

$$L = \frac{2.303 \log (0.01)}{-0.042} = \underline{110 \text{ cm}}$$

for 3 log removal, N/No = 0.001, $\lambda = 0.042$ cm^{-1}

$$L = \frac{2.303 \log (0.001)}{-0.042} = \underline{165 \text{ cm}}$$

These could represent practicable designs, if the sand is uniform in size.

7.18 **In summary:**

(i) single oocysts are too small to be strained out by sand filters;

(ii) single oocysts are near the size for minimum removal efficiency;

(iii) if oocysts reach a sand surface they should attach;

(iv) depth filtration implies logarithmic removal, but the filtrate never reaches a zero concentration of oocysts;

(v) aggregation of oocysts (clumping) brings little advantage;

(vi) surrogate (chlorella) data indicate that 3 log removal is possible with very deep filters of *uniform* sand of about 0.7mm size;

(vii) the above remarks concern free oocysts. If they are flocculated, with aluminium and ferric hydroxides, by preflocculation-clarification, direct filtration or contact filtration their removal is dictated by the filtration of the hydroxide flocs (containing oocysts). For this the waterworks process technology is well-established (see Table VIII.2).

Multiple layer filters

7.19 To avoid the excessive clogging of the upper layers of a uniform (or single material) filter, which is a consequence of the logarithmic removal with depth, many filters employ more than one material in layers. Such designs aim to introduce the water being filtered to progressively finer grains as it passes through the filter depth. To maintain this layered format of coarse grains over fine grains, during the backwashing process, the upper coarser grains must be significantly less dense than the lower finer grains. A typical three-layer filter would be arranged as in Table VIII.1).

Table VIII.1   Typical Three-Layer Filter Media Arrangement

Layer	Material	Size	Density	Filter coefficient	Depth
		mm	kg/m^3	cm^{-1}	cm
top	anthracite	1·2	1,400	0·01	30
middle	sand	0·63	2,650	0·08	18
bottom (support media below)	garnet	0·32	4,000	0·18	12
				Total	60cm

Table VIII.2   Survey of filtration plants in the USA for the presence of oocysts in the filtrate*

No. of filtration plants Filter Type	(All using prior Flocculation —Sedimentation) = 28		
	No. Observed	No. Positive (oocysts in filtrate)	Raw Water Oocyst Count
Sand	5	3	2540/100 l
Dual media	4	1	310/100 l
Mixed media	6	2	77/100 l
GAC (Granular Activated Carbon)	13	8	880/100 l

*Le Chevallier *et al*, 1989.

7.20   By summing the effects of the three layers, shown in Table VIII.1, it gives an overall 2 log removal. Similar calculations are feasible for two layer filters such as anthracite/sand or activated carbon/sand. There is no evidence that different granular filtration materials are significantly different, size for size, in their removal of small particles. There are marginal advantages in using slightly angular, rather than spherical, grains.

7.21   All such calculations, as those above, are highly speculative until more definitive data about oocysts, or verified surrogates, are available. Very little field data are published, although a recent survey by Le Chevallier *et al* (1989) gave the limited observations in the USA in Table VIII.2, where the waters being filtered had been clarified by prior flocculation — sedimentation processes.

7.22   It is difficult to interpret this small data set, for although it appears to show greater reliability of dual and mixed media filtration, the raw water oocyst numbers may be the dominant factor. No good correlations could be established between oocyst numbers and measurements of turbidity, coliform and faecal coliforms in the raw water. A few cases of direct filtration (prior flocculation but no sedimentation) were reported as satisfactory, but without detail. The final effluent (water passing into supply) for the 28 observed plants had 11 positive for the presence of cryptosporidium with number of oocysts ranging from 0.1 to 47 per 100 l.

7.23   Inspection of these filtration processes showed no correlation between the presence or absence of oocysts in the filtrate, the operational parameters such as initial filtration to waste, use of surface wash, the observed condition of the filter and run time. Many of the waterworks recycled backwash water, but no details were available.

7.24   It may be concluded that, at present, no rapid filtration process can be relied upon totally to remove oocysts, even with good prior flocculation, particularly if raw water source numbers are high. Although claims have been made for complete removal by filters, spiked with oocysts, it is necessary to examine such claims critically, particularly with respect to filtrate sampling and counting.

Wormholes

7.25   Observations by Baumann and Ives (1987) have revealed openings in rapid filters of 100 to 1,000μm size, which persist deep into the filter media. These openings are flow channels which connect the larger pores consequent upon the random arrangement of grains in the filter. Not only do they persist to depths of about 300mm, they also persist and even enhance in time, as neighbouring regions of the filter become progressively clogged. These wormhole like channels can readily transport unfiltered material deep into the filter, posing a hazard to the filtrate quality. Flocculent material has been observed significantly larger than a pore opening, to deform and enter a wormhole channel without blocking it.

7.26   Cracks have been observed in some poorly maintained filters, particularly at the walls. These may be due to wall streaming of the flow, or poor backwashing which leaves residual lumps of floc and sand, which grow into mudballs, or disturbance of the underdrains and support gravel. These are well documented malfunctions which are avoidable by good design and operation. Nevertheless, they exist, and any such filters can allow passage of unfiltered water into the filtrate.

7.27   These observations cast further doubt on any reliance upon rapid filters to act as a reliable barrier against the passage of oocysts.

Dislodgement

7.28   Whether attached to a grain surface individually, or in a floc, deposits of oocysts may be dislodged during filtration. Shear stresses build up in the filter pores as they become narrowed by accumulating deposits. Such detachment phenomena have been observed (but not for oocysts) when a filter is well-loaded with deposits towards the end of its filter run.

7.29   In addition, detachment is likely when filtration flow rates are increased, as this causes an increase in pore shear stress. Any upward change in flow rate should be made slowly particularly if it is made well into the filter run. Such increases may be consequent upon increased demand on the waterworks output, or the transfer of load when a filter is taken out of service for backwash. The smaller the number of filters on the works, the more critical is this latter factor.

7.30   No observations have been reported of the dislodgement of oocysts from filters. Any dislodgement of deposited material which affects the filtrate quality should be detected by turbidity monitors on each filter.

7.31   However, it has been inferred from the Carrollton incident that the overnight shut down of the deposit-loaded filters, and their subsequent restart without washing could have led to massive dislodgement of oocyst-containing deposits into the filtered water, as the filters were increased in flowrate from zero to their full operating rate during the morning restart. Thirty five potable waters were sampled in the USA of which 17 per cent were positive for oocysts. The geometric average was 0.11 oocysts/100 l including negatives, whereas the water supply in Carrollton peaked at 63 oocysts/100 l (Rose, 1989).

Initial restart conditions

7.32   Apart from restart without backwashing as mentioned above, there are initial conditions when a filter is put back into service, which adversely affect filtrate quality. These are due to displacement of residual washwater, and the lower efficiency of clean filter media, compared with partly deposit-loaded ("ripened") filter grains. (Amirtharajah *et al*, 1980). Two remedies are available if this initial filtrate deterioration is significant. One is to filter to waste initially, until the filtrate quality is acceptable. The other is to restrict the rate of flow though the filter ("slow start") until filtrate quality is acceptable. The former procedure wastes water, which has been treated; the latter requires an additional programming of the flow controller. Inspection of 14 water treatment plants in the USA showed no significant difference with regard to positive transmission of oocysts to the filtrate, whether filter to waste was employed or not. (Le Chevallier *et al*, 1989).

7.33   Some suggestions have been made that better initial filtrates will be obtained if polymer filter aid is added to the final backwash rinse.

Backwashing

7.34   Whatever backwashing procedure is adopted, its objective is to concentrate the deposit from the filter into the minimum volume of washwater, leaving the filter grains essentially clean. The volume of washwater required depends on the nature of the deposits, the sizes and densities of the filter grains, and theoretically on the water temperature (although this is rarely taken into account in practice).

7.35   If the volume of washwater is 2 per cent of the filtered water, than a concentration of 50 to 1 of deposit material results in the washwater. Excellent removal of oocysts by a filter, followed by an excellent removal of deposited oocysts by the washwater, results in a very hazardous suspension.

7.36   In a survey of 15 water treatment plants, 40 per cent of the backwash waters were positive for oocysts, with a geometric mean value of 2100 oocysts/100 l, and a maximum of 10^4 oocysts/100 l. Because they are extremely dirty, such backwash samples are difficult to evaluate. (Rose, 1989).

7.37   The hazard of high oocyst concentrations in backwash/floc sludge water is only expected to be significant when the raw water itself contains high numbers of oocysts. It is a matter of discussion therefore, whether it is necessary to treat such water all the time, to remove/kill oocysts before recycling. It is a critical point in the water treatment process, because if oocysts are present in the raw water, their concentrations will be magnified in the backwash/floc sludge. This may be a good point at which to monitor regularly, in spite of the problems of the very dirty water.

7.38   Backwash water is frequently combined with floc sludges from the clarification-settlement stage, and the whole is allowed to settle without disturbance. The supernatant water from such sedimentation may contain non-settling material, including free oocysts, due to the violent agitation of backwashing, and turbulent flow transport of the sludge sedimentation tanks. Also, the settled sludge would be expected to contain large numbers of oocysts. Both supernatant and sludge would be hazardous with oocysts and recycling to the water treatment inlet is undesirable.

7.39   As even 2 per cent of product water is valuable, recycling of the supernatant is economically attractive. It remains to be seen if this water can be processed to eliminate oocysts. Similarly the sludge has to be disposed of, hygienically. It may be possible to disinfect it with massive concentrations of disinfectants, which are otherwise unacceptable in potable water treatment. (See Section 10). No published data on backwash water treatment are available, with respect to oocysts.

8 Slow Sand Filtration

8.1 Normally, no chemicals are added to condition particles in suspension entering slow sand filters. Generally, flocculent aggregates derived from flocculation with aluminium or ferric salts would clog the fine sand, and could interfere with the biological processes which are important in slow sand filtration.

8.2 The fine sand is mixed in size, which ranges from 0.15 mm to 0.35 mm. Nevertheless, the pores are still quite large (about 60 µm), relative to the particles to be removed (less than 1µm to 20 µm), and straining is unlikely for oocysts of about 4 µm diameter. Although there is some filtration in depth, as in rapid filtration, the vital process of slow sand filtration is the formation of a biologically active layer (the "*schmutzdecke*") in the top 2 cm of the sand. This provides an effective surface filtration of very small particles, including many bacteria, and would retain most oocysts. Typical rates of flow are 0.1 to 0.3 metres/hour (compare 5–15 m/h in rapid filters).

8.3 Any particles which pass through the *schmutzdecke* may be retained in the remaining depth of the sand by the same mechanisms (sedimentation, Brownian diffusion, hydrodynamic and surface physico-chemical attraction) as exist for rapid sand filtration. These mechanisms are considerably enhanced by the smaller pore sizes (about one-third) by the specific surface (about $2\frac{1}{2}$ times) and the slower rate of filtration (about one-fiftieth) in slow sand filters. The particles in suspension are in the vicinity of any single grain surface for about 4 to 5 seconds compared with about one-third of a second in rapid filters.

8.4 Consequently, the efficiency of removal for oocysts is substantially better in slow sand filters, except that the oocysts are likely to be free particles and not part of larger floc aggregates as with chemically coagulated suspensions being rapid filtered. A logarithmic decline in numbers with depth is to be expected, with a few oocysts passing into the filtrate.

The biological layer
(schmutzdecke)

8.5 The biological layer in the upper 2 cm of sand is dominated by aerobic bacteria which produce extracellular biopolymers which provide a sticky network among the sand grains, causing the retention of many suspension particles including bacteria. It is, therefore, probably effective in removing oocysts, but since the *schmutzdecke* structure is not uniform, there are pores through which some particles pass. The rate of growth of these bacteria is dependent on the organic content of the water, and its temperature as they are more active in warmer water. The bacterial layer is colonised by protozoa which graze the surface, and furthermore insect larvae (particularly chironomids) flourish on this biological, oxygen rich surface. The oxygen is derived from the incoming water (in equilibrium with air), and frequently enhanced by photosynthetic oxygen from algae in the supernatant water and from algae (filamentous green algae and diatoms) on the *schmutzdecke* surface. The algal activity is strongly dependent on the sunlight, the clarity of the supernatant water, and the mineral (eutrophic) content of the water.

8.6   It is possible that some oocysts may be ingested by predators, but it is to be expected that a high concentration of oocysts would be retained in the *schmutzdecke* if they reach the slow filters in large numbers. This creates a problem at the cleaning stage.

Cleaning and resanding

8.7   The growth of the *schmutzdecke* and its retention of suspension particles creates a loss of permeability in the top layer of sand, so that after some weeks (fewer in the summer, longer in the winter) the required rate of flow cannot be maintained, and a head loss of 1 to 3 metres, depending on the design, is incurred across the filter sand.

8.8   The filter is taken out of service, drained down, so that the top 2–3 cm can be skimmed and removed from the filter. These skimmings contain a high concentration of the impurities removed from the water, and would include a high number of oocysts if they were present in the water flowing into the slow sand filters. The skimmings are washed immediately to clean the sand grains for re-use, separating the retained solids into a very dirty washwater stream, contaminated with various microorganisms.

8.9   It is therefore advisable to instruct the workforce who operate skimming and washing procedures in necessary hygiene practices when cleaning slow sand filters during or following a cryptosporidium incident. The practice of lagooning the washwater, and returning the lagoon supernatant to the water treatment works inlet may, therefore, seed the inlet water with high concentrations of oocysts, and perpetuate a cycle of retention, return and possible passage into the filtrate.

8.10   As oocysts retain their viability in water for a few months, they continue to pose a hazard, and their return from washwater, to the slow filter inlet may allow some to pass through into supply.

8.11   A further hazard arises from the disposal of the lagoon sludge which, having settled from the washwater, contains a concentration of dirt, microorganisms and oocysts which were retained in the *schmutzdecke*. This, however, can be disposed to a designated tip site, suitably protected.

8.12   After about 2–3 years (approximately 15 times) of successive skimming, the sand in a filter will approach its minimum thickness, about 30 cm, and resanding becomes necessary. There is little hazard in the procedure, if the sand was cleaned effectively when skimmed. A few residual oocysts may not be viable after a long period of semi-dry storage, so are unlikely to be a hazard.

Summary and Conclusions

8.13   The removal of cryptosporidial oocysts from water by slow sand filters is expected to be more efficient than with rapid filters, although the latter are assisted by prior chemical flocculation.

8.14   Due to the slow flowrate being about one-fiftieth, and the mean sand size about one-half, of rapid filtration, the filter coefficient would be about 100 times that of rapid filters (see Section 7). Therefore, if the sand is homogeneous, a few centimetres of depth would produce 3 log removal. Consequently, the minimum depth of 30 cm maintained by good cleaning/resanding practices would assure a good removal of oocysts by depth filtration alone. If this is enhanced by the *schmutzdecke* contributing about 2–3 log removal, an overall efficiency of about 5–6 log removal may be expected. This is the figure which is discussed in the USA, to provide protection against giardia cysts and cryptosporidial oocysts.

8.15   Failure to maintain a minimum homogeneous depth of 30 cm, or the appearance of "wormholes" (Section 7.25–7.27), may vitiate this high removal performance. It has been reported (Toms & Bayley, 1988) that certain unicellular algae of similar sizes to oocysts have penetrated slow sand filters, when high numbers have appeared in the water to be filtered. So the barrier against the penetration of oocysts into the filtrate cannot be regarded as absolute.

8.16   The recycling of washwater from slow sand cleaning, amounting to about 1 per cent of the throughput flow, has to be critically reviewed if the presence of large numbers of oocysts is suspected. Technologies of supernatant water treatment may have to be introduced (see Section 9).

9 Washwater and Sludge Disposal

Sedimentation and supernatant recycling

9.1 Waste water from water treatment derives principally from filter washing and floc sludge removal from clarifiers. This is usually combined in treatments which involve chemical (Al or Fe) flocculation and rapid filtration, and amounts to 1–3 per cent of the total flow. In the case of slow sand filtration, the waste water is dominantly washwater from primary filters (or occasionally microstrainers) and from the skimmed sand washing.

9.2 Because the retained solids have been aggregated during the settling/flotation/filtration processes they settle quite readily in sludge tanks (lagoons) and the supernatant water can be pumped away, leaving a thickened sludge concentrate. Both the supernatant and the sludge concentrate will contain the impurities which have been retained from the treated water.

9.3 If the waste water is 2 per cent of the total flow, and the water treatment processes are efficient, the impurities will be concentrated 50 times in the waste water. It is not known how these will partition between the supernatant and the sludge, although presumably the greater fraction will be in the sludge. If the partitioning is one-fifth supernatant and four-fifths sludge, it still means a 10 times concentration of impurities in the supernatant.

Treatment of supernatant

9.4 The waste water is usually recovered as far as possible by recycling the supernantant water to the treatment works inlet. There its dilution and subsequent treatment with the raw water normally ensures that its recovery is satisfactory. However, with oocysts present, the situation is transformed to become potentially dangerous. As it is known that some oocysts will pass through conventional treatment processes, and that normal chlorination will not kill them, this hazard is compounded by the recycling of waste water containing oocysts. Consequently, the treatment of recycled supernatant water during a cryptosporidium incident has to be considered.

9.5 It is possible to filter the recycling supernatant water by specialised processes because of the relatively small flows that are involved. Such processes include membrane filtration, diatomite filtration, or cartridge filtration, as are used in smaller scale industrial solid-liquid separation. Little experience is available regarding their use in recycled water, for the removal of oocysts, but the separation sizes required in industrial liquid processing indicates that oocysts of 4 μm diameter should be retained (Purchas, 1971; Svarovsky, 1990).

9.6 There still remains the problem of disposal of the concentrate from these units, but it would usually be only a few per cent of the recycled supernatant water. Such concentrates, containing retained oocysts may be returned to the lagoon settled sludge.

9.7 Alternatively, the recycled supernatant could be treated with a disinfectant which is lethal to oocysts. As chlorine concentrations of between 8,000 and 16,000 mg/1 have been reported as necessary to kill oocysts (see Section 10) the use of chlorine is inappropriate. Ozone, or even chlorine dioxide, may be effective although by-product formation in such relatively dirty water (presumably containing organics removed by flocculation) may create problems (see Section 10).

Thickened sludge disposal

9.8 The thickened sludge from the waste water settling lagoons should be treated as a microbiologically hazardous waste, if the water originally contained oocysts. If it is disposed of, as a slurry to a landfill, the precautions at the landfill site (handling, personnel protection, ground water protection, security) would need special care.

9.9 If the sludge is thickened or dewatered on site, by conventional techniques, such as centrifuging, filter pressing, vacuum filtration, then further considerations apply. The handling personnel must be protected, the liquid stream could be returned to the lagoon supernatant, the dewatered sludge could be disposed to landfill, with the precautions outlined above. If the sludge can be incinerated, its hazard is removed. If the sludge can be taken to a sewage works aneaerobic digester, its hazard would be greatly lessened, although the thermophilic temperatures of digesters (40–45°C) would not be sufficient to pasteurise the oocysts. It is not known if long periods (30–60 days) in an anaerobic atmosphere would kill the oocysts.

Summary and conclusions

9.10 Separation of waste water into a supernatant for recycling and a thickened sludge for disposal follows conventional processing.

9.11 If oocysts are present both the supernatant and the sludge are hazardous as they will contain concentrations of oocysts which have been removed in the water treatment processing.

9.12 The supernatant, if recycled, should be treated by specialised filtration techniques or disinfection. Chlorine is an ineffective disinfectant for oocysts, and ozone or chlorine dioxide may be suitable.

9.13 The sludge treatment and disposal must be handled with the care appropriate to a microbiologically hazardous waste.

10 Disinfection

10.1   Normal water treatment practice includes disinfection as the final barrier against pathogens, and as a means of maintaining a small disinfecting residual in the distribution system. It is evident that this barrier has been breached by cryptosporidial oocysts, and that disinfection has to be reassessed with respect to oocysts in water.

10.2   The minimum infective dose of *Cryptosporidium parvum* oocysts for humans is not yet known. Comparisons with other parasitic organisms have suggested between 1 and 10, per ingestion. Among significant factors are the virulence of cryptosporidium and human susceptibility.

10.3   A further uncertainty is whether oocysts counted by current monitoring techniques are viable or not, also whether the oocysts are *C. parvum* (human pathogenic) or some other species which are only bird or fish pathogenic. These are separable by refined and skilled parasitological methods, but current water monitoring methods would not necessarily differentiate them.

10.4   It is, therefore, desirable to aim at the lowest possible number of oocysts, after disinfection with procedures originating from well-defined laboratory experiments where viability and unequivocal identification are controlled.

10.5   The use of disinfectants in water treatment is based on their effectiveness against microorganisms (principally a function of their chemical/biochemical interactions) with disinfectant concentration (C mg/l) and time of contact (T min) as major variables. Chick's Law is a first-order response of microorganism die-off with respect to time, after some short period of activation, possibly due, among other things, to the penetration of the disinfectant to the microorganism's cell metabolism. The rate constant of Chick's Law has been shown to be responsive to disinfectant concentration (faster with higher concentrations) so that a given microorganism kill can be achieved by a combination of concentration and time. This is usually written:

$$C^n T = \text{constant}$$

10.6   The power n relates to the particular biochemistry of the disinfectant and the cell material (wall, enzyme metabolism, secretion of protective extracellular chemicals, etc). Both n and the constant are also dependent on the disinfectant chemistry (eg pH, daughter products, etc) and temperature. In most water works applications, the value of n is taken as unity, although this is based on experience with chlorine and coliform organisms.

10.7   Bearing this in mind, and the simplifications implied in CT = constant (ie concentration and time are inter-changeable), any data quoted in the following review must be evaluated with caution.

173

Chlorination

10.8 From at least two outbreak experiences (Carrollton and Swindon/Oxfordshire) it is evident that routine terminal disinfection with chlorine is ineffective against oocysts. Figures ranging from about 8,000 to 16,000 mg/1 as free chlorine, have been stated as necessary to kill all oocysts. These data (Smith *et al* 1989) were obtained with oocysts at concentrations of 10^3/ml added to series of free chlorine concentrations from 1 to 16,000 mg/1 at pH values of 6, 7 and 8, and at temperatures of 5°C and 20°C, with contact times of 4, 12 and 24 hours. Cyst viability was estimated by excystation and subsequent microscopy. At pH6 and 7, 8,000 mg/1 of free chlorine eliminated oocyst viability after 24 hours at both temperatures, but not at pH8. With 16,000 mg/1 for 24 hours, irrespective of pH and temperature, the viability dropped to zero. These values are based on laboratory observation, but nevertheless they indicate that chlorination at concentrations which are feasible in water treatment practice is not a practicable process to eliminate oocysts.

10.9 Additional information (Sterling *et al,* 1989) based on laboratory experiments with oocysts from calves, at 25°C, pH7 has shown that 80 mg/1 free Cl_2 reduced excystation to zero, after 120 min contact (CT = 9600). Parallel experiments on infection of mice, gave 99 per cent. (2 logs) inactivation of oocysts in 90 min at 80 mg/1 free Cl_2 (CT = 7,200). The danger of assuming that C and T are equally interchangeable is illustrated by further data, in the same experimental series, where the applied dose was 4.8 mg/1 of free Cl_2 (closer to what might be considered practicable in water treatment, except for the production of chlorine compounds such as trihalomethanes THM). In this case there was an immediate *enhancement* of excystation to 140 per cent of the zero dose excystation numbers. This eventually fell back to 100 per cent after 240 min. Consequently low-level chlorination appears to be disadvantageous and simple substitution of C and T cannot be justified until proven. For example, if CT = 7,200 (based on C = 80 mg/1 T = 90 min) is effective, it is not acceptable to provide C = 5mg/1 and T = 1,440 min (24hr).

10.10 Chloramination, reported by the same authors, at 80 mg/1 NH_2Cl (monochloramine) required 120 min contact (CT = 9,600) to stop excystation, but mouse infectivity* showed less effect. The 80 mg/1 applied for 90 min (CT = 7,200) to compare with free chlorine, produced only 90 per cent inactivation (1 log).

Chlorine dioxide

10.11 High concentrations of chlorine dioxide (ClO_2) or compounds containing ClO_2 have been reported as effective in veterinary laboratory procedures, for killing oocysts (Peeters 1989). Between 9 and 13 neonatal mice* were inoculated intragastrically with 0.1 ml of samples containing 10^4 oocysts/ml. After 7 days the mice were sacrificed and the homogenised gut was examined for oocysts in 1mm³ (10^{-3} millilitre) in a haemocytometer. The untreated inoculum (10^4 oocysts/ml) was 100 per cent infective. Inactivation effective between 1 and 2 logs (90 per cent–99 per cent) was obtained as in Table VIII.3.

Table VIII.3 Inactivation of oocysts by chlorine dioxide, in veterinary laboratory procedures, using mouse tests.

Cholorine Dioxide Initial (C) mg/1	Final mg/1	Contact Time Min	CT	Inactivation per cent
0.31	0.07	16	5	97
0.43	—	15	6.5	93.5
0.43	0.22	30	12.9	94.3

*There may be variations in mouse response depending on the mouse strain, methods of oocysts introduction, laboratory techniques etc.

10.12 The laboratory work of Sterling et al (1989) using oocysts from calves, demonstrated that 0.6 mg/1 as ClO_2 was almost ineffective in reducing excystation over 60 min. But an increased dose of 1.3 mg/1 ClO_2 produced almost zero excystation after 60 min (CT = 78). However, the ClO_2 concentration could not be maintained over the 60 min, and fell to 0.4 mg/1 at the end of the period. Mouse infectivity showed that the initial C times the contact T (78) produced 90 per cent inactivation of the oocyst infectivity (1 log). It might be more justified to take the average C (since the data do not allow a time integration) which is C_{av} = 0.85 mg/1, over 60 min to give C_{av} T = 51 to produce 1 log reduction in mouse infectivity. It can be seen that these are rather higher than the Peeters data.

10.13 As 1 log reduction is unlikely to be sufficient as a safeguard in water supply, further work is desirable to find what CT values are needed to provide 2 and 3 log reductions in infectivity. The low response from the lower ClO_2 concentration, is a warning against assuming interchangeability of C and T, and against extrapolation of dose — response data. Also see the note on Table VIII.5 regarding limits allowable for residual ClO_2 in drinking water.

Ozone

10.14 The positive results from Peeters (1989) for ozone, has encouraged serious consideration of O_3 as a potential practical disinfectant for water containing oocysts. The test method involved intra-gastric inoculation of neonatal mice, which were assessed 7 days later for oocyst infection. Complete inactivation was found as in Table VIII.4. These results have been confirmed in UK experiments using in vitro excystation (Casemore 1989).

Table VIII.4 Ozone concentrations and contact times to eliminate infectivity of oocysts in mouse tests
(Peeters 1989)

Oocyst Concentration No/ml	Ozone Conc Initial (C) mg/l	Final	Time of Contact T min	CT
10^4	1.11	0.77	6	6.7
5×10^5	2.27	1.49	8	18.2

10.15 Control was established with the mice receiving 0.1 ml of 10^4 oocysts/ml being 100 per cent infected. The numbers of mice tested varied between 4 and 13, for each ozone dose and various contact times.

10.16 Similar experiments to these for chlorine were reported by Sterling et al (1989) for ozone applied to calf-derived oocysts in water. Preliminary experiments compared excystation with vital dye staining techniques, and mouse infectivity tests. The vital stains were inconclusive, except that they revealed that some oocysts were initially damaged by O_3 (at 1.8 mg/1), but later recovered and responded to the dyes. Mouse infectivity tests appeared to be the most reliable. Using excystation, the 1.8 mg/1 O_3 produced the lowest excystation after 3 min (CT = 5.4), but after 10 min there was evidence of increased excystation, as measured by empty oocyst shells, but no sporozoites were observed. Pre-ozonation may damage oocysts; observations on giardia cysts (Wallis et al, 1989) showed protein leakage due to ozone damage.

10.17 Applying, and maintaining a residual of 1 mg/1 O_3, excystation was totally suppressed by 5 min contact (CT = 5). Parellel mouse infectivity tests required 10 min contact (CT = 10) to produce 99 per cent (2 log) inactivation.

10.18   These most encouraging results with O_3 in laboratory bench scale experiments require some further validation, in continuous flow pilot plant studies. In such studies, reliable methods of O_3 concentration are required (indigo method is strongly supported by USA researchers) as well as observations on ozone chemistry to determine how much of the O_3 is available for disinfection and how much has reacted with organic matter. Also O_3 by-products may contain peroxides, which may act as disinfectants. The contact time, in a flowthrough contactor column, is not a simple plug flow displacement time, but requires tracer testing to determine the residence time distribution. From residence times, some investigators report the 10 percentile ($t_{10} = T$), others t_{50} and others the modal time. Some agreed definition of T is required for flowthough contactors. It is also not clear what is the effect of temperature on O_3 inactivation of oocysts.

10.19   Ozone by-products are not the subject of this report, but attention must be drawn to the effects of ozonation on the water chemistry, if it is to be adopted for oocysts inactivation. The following list indicates the principal ozone by-products of current concern in water treatment (not all are produced at the same time): —

Aldehydes and ketones; quinones, oxidised phenolics; epoxides, products of PAH (polycyclic aromatic hydrocarbons); organic peroxides, hydrogen peroxide; organic bromides and iodides; bromate, iodate; oxidised organic nitrogen compounds, amino groups in humics; organic nitrites; multifunctional higher molecular weight compounds; assimilable organic carbon; acidic carcinogenic compounds. (Glaze, 1989).

10.20   This formidable list indicates that O_3 cannot be regarded simply as a terminal disinfectant; it may be necessary to place it in the treatment sequence so that subsequent adsorption, or further chemical treatment can minimise the adverse effect of ozone by-products.

Hydrogen peroxide

10.21   In laboratory experiments oocysts have been killed with applications of 1,000 to 29,000 mg/1 H_2O_2, but no controlled experiments have been reported where inactivation has been measured as a function of concentration and time of contact. If the above range is indicative, H_2O_2 does not appear to be promising for water supplies. (See also Blewett, 1989).

10.22   It has been noted that peroxides are by-products of ozonation, so they may contribute some effect to oocyst inactivation. Pilot scale tests are planned (Scott *et al*, 1989) on the inactivation of *Giardia muris* with a mixture of O_3 and H_2O_2 in 1.0:0.2 weight ratio. However the greater susceptibility of giardia cysts to disinfectants makes any such experiments difficult to assess in relation to cryptosporidium. Typically giardia requires about one-tenth of the CT values which are needed for inactivation of cryptosporidium.

Other oxidants

10.23   Occasionally other oxidants such as potassium permanganate, and iodine have been used in the disinfection of water. There is no information on the effect of other oxidants on oocysts, in relation to drinking water treatment.

Ultraviolet radiation

10.24 The use of UV radiation has grown in relation to disinfection of water containing intestinal bacteria. Larger units have enabled the application of UV disinfection to move from small-scale local installations in consumers' premises, to consideration for small public supplies.

10.25 The effect of UV on oocysts is unknown, but consideration would have to be given to the effects of wavelength within the UV band, and the energies required.

10.26 Other radiations within the electromagnetic spectrum may be considered, of which gamma wavelengths may be effective, as their biocidal effects are used in applications outside drinking water treatment.

Discussion

10.27 The most recent data appear to be from Smith *et al* (1989) and Sterling *et al* (1989) with excystation and mouse infectivity inactivation tests. These have been conducted with the disinfectant applied at a given pH and temperature, and presumably defined water chemistry. Therefore, these variables require exploration. In addition, some of the tests have not shown the interchangeability of C and T to provide a required CT value. Therefore the relationshiop $C^n T = const$ may need evaluation, and the dependence of n on pH, temperature, etc.

10.28 Bearing these limitations in mind, the following Table VIII.5 indicates some oocyst inactivation results, from which ozone and chlorine dioxide appear the most promising.

Table VIII.5 Inactivation of *Cryptosporidium parvum* oocysts in water by various disinfectants tested by mouse infectivity

Disinfectant	Inactivation	CT Value
Ozone	99%	5–10 (Peeters. Sterling)
Chlorine dioxide*	90%	78 ($C_{av}T = 51$) (Sterling)
Chlorine**	99% 100%	7,200 (Sterling) 23×10^6 (Smith) pH-6–8: 5–20°C
Monochloramine**	90%	7,200 (Sterling)

*A limit is placed on the concentration of CLO_2 as a residual of CLO_2 + chlorite + chlorate must not exceed 0.5 mg/1 as CLO_2. There is a danger that residuals may interact with certain pipe linings to form polycyclic aromatic hydrocarbons (PAH).
**Subject to limits imposed by THM (trihalomethane) formation.

11 Distribution Systems

Pipe Reticulations

11.1 The normal management of the distribution pipe network should involve no hazard from cryptosporidial oocysts, except possibly in emergency conditions. If oocysts enter the distribution system from the treatment works they are most unlikely to be retained in the pipes and will be displaced from the pipework system by the normal flow conditions.

11.2 It is well known that distribution pipe networks leak, although the detailed leakage pattern is not always well known. Because of positive pressure these leaks are outward and present no health hazard. However, if due to some emergency (pipe burst, very high firefighting demand) the pressure should drop to below the pipe datum, it is feasible that local ground water may be drawn into the pipe. Since most sewers leak outwards, there is a remote possibility of sewage water contaminating drinking water under these unusual conditions of low pressure. This is analogous to the problem of backsiphonage, except that the presence of cryptosporidiosis in the population should alert water supply authorities to monitor any emergencies carefully.

11.3 In the case of mains repairs or replacements, the protocols for disinfecting pipes before putting them back into service are well set-out in Operational Guidelines for the Protection of Drinking Water Supplies (WAA, September 1988). These guidelines propose 20 mg/l of free chlorine for 24 hours for new mains, but may be changed to 50 mg/l for 30 minutes for repaired mains. If these procedures are impracticable then surfaces should be disinfected with 1,000 mg/l chlorine solution.

11.4 If oocysts are suspected to be present (the 1985 outbreak of giardiasis in Bristol indicated vulnerability of distribution systems) then such routine disinfection with chlorine is no certain safeguard. As discussed in paragraph 10.8, chlorine concentrations of more than 8,000 mg/l are needed to kill oocysts.

11.5 There should be discussions with the authors of Operational Guidelines, and experts on cryptosporidium, to determine if new protocols of disinfection and sampling for distribution systems should be established if cryptosporidiosis is evident in the population, or oocysts are suspected in the treated water supply from the waterworks.

Service Reservoirs

11.6 Good practice regarding the maintenance of service reservoirs and water towers should ensure their hygienic safety. Service reservoirs, particularly roofs, may leak inwards, consequently the grazing of grassed roof covers by livestock should be discouraged. This has been policy for some time, but it is underlined by the risk of livestock suffering from cryptosporidiosis contaminating the ground. Leakage in of oocysts poses a particular risk to the population served by a treated water reservoir, as there is no further barrier to the oocysts reaching consumers' taps.

178

11.7 After commissioning service reservoirs, following construction or maintenance, the disinfection procedures which are recommended to obtain 20 mg/l free chlorine residual, represent no safeguard if oocyst contamination is suspected. As for pipe reticulations above, a revision of the disinfection protocol will be needed.

References

Amirtharajah, A. and Wetstein, D. P. (1980) Initial degradation of effluent quality during filtration. J. Amer. Wat. Wks. Ass. **72,** 518-524.

Baumann, E. R. and Ives, K. J. (1987) The evidence for wormholes in deep bed filters. Proc. Filtech. Conf. Utrecht, September 1987, Vol. 1, 151—164. The Filtration Society, University of Loughborough, UK.

Blewett, D. A. (1989) Disinfection and oocysts in Cryptosporidiosis. Proc. 1st Internat. Workshop, September 1988, 107—115. The Animal Diseases Research Association.

Casemore, D. P. (1989) Personal Communication to Dept. of Environment, December 1989. Public Health Laboratory, Glan Clwyd Hospital, Clwyd LL18 5UJ.

Colbourne, J. S. (1989) Thames Water Authority's experience with *Cryptosporidium.* Amer. Wat. Wks. Ass. 1989 Water Quality Technology Conference, November 1989, Philadelphia.

Glaze, W. H. (1989) Identification and occurrence of ozonation by-products in drinking water in "Analytical Methods for the Measurement of Ozone Residual and Ozonation By-products", Seminar of Amer. Wat. Wks. Ass. Research Foundation, November 1989, Philadelphia. (See also: Glaze *et al* (1989) Env. Sci. & Tech. **23,** 838–847).

Ives, K. J. (1956) Electrokinetic phenomena of planktonic algae. Proc. Soc. Wat. Trtmt. Exam. **5,** 41–58.

Ives, K. J. (1962) Filtration using radioactive algae. Trans. Am. Soc. Civ. Engrs. **127,** (III) 372–390.

Le Chevallier, M. W., Norton, W. and Lee, R. G. (1989) Distribution of *Giardia* and *Cryptosporidium* in surface water. Amer. Wat. Wks. Ass. 1989 Water Quality Technology Conference, November 1989, Philadelphia.

Logsdon, G., Mason, L. and Stanley, J. B. (1988) Troubleshooting an existing treatment plant. Am. Wat. Wks. Ass. Annual Conference, June 1988, Orlando, Florida, 17pp.

Peeters, J. E., Mazas, E. A., Masschelein, W. J., Maturana, I. V. M. de., and Debacker, E. (1989) Effect of disinfection of drinking water with ozone or chlorine dioxide on survival of *Cryptosporidium parvum* oocysts. Appl. & Env. Microbiol 1989; vol 55 no 6: 1519-1522.

Purchas, D. P. (1971) Industrial Filtration of Liquids, 2nd Ed. Leonard Hill, London.

Rose, J. B. (1989) Survey of waters for *Cryptosporidium* and *Giardia.* Amer. Wat. Wks. Ass. 1989 Water Quality Technology Conference, November 1989, Philadelphia.

Scott, K. N., Wolfe, R. L., Stewart, M. H. and McQuire, M. J. Pilot scale evaluation of peroxone and ozone for disinfection of *Giardia muris.* Amer. Wat. Wks. Ass. 1989 Water Quality Technology Conference, November 1989, Philadelphia.

Smith, H. V., Smith, A. L., Girdwood, R. W. A. and Carrington, E. G. (1988) The effect of free chlorine on the viability of *Cryptosporidium* spp oocysts. WRc Publication PRU 2023-M, Water Research Centre, Medmenham, 39pp.

Sterling, C.R., Korich, D. G., Mead, J. R., Madore, M. S. and Sinclair, N. A. (1989) Chlorine and ozone inactivation of *Cryptosporidium* oocysts. Amer. Wat. Wks. Ass. 1989 Water Quality Technology Conference, November 1989, Philadelphia.

Svarovsky, L. (Ed.) (1990) Solid-Liquid Separation, 3rd Ed. Butterworths, London.

Toms, I. P. and Bayley, R. G. (1988) Slow sand filtration: an approach to practical issues in "Slow Sand Filtration" N. J. D. Graham (Ed.), Ellis Horwood, Chichester.

Wallis, P. and Van Roodselaar, A. (1989) Inactivation of *Giardia* cysts in a pilot plant using chlorine dioxide and ozone. Amer. Wat. Wks. Ass. 1989 Water Quality Technology Conference, November 1989, Philadelphia.

Water Authorities Association (1988) Operational Guidelines for the Protection of Drinking Water Supplies. WAA, London, 26pp.

Yao, K. M., Habibian, M. T. and O'Melia, C. R. (1971) Water and waste water filtration: concepts and applications. Environ. Sci. Technol. **5,** 1105-1112.

Part II – Paper IX

The Effect of Free Chlorine on the Viability of *Cryptosporidium* Sp Oocysts Isolated from Human Faeces.

H. V. Smith*, A. L. Smith*, R. W. A. Girdwood* and E. G. Carrington
*Scottish Parasite Diagnostic Laboratory, Stobhill Hospital, Glasgow

Research report commissioned and first published by WRc, Medmenham, February 1989, and reproduced by kind permission of the Director.

Summary

I   Objectives

To estimate the level of free chlorine required to inactivate oocysts of *Cryptosporidium* sp in potable water and to evaluate the use of fluorogenic dyes as a method for estimating the viability of the oocysts.

II   Reasons

An increasing awareness of the risks of *Cryptosporidium* oocysts contaminating water sources indicated the need to extend earlier studies which investigated the control and identification of *Giardia intestinalis* cysts.

III   Conclusions

The study showed that *Cryptosporidium* oocysts are considerably more resistant to free chlorine than other enteric protozoan cysts, such as *Giardia lamblia*. The levels of free chlorine required to completely inactivate the oocysts were far in excess of levels that can be practically obtained in water, even in the repaired main situations. The fluorogenic dyes used were not a satisfactory indicator of viability.

IV   Recommendations

It is recommended that the studies are extended to evaluate the efficiency of water treatment processes such as coagulation, sedimentation and rapid and slow sand filters at removing *Cryptosporidium* oocysts and *Giardia* cysts from influent water.

V   Resume of Contents

A pool of *Cryptosporidium* sp oocysts was purified from human faeces using 5 per cent formalin-ether concentration followed by discontinuous sucrose density gradient centrifugation. The pool of purified oocysts, was subjected to various levels of free chlorine in demand free water at pH6, pH7 or pH8 at 5°C or 20°C for time periods up to 24 hours. *Cryptosporidium* sp oocyst viability was only reduced to zero after 24 hours exposure to between 8,000 and 16,000 mg/l of free chlorine, independent of pH or temperature.

A range of histological stains was evaluated as an aid to enumeration of *in vitro* excystation, however, none proved to be as useful as the observation of wet films using Nomarski differential interference contrast microscopy.

Contents

Introduction

Cryptosporidium spp (Tyzzer 1907) are coccidian parasites, belonging to the class Sporozoasida, which have only been recognised recently as human pathogens (Meisel *et al* 1976; Nime *et al* 1976). The classification of *Cryptosporidium* spp is still controversial. Levine (1984) concluded that there were four separate species, one for each vertebrate class. However, Upton and Current (1985) concluded that there were two species infecting mammals, *C.Parvum* and *C.Muris,* although there is little information as to whether *C.Muris* infects humans.

Cryptosporidium spp are widely distributed in nature and infect a wide range of animal hosts. It is therefore possible that zoonotic reservoirs can be involved in human infection (Angus 1983, Fayer and Ungar 1986). Human infection which is usually by the faecal-oral route can be asymptomatic. Infected humans can continue to excrete oocysts for long periods following the cessation of symptoms. *Cryptosporidium* spp oocysts are smaller (4–6 μm) than the oocysts of other coccidian parasites, and their small size enables them to be aerosolised and transported long distances. All coccidian oocysts, including *Cryptosporidium* spp oocysts, are extremely resistant to a wide range of environmental pressures and can persist in the environment. There is therefore, a clear potential for the transmission of *Cryptosporidium* spp oocysts via the water route.

A waterborne outbreak of cryptosporidiosis which was caused by sewage contamination of a chlorinated well occurred in San Antonio, Texas (D'Antonio *et al* 1985). An outbreak of human cryptosporidiosis in the West of Scotland in April, 1988 was believed to be waterborne. The Scottish Parasite Diagnostic Laboratory (SPDL) demonstrated *Cryptosporidium* spp oocysts in both raw and potable water supplies using a variety of staining techniques including Giemsa, cold Zeihl-Neelsen, auramine phenol and fluorescent monoclonal antibody (Smith *et al* 1988a 1989). Madore *et al* (1987) using techniques for the detection of *Cryptosporidium* spp oocysts from large volumes of sewage and water by filtration, detected high numbers in raw sewage (5 180/litre) and in treated sewage (1 300/litre). In surface waters, oocysts numbers were found to vary between 0.8 and 5,800 per litre, and the presence of oocysts was also demonstrated in two filtered water supplies. In another study, Ongerth and Stibbs (1987) demonstrated *Cryptosporidium* spp oocysts in eleven samples (100 per cent) from six rivers in the Western USA.

There is only a limited literature with regard to the effect of disinfectants, including chlorine, on the viability of *Cryptosporidium* spp. All of the reported studies (Angus *et al* 1982; Campbell *et al* 1982; Pavlasek 1984) concentrated on the use of commercial disinfectants and found that most of those tested including 3 per cent sodium hypochlorite, were unable to kill the *Cryptosporidium* spp oocysts, as shown by infection of mice. Campbell *et al* (1982) tested the widest range of disinfectants on oocysts isolated as intestinal homogenates from infected rats and found that only two of the disinfectants tested namely 10 per cent formol saline and 5 per cent ammonia were effective after exposure for 18 hours. There has been no study on the effectiveness of disinfectants used in water treatment to kill oocysts.

This study reports the effects of free chlorine levels on the viability of *Cryptosporidium* sp oocysts in chlorine-demand free tap water at pH6, 7 and 8 and at temperatures of 5°C and 20°C over periods of up to 24 hours and is complementary to a similar study using *Giardia intestinalis* cysts (Smith *et al* 1988b). It also investigated the use of the fluorogenic dyes, fluorescein diacetate (FDA) and propidium iodide (PI), as an alternative method for estimating the viability of *Cryptosporidium* sp oocysts.

2 Materials and Methods

Detection of positive samples

2.1 Human stool samples were concentrated by the formol-ether technique (Allen and Ridley 1970), air dried on microscope slides and fixed for 3 minutes in methanol. The slides were then stained using the auramine-phenol (Lempert) technique described by Casemore *et al* (1985).

Purification of oocysts from faecal samples

2.2 The purification of oocysts from a pool of twenty faeces samples from known positive patients was performed by diluting the faeces with distilled water, followed by filtration through a series of sieves with a minimal exclusion range of 50 μm. The filtrate was mixed with an equal volume of 10 per cent formalin, and overlaid with diethyl ether in 50 ml centrifuge tubes. The contents of the tubes were mixed thoroughly by shaking and then centrifuged at 900 g for 3 minutes. The supernatant was discarded and the pellet washed with distilled water thrice before being resuspended up to 12.5 ml in distilled water. Further purification of oocysts was performed according to the protocol of Woodmansee (1987). Briefly, this involved the layering of 12.5 ml of oocyst suspension over a three layer discontinuous sucrose gradient consisting of 12.5 ml of cold sucrose solution at a specific gravity of 1.02 g/ml (upper layer) underlaid by 25 ml of 1.09 g/ml sucrose solution (middle layer) and 12.5 ml of 1.18 g/ml sucrose solution (lower layer). Gradients were centrifuged at 900 g for 15 minutes and 1.09 g/ml fraction was recovered and diluted four fold with distilled water (Woodmansee used Dulbecco's phosphate buffered saline). The oocysts were concentrated by centrifugation at 900 g for 10 minutes. The sucrose gradient separation was repeated if it was considered that the oocyst suspension still contained too much contaminating matter.

Purified oocysts were stored at 4°C in distilled water. Counts prior to use were made using a haemocytometer.

Excystation of *Cryptosporidium* sp oocysts

2.3 Prior to excystation, oocysts must be sporulated, and this was checked by examination by Nomarski blc microscopy (magnification × 400) when up to 4 crescentic sporozoites could be seen within an oocyst.

The following two step excystation procedure for *Cryptosporidium* sp was performed by following the method obtained from Dr V McDonald (London School of Tropical Medicine and Hygiene). Equal volumes of the oocyst suspension (1×10^4 oocysts) and Balanced Salt Solution with Hank's Salts (HBSS, Flow Laboratories, Scotland) were incubated for 1 hour at 37°C. The oocysts were pelleted by centrifugation (1,000 g, 10 minutes) and the supernatant discarded. The pellet was then resuspended in 100 μl HBSS, 50 μl 0.8 per cent bovine bile salts (Sigma B8381) in Eagles Minimal Essential Medium with Hanks Salts (HMEM) and 50 μl of 0.44 per cent sodium bicarbonate (freshly made). This mixture was incubated for 1 hour at 37°C, and following centrifugation (900 g, 5 minutes) the supernatant was discarded and the pellet resuspended in

20 µl of HMEM. The efficiency of excystation was measured by counting both excysted oocysts (EO) and intact oocysts (IO) using a haemocytometer at a magnification of × 400. Percentage excystation was calculated using the following formula, after between 100–200 oocysts had been counted;

$$\% \text{ excystation} = \frac{EO}{EO + IO} \times 100$$

The effect of free chlorine on *Cryptosporidium* sp oocyst viability in water

2.4 Sodium hypochlorite was diluted with demand-free tap water to give a stock solution of chlorine which was then adjusted to pH6, 7 or 8 with 0.1 M HC1 and left overnight at 4°C in the dark. The free and combined chlorine levels were determined by the DPD technique described by Palin (1967) using the DPD solutions A, B and C (Wallace and Tiernan, Kent). The three chlorine solutions (pH6, 7 and 8) were diluted with demand-free tap water at the respective pH to give a series of free chlorine concentrations from 1 mg/1 to 16,000 mg/1 in final volumes of 10 ml. The oocyst suspension was added to each of these chlorine concentrations to give a final concentration of 1×10^3 oocysts/ml. Prior to the addition of the purified oocyst samples to the chlorinated water, the oocyst suspension was reduced in volume as much as possible. The chlorine demand of the oocyst suspension was calculated and found to be below 0.1 mg/1. This was taken into account when the final chlorine solutions were made up. A stock of *E coli* of faecal origin (NCTC No 9001) maintained by overnight incubation in 10 ml of Tryptone soya broth (CM129, Oxoid) at 37°C and washed three times in sterile phosphate buffered saline was added at approximately 1×10^3 organisms/ml to the experimental tubes. Control tubes containing oocysts, demand-free water with no added free chlorine, at each pH and temperature, were also included.

The experiments were performed at 5°C or 20°C and incubated over contact time intervals of 4 hours, 12 hours and 24 hours. At the termination of each experiment 1 ml of 1.0 per cent sodium thiosulphate was added to each experimental tube to inhibit the action of the chlorine. The tubes were then centrifuged at 900g for 5 minutes and the supernatant discarded. This wash with sodium thiosulphate was repeated and followed by 2 washes with chlorine-free water. The level of sodium thiosulphate used in this study was non-toxic to *Cryptosporidium* sp oocysts used (data not shown). In each experiment at least 4 extra tubes (containing oocysts) were included. These were used to determine residual chlorine levels at the end of each time period. The final pellet of oocysts was resuspended in 0.5 ml of HBSS and oocyst viability was estimated using the *in vitro* excystation protocol described earlier. The presence of viable coliforms in each tube was also tested by plating out a loopfull of the test suspension on MacConkey's medium and counting the resultant colonies after incubation at 37°C overnight.

The use of various stains in the quantification of excystation of *Cryptosporidium* sp oocysts

2.5 A batch of oocysts was excysted according to the above protocol, after which the final volume was reduced to 20 µl. Five µl aliquots were air dried onto multispot microscope slides. After fixation in methanol and washing for 15 minutes in tap water these were stained with auramine-phenol, Giemsa (Diff-Quik), Field's stain or a fluorescein conjugated monoclonal antibody (Northumbria Biologicals Ltd) according to the protocols given below.

Auramine-phenol staining of *Cryptosporidium* sp oocysts.

1. Stain in auramine-phenol for 5 minutes.
2. Rinse in tap water.
3. Counter-stain in cold carbol fuchsin for 10 seconds.
4. Rinse in tap water.

5. Allow slide to dry and view using a fluorescence microscope and FITC filters at × 250 and × 400 magnification.

Giemsa (Diff-Quik (Travenol Laboratories)) staining of *Cryptosporidium* sp oocysts.
1. Stain for five to eight seconds in Diff-Quik solution A.
2. Stain for five to eight seconds in Diff-Quik solution B.
3. Air dry slide and view under oil immersion (× 1,000) by light microscopy.

Field's staining of *Cryptosporidium* sp oocysts.
1. Stain for five seconds in Field's solution A.
2. Rinse with tap water.
3. Stain for five seconds in Field's solution B.
4. Rinse with tap water.
5. Air dry slide and view by light microscopy at × 1,000 under oil immersion.

Fluorescein conjugated monoclonal antibody (MAb) detection of *Cryptosporidium* sp oocysts.
1. Wash with 0.1 M phosphate buffered saline (5 minutes).
2. Apply 5 µl of FITC labelled monoclonal antibody to sample and incubate at 37°C for 30 minutes in a humid chamber.
3. Wash with 0.1 M phosphate buffered saline three times (5 minutes each wash).
4. Air dry slide and view using a fluorescence microscope using FITC filters at × 250 magnification.

In addition 1×10^4 oocysts were incubated on ice, which reduced their metabolic activity, for 10 minutes, 30 minutes and 120 minutes with 5 ml volumes of 2 per cent or 5 per cent sodium hypochlorite solution. The oocysts were recovered by centrifugation (900 g for 5 minutes), washed three times and resuspended in 40 µl in PBS. These were then air dried on multispot slides (5 µl/well), fixed and then incubated with fluorescein conjugated MAb according to the above protocol.

The use of fluorogenic vital dyes to determine *Cryptosporidium* sp oocyst viability

2.6   Two fluorogenic vital dyes were investigated fluorescein diacetate (FDA; Sigma F5502) and propidium iodide (PI; Sigma P4170). Fluorescein diacetate is a fluorescein ester which has been shown to enter a wide range of living cells (Schupp and Erlandson 1987). Propidium iodide is not known to traverse intact cell membranes and according to Horan and Kappler (1977) only cells with disrupted or broken membranes can be stained with PI. These dyes have been used simultaneously to determine cell viability (Jones and Senft 1985). A stock solution of FDA at 10 mg/ml in acetone and a working solution of PI at 1 mg/ml in Dulbecco's phosphate-buffered saline (DPBS) pH7 were prepared. Stock and working solutions were kept at 4°C in the dark. Working solutions of FDA were made up by diluting the stock solution 1:1,000 in DPBS. To 1×10^5 oocysts, 100 µl or 1,000 µl of FDA and PI working solutions were added simultaneously and incubated at 37°C for 10 minutes, in the dark, to prevent quenching. The oocysts were then pelleted by centrifugation (900 g; 10 minutes) and the supernatant reduced to approximately 20 µl by aspiration. The fluorescence exhibited by FDA excited at 490 nm is apple green, and by PI bright orange/red when excited at 554 nm, emitting at 583 and 610 nm respectively.

The results obtained by fluorescent viability counts were compared, in triplicate on three isolates, with those obtained by *in vitro* excystation as described above.

3 Results

Purification of oocysts from faecal samples

3.1 The study showed that *Cryptosporidium* sp oocysts could be purified from human faeces using filtration, formalin-ether concentration and discontinuous sucrose gradient centrifugation. Oocysts retained high levels of viability as shown by *in vitro* excystation. The mean control excystation value for the pool of purified oocysts was 35.43 per cent $\pm$ 6.82 SD. The control excystation values were highly variable, but this was not influenced by the storage of oocysts in water at different pH values (6, 7 or 8) or temperatures (5°C or 20°C) for up to 24 hours (chi-square analysis (P $<$ 00.5)). Storage of oocysts in distilled water at 4°C with gentamicin sulphate (0.08 mg/ml) and vancomycin (20 mg/ml) to reduce bacterial contamination did not reduce the viability of the oocysts over an eight-week period.

The effect of free chlorine on *Cryptosporidium* sp oocyst viability in water

3.2 The results are shown in Figures IX.1 to IX.6 and in the Appendix. Excystation levels are expressed as percentages of excystation obtained from oocysts simultaneously maintained under the same conditions but in the absence of chlorine (control). During the experiments excystation levels were assessed by counting intact and empty (excysted) oocysts using Nomarski differential interference microscopy at x 400 magnification. Intact oocysts are refractile objects of 4–6 μm diameter, whereas excysted oocysts are non-refractile except for the oocyst wall and a refractile body within the empty oocyst.

Figures IX.1 and IX.2 demonstrate that incubation for 4 hours with free chlorine concentrations of 1 to 200 mg/l did not reduce excystation levels significantly below those of mean control excystation, irrespective of pH or temperature. However, at 1,000 mg/l of free chlorine oocyst viability decreased to between 50.72 and 79.00 per cent of control levels but no significant trend was apparent with regard to temperature or pH. With higher free chlorine levels oocyst viability decreased to between 14.90 per cent and 27.29 per cent, at concentrations of 16,000 mg/l, over a four-hour period.

When oocysts were treated with chlorinated water at 5°C for 12 hours (Figure IX.3), the excystation levels began to decrease at free chlorine concentrations of 100 mg/l and above at pH6, pH7 and pH8. Excystation levels continued to fall with increasing free chlorine concentrations, and at 16,000 mg/l excystation levels of between 10.07 per cent and 14.39 per cent were obtained. When oocysts were incubated at 20°C for 12 hours (Figure IX.4), the observed excystation levels began to fall significantly after treatment of the oocysts with 50–200 mg/l of free chlorine irrespective of pH. After treatment for 12 hours with 1,000 mg/l of free chlorine excystation levels had fallen to 66.70 per cent, 72.31 per cent and 76.57 per cent at pH6, pH7 and pH8 respectively. When the oocysts were incubated with 16,000 mg/l of free chlorine at 20°C excystation levels fell to between 10.08 per cent and 15.80 per cent similar to those observed for the 12-hour treatment at 5°C.

Figure IX.5 shows the observed excystation levels after 24 hours incubation at 5°C with various free chlorine concentrations. Excystation levels in the experimental tubes remained similar to those of control organisms at free chlorine concentrations below 50 mg/l. Excystation levels fell to between 54.60 per cent and 62.37 per cent at 100 mg/l. At 1,000 mg/1 free chlorine oocyst excystation was reduced to 38.10 per cent, 46.03 per cent and 51.02 per cent at pH6, pH7 and pH8 respectively, and no signficant influences of pH on free chlorine efficacy were evident. The incubation of oocysts at 5°C for 24 hours with 16,000 mg/l of free chlorine reduced *in vitro* excystation to zero irrespective of pH. At 8,000 mg/l free chlorine and pH8, 1.5 per cent excystation was observed whereas at pH6 and pH7 zero excystation was observed. Incubation of oocysts with increasing levels of free chlorine for 24 hours at 20°C produced an oocyst survival pattern similar to that obtained at 5°C. At pH6 and pH7 a small proportion of oocysts excysted after 24 hours at 20 °C and 8,000 mg/l of free chlorine whereas no excystation was detected at pH8. This is in contrast to the result obtained for incubation with 8,000 mg/l of free chlorine for 24 hours at 5°C. Treatment of oocysts with 16,000 mg/l of free chlorine for 24 hours at 20°C again produced zero excystation, irrespective of pH.

The use of stains to facilitate the quantification of levels of excystation of *Cryptosporidium* sp oocysts

3.3 In an effort to simplify the differentiation of excysted and unexcysted oocysts from other possible contaminants such as yeasts various stains were investigated. The fluorescent stain, auramine-phenol was not suitable due to the absence of observable internal morphology within intact oocysts. Thus it was impossible to determine whether any particular oocyst has excysted or not. Intact and excysted oocysts could be observed when Giemsa (Diff-Quik), Field's stain and fluorescent monoclonal antibody (mAb) techniques were used. However, unstained or poorly stained ("ghost") forms were commonly found when the Giemsa (Diff-Quik) or Field's stains were used and the excysted or unexcysted nature of these oocysts could not be determined. Within some of these "ghost" oocysts, up to four refractile sporozoite-like objects could be visualised using Nomarski microscopy. When the fluorescent mAb was used, it was possible to differentiate ruptured oocysts from intact oocysts, but no internal morphology could be determined. The mAb technique was less sensitive than direct observation using Nomarski microscopy, in that some oocysts which had excysted (as viewed by Nomarski microscopy) were not obviously ruptured.

The effect of sodium hypochlorite treatment of the oocysts on their recognition by a fluorescent mAb

3.4 Table IX.1 shows the results obtained when oocysts were incubated on ice with 2 per cent or 5 per cent sodium hypochlorite for 10 minutes to 2 hours and then probed using the fluorescent monoclonal antibody. The mAb still recognised hypochlorite-treated oocysts even after 2 hours incubation with either concentration of sodium hypochlorite. However, the intensity of fluorescence in all cases was markedly reduced when compared with untreated oocysts.

Table IX.1 Studies on the surface of sodium hypochlorite-treated oocysts using a fluorescent monoclonal antibody

Sodium hypochlorite treatment at 4·C	Oocyst fluorescence	Intensity of fluorescence
Control	Yes	+++
2 per cent 10 minutes	Yes	+
2 per cent 60 minutes	Yes	+
2 per cent 120 minutes	Yes	+
5 per cent 10 minutes	Yes	+
5 per cent 60 minutes	Yes	+
5 per cent 120 minutes	Yes	+

+++ = Strong fluorescence
+ = Weak fluorescence

The use of fluorogenic vital dyes to determine *Cryptosporidium* sp oocyst viability

3.5 The fluorogenic vital stains FDA and PI were evaluated in an attempt to improve the speed and accuracy of assessing the viability of *Cryptosporidium* sp oocysts. The results of this study are shown in Table IX.2. No oocysts were found to be FDA positive and only low percentages were PI positive. A further experiment showed that even when treated with 2 per cent sodium hypochlorite for 10 minutes at 4°C prior to staining, no oocysts were FDA positive and the percentages of PI positive oocysts were 21.74 per cent, 25.50 per cent and 26.00 per cent after three replicate experiments. These results were not significantly different to those obtained for untreated oocysts.

Table IX.2 The use of FDA/PI vital staining as an indicator of the viability of *Cryptosporidium* sp oocysts

Sample*	% FDA positive oocysts	% PI positive oocysts	% excystation
1/100 μl	0.00	15.00	33.05
2/100 μl	0.00	31.11	42.57
3/100 μl	0.00	16.67	43.75
1/1 ml	0.00	23.07	33.05
2/1 ml	0.00	25.45	42.57
3/1 ml	0.00	25.00	43.75

*Three samples of oocysts were used in this experiment, the amount of FDA and PI working solutions used are given after the sample number.

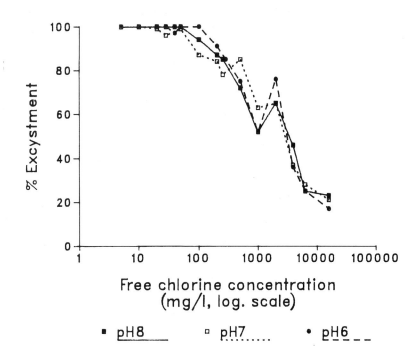

Figure IX.1 The effect of free chlorine on the viability of
Cryptosporidium sp oocysts after 4 hours incubation at 5°C

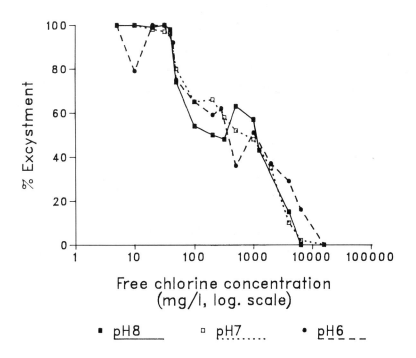

Figure IX.6 The effect of free chlorine on the viability of
Cryptosporidium sp oocysts after 24 hours incubation at 20°C

4. Discussion

Purification of oocysts from faecal samples

4.1   The purification of *Cryptosporidium* sp oocysts from human faeces by filtration, formalin-ether concentration and a discontinuous sucrose gradient provided large numbers of relatively uncontaminated oocysts for use in the chlorination experiments. The use of the formalin-ether concentration technique removed contaminating lipids from the pooled faecal sample, which may have increased the effectiveness of the discontinuous sucrose gradients. Also, pre-treatment with formalin reduced bacterial and fungal growth.

The use of sucrose gradients for further purification of the oocyst suspension reintroduced some yeasts and bacteria from the environment. As it was impractical to perform this step under aseptic conditions some of the initial advantages of formalin treatment were lost. However, the numbers of bacterial contaminants were greatly reduced by the addition of antibiotics (gentamicin and vancomycin) to the final oocyst solution. The addition of these antibiotics to the stock oocyst suspension did not reduce the observed excystation levels over a period of eight weeks.

Excystation of *Cryptosporidium* sp oocysts

4.2   The excystation of the pool of *Cryptosporidium* sp oocysts averaged 35.43 per cent. $\pm$ 6.82 per cent. SD with a range of 25.00 per cent. to 51.79 per cent. over 42 excystations. This variability of observed values of excystation could have been due to a number of factors, including slight differences in the excystation solutions, the excystation protocol giving variable values of excystation or the assessment of levels of excystation being too subjective. It seems most likely that variability is related to the latter two. The microscopic differentiation of oocysts from yeasts can, at times, be very difficult and time consuming.

The use of various stains to facilitate the quantification of levels of excystation of *Cryptosporidium* sp oocysts

4.3   Various stains were investigated to assess whether they could both decrease the subjectivity and increase the speed of enumerating percentage excystation. The fluorescent stain auramine-phenol was not suitable for differentiation of excysted and intact oocysts because no internal morphology could be distinguished. The Giemsa stain was much more useful because not only did the oocyst wall stain (pale blue) but metachromatic sporozoites could also be seen within intact oocysts. Therefore, this stain enabled differentiation of intact and excysted oocysts as well as staining excysted sporozoites. However, a variable proportion of oocysts did not stain in the manner described above and appeared as "ghost" forms. This significantly reduced the usefulness of this stain especially when excystation levels were low. Similar results were also obtained with the related Field's stain, therefore neither Field's nor Giemsa stains fulfilled the requirements of this study.

The fluorescein conjugated monoclonal antibody (Northumbria Biologicals) was also tested on excysted oocysts. It was possible to differentiate ruptured from intact oocysts, but there were problems associated with this technique. Not all excysted oocysts were obviously ruptured, when viewed by Nomarski microscopy, and these could not be differentiated from unexcysted oocysts when the mAb technique was used. In addition, some unexcysted oocysts (highly refractile when viewed by Nomarski microscopy) were damaged and unlikely to be capable of excystation. The possible misinterpretation of damaged oocysts as excysted oocysts may have resulted in false positive results since only the oocyst wall was visible and no internal oocyst morphology could be recognised. In addition the fluorescent mAb is specific for epitopes on or in the oocyst wall and does not recognise epitopes expressed by excysted sporozoites.

The effect of free chlorine on the viability of *Cryptosporidium* sp oocysts in water

4.4   Free chlorine levels of up to 300 mg/l were ineffective after treatment for 4 hours at reducing oocyst viability. Further increases in free chlorine concentration began to reduce the observed excystation values, but incubation of oocysts with 16,000 mg/l over 4 hours failed to destroy completely oocyst viability.

After 12 hours exposure at 20°C to free chlorine concentrations of between 50 mg/1 and 200 mg/l, viability was reduced by approximately 30 per cent. When the free chlorine concentration was increased to 16,000 mg/l relatively low (10 per cent to 16 per cent) excystation levels were obtained after 12 hours incubation at 5°C or 20°C. However, these viability values would still be significant in the event of environmental contamination.

When the contact time was increased to 24 hours, the excystation values did not fall appreciably until free chlorine levels of 50 mg/l or greater were used at either 5°C or 20°C. Even though excystation values fell, they still remained above 38 per cent of control excystation values after treatment with 1,000 mg/l, irrespective of pH or temperature. As the free chlorine concentrations were increased further, excystation decreased, reaching zero at free chlorine concentrations of between 8,000 mg/l and 16,000 mg/l after 24 hours at either 5°C or 20°C. However, although at pH6 and 7, 8,000 mg/l was sufficient to eliminate oocyst viability it was not effective at pH8 irrespective of temperature.

It is difficult to interpret the overall results due to the inherent variability of *in vitro* excystation measurement coupled with the low efficacy of free chlorine as a disinfectant for the oocysts. There were no clear trends towards a decrease of oocyst viability after incubation with respect to pH level or temperature with increasing free chlorine concentrations. *Cryptosporidium* sp oocysts have considerable resistance to the effects of free chlorine, independent of the effects of pH or temperature.

This phenomenon is evident from the results presented here, and from many published excystation (Reduker and Speer (1985) and Woodmansee (1987)) and oocyst cleaning (Brasseur *et al* (1988)) protocols. The concentration of sodium hypochlorite and the contact time varied considerably, from 1.05 per cent and 1.75 per cent (w/v) for 12 minutes on ice (Reduker and Speer 1985a), 5.25 per cent for 5 minutes on ice (Woodmansee 1987) and 10 per cent for 15 minutes at room temperature (Brasseur *et al* 1988). In all of the above studies either high excystation rates, up to 80 per cent, (Reduker and Speer 1985a; Woodmansee 1987) or infection in immunodeficient rats (Brasseur *et al* 1988) occurred after sodium hypochlorite treatment of oocysts.

The effect of various commercial disinfectants on the viability of *Cryptosporidium* sp oocysts obtained from gut homogenates of laboratory mice and rats was studied by Campbell (1983). *Cryptosporidium* sp oocysts were incubated with a final concentration of 3 per cent sodium hypochlorite for 18 hours at 4°C which did not prevent infection in mice after oral inoculation. However, the high concentration of protein made it impossible to calculate the free chlorine levels. It is also likely that a proportion of oocysts would be immersed in the homogenate, affording them a degree of protection from the action of free chlorine. It can only be concluded that the oocysts were incubated for 18 hours with an unknown amount of free chlorine and still retained viability as shown by both histological evidence of infection and oocyst shedding by the inoculated mice. The only commercial disinfectants found to destroy oocyst viability were 10 per cent formal saline and 5 per cent ammonia after 18 hours incubation at 4°C.

The effect of sodium hypochlorite treatment on the recognition of *Cryptosporidium* sp oocysts by staining techniques

4.5   Further studies on the use of this mAb to detect chlorine treated oocysts, involved the incubation of oocysts with 2 per cent or 5 per cent sodium hypochlorite, on ice for varying periods of time. The mAb still recognised the surface of oocysts treated at either hypochlorite concentration for two hours, indicating that the epitope recognised by the mAb was still exposed on the oocyst surface and not denatured by hypochlorite treatment. However, the fluorescence observed after oocysts had been subjected to sodium hypochlorite treatment was considerably reduced in intensity.

Reduker *et al* (1985) described the ultra-structure of the oocyst wall as consisting of two distinct layers. The outer layer was irregular in thickness (average 10 nm) and the inner layer comprised of an outer zone (11.6 nm) and an inner zone (25.8 nm). The incubation of oocysts with 1.75 per cent sodium hypochlorite for 12 minutes in an ice bath led to thinning, perforation or removal of the outer layer of the treated oocyst wall and occasionally the outer zone of the inner layer appeared to be removed. This treatment did not affect the inner zone of the oocyst. Thus, it is reasonable to suggest that up to 2 hours treatment with either 2 per cent or 5 per cent sodium hypochlorite thinned or removed the outer layer of the oocyst. Therefore, the continued binding by the mAb indicates that the outer wall was not completely removed, or the epitope is present on more than the outer layer of the oocyst wall or that a cross-reacting epitope is expressed after sodium hypochlorite treatment. The reduced fluorescence of the treated oocysts may be due to hypochlorite modification of the epitope or a decrease in its expression density on the hypochlorite-treated oocyst.

The fluorogenic vital stains fluorescein diacetate (FDA) and propidium iodide (PI) were evaluated for their use as indicators of viability of *Cryptosporidium* sp. oocysts. Fluorescein diacetate is a fluorescein ester which has been shown to enter a wide range of living cells including *Giardia muris* cysts (Schupp and Erlandson 1987) via a diffusion gradient and is then catalysed by non-specific esterases. It releases free fluorescein which accumulates within the cells (Rotman and Papermaster 1966, Hoffman and Sernetz 1983). Propidium iodide is a fluorochrome which binds specifically to double-stranded nucleic acids. Upon intercalation there is approximately a 25 fold increase in fluorescence emission at 610 nm, when the maximum excitation peak occurs at 530 nm (Barni *et al* 1981). Propidium iodide is not known to traverse intact cell membranes and according to Horan and Kappler (1977) only cells with disrupted or broken membranes can be stained with PI. In other experiments we have found that FDA/PI staining of *G. intestinalis* cysts does not correlate with *in vitro* excystation as a measure of viability (Smith *et al* 1988c, Smith and Smith, 1989), although both FDA and PI do stain a proportion of cysts.

In the present study, FDA did not stain any *Cryptosporidium* sp oocysts and PI only stained a small proportion of oocysts. Again, the use of these vital stains did not correlate with the estimates of viability as shown by *in vitro* excystation of the oocysts. It may be that the intact oocyst wall is not sufficiently permeable to allow entry of FDA or PI. However, some non-viable oocysts may have a ruptured oocyst wall, thus allowing PI to gain entry into the oocyst and stain the dead sporozoites. It is more likely that the absence of FDA staining is due to the inability of FDA to penetrate the oocyst wall and not to the absence of detectable esterase activity within the sporozoite.

It is notable that the pre-treatment of oocysts with 2 per cent sodium hypochlorite for 10 minutes at 4°C, which removes or perforates the outer layer of the oocyst wall (Reducker *et al* 1985), did not permit entry of either FDA or PI into larger numbers of oocysts. If the oocyst wall is responsible for preventing the ingress of FDA and PI the capacity to exclude FDA or PI could reside in the inner layers of the oocyst wall. There are similarities in the structure or composition of the outer two layers of the wall as shown by the continued expression of the mAb epitope. However, there are also differences as shown by the reduced fluorescence when using the mAb on hypochlorite-treated oocysts and this difference may, in part, be responsible for the exclusion of FDA and PI.

5 Conclusions

5.1 *Cryptosporidium* sp oocysts are extremely resistant to damage by free chlorine in water, with resistance much higher than that described for other enteric protozoan cysts such as *Giardia intestinalis*.

5.2 The levels of free chlorine necessary for complete reduction in oocyst viability are far in excess of attainable levels of free chlorine in water even in a repaired mains situation.

References

Allen, A V H and Ridley, D S (1970) Further observation on the formol-ether concentration technique for faecal parasites. *Journal of Clinical Pathology* 23, 545–546.

Angus, K W, Sherwood, D, Hutchinson, G and Campbell, I (1982) Evaluation of the effect of two aldehyde based disinfectants on the infectivity of faecal *Cryptosporidium* for mice. *Research in Veterinary Science* 33, 379–381.

Angus, K W (1983) Cryptosporidiosis in man, domestic animals and birds: a review. *Journal of the Royal Society of Medicine* 76, 62–70.

Barni, S, de Piceis Polver, P, Gerzeli, G, and Nano, R (1981) Propidium iodide as a probe for the study of chromatin thermal denaturation *in situ*. *Histochemical Journal* 13, 781–791.

Brasseur, P, Lemeteil, D and Ballet, J J (1988) Rat model for human cryptosporidiosis. *Journal of Clinical Microbiology* 26, 1037–1039.

Campbell, I, Tzipori, S, Hutchison, G and Angus K W (1982) Effect of disinfectant on survival of *Cryptosporidium* oocysts. *Veterinary Record* 111, 414–415.

Casemore, D P, Armstrong, M and Sands, R L (1985) Laboratory diagnosis of Cryptosporidiosis. *Journal of Clinical Pathology* 38, 1337–1341.

D'Antonio, R G, Winn, R E, Taylor, J P, Justafson, T L, Current, W L, Rhodes, M M, Gary, G W and Zajac, R A (1985). A waterbourne outbreak of cryptosporidiosis in normal hosts. *Annals of Internal Medicine* 103, 886–888.

Fayer, R and Ungar, B L P (1986) *Cryptosporidium* spp and Cryptosporidiosis. *Microbiological Reviews* 50, 458–483.

Hoffman, J and Sernetz, M (1983) A kinetic study on the enzymatic hydroysis of fluorescein diacetate and fluorecein di-beta-D-galactopyranoside. *Analytical Chemistry* 36, 409–413.

Horan, P K and Kappler, J W (1977) Automated fluorescent analysis for cytotoxicity assays. *Journal of Immunological Methods* 18, 309–316.

Jones, K H and Senft, J A (1985) An improved method to determine cell viability by simultaneous staining with Fluorocein diacetate and Propidium iodide. *Journal of Histochemistry and Cytochemistry* 33, 77–79.

Levine, N D (1984) Taxonomy and review of the coccidian genus *Cryptosporidium* (Protozoa, Apicomplexa). *Journal of Protozoology* 31, 94–98.

Madore, M S, Rose, J B, Gerba, C P, Arrowood, M J and Stering, C R (1987) Occurrence of *Cyrptosporidium* oocysts in sewage effluents and selected surface waters. *Journal of Parasitology* 73(4), 702–705.

Meisel, J L, Perera, D R, Meligro, B S and Rubin, M D (1976) Overwhelming watery diarrhoea associated with *Cryptosporidium* in an immunosuppressed patient. *Gastroenterology* 70, 1156–1160.

Nime, F A, Burek, J D, Page, D L, Holscher, M A and Yardley, J H (1976) Acute enterocolitis in a human being infected with the protozoan *Cryptosporidium. Gastroenterology* 70, 592–598.

Ongerth, J E and Stibbs, H H (1987) Identification of *Cryptosporidium* oocysts in river water. *Applied and Environmental Microbiology* 53, 672–676.

Palin, A T (1967) Methods for the determination, in water, of free and combined available chlorine, chlorine dioxide and chlorite, bromide, iodine and ozone, using diethyl-p-phenylene diamine. *Journal of the Institution of Water Engineers and Scientists* 21, 537–547.

Pavlasek, I (1984) Effect of disinfectants on infectiousness of oocysts of *Cryptosporidium* spp. *Ceskoslovenska Epidemiologie Mikrobiologie Immunology* 33, 97–101.

Reducker, D W and S Peer, C A (1985) Factors influencing excystation in *Cryptosporidium* oocysts from cattle. *Journal of Parasitology* 71, 112–115.

Reducker, D W, Speer, C A and Blixt, J A (1985) Ulstrastructural changes in the oocyst wall during excystation of *Cryptosporidium parvum* (Apicomplexa; Eucoccidiorida). *Canadian Journal of Zoology* 63, 1892–1896.

Rotman, B and Papermaster, B W (1966) Membrane properties of living mammalian cells as studied by enzymatic hydrolysis of fluorogenic esters. *Proceedings of the National Academy of Science USA* 55, 134–141.

Schupp, D G and Erlandson, S L (1987) A new method to determine *Giardia* cyst viability: Correlation of Fluorocein diacetate and Propidium iodide staining with animal infectivity. *Applied and Environmental Microbiology* 53, 704–707.

Smith, H V, McDiarmid, A, Gilmour, R A and Smith, A L (1988a) Detection of *Cryptosporidium* spp oocysts in water. *Transactions of the Royal Society of Tropical Medicine and Hygiene* 82,942.

Smith, H V, Smith, A L, Girdwood, R W A and Carrington, E G (1988b) The effect of free chlorine on the viability of *Giardia lamblia* cysts. Water Research Centre PRU 1875-M.

Smith, A L, Gilmour, R A and Smith, H V (1988c) The effect of free chlorine on the viability of *Giardia lamblia* cysts as determined by *in vitro* excystment and fluorogenic dye incorporation. *Transactions of the Royal Society of Tropical Medicine and Hygiene* 82,941.

Smith, H V, McDiarmid, A, Smith, A L, Hinson, A and Gilmour, R A (1989). An analysis of staining methods for the detection of *Cryptosporidium* spp, oocysts in water-related samples. *Parasitology* 99, 323–327.

Smith, A L and Smith H V, (1989) A comparison of fluorescein diacetate and propidium iodide staining and *in vitro* excystation for determining *Giardia intestinalis* cyst viability. *Parasitology* 99, 329–331.

Tyzzer, E E (1907) A sporozoan found in the peptic glands of the common mouse. *Proceedings of the Society of Experimental Biology and Medicine* 5, 12–13.

Upton, S J and Current, W L (1985) The species of *Cryptosporidium* (Apicomplexa: Cryptosporidiidae) infecting mammals. *Journal of Parasitology* 71, 625–629.

Woodmansee, D B (1987) Studies of *in vitro* excystation of *Cryptosporidium parvum* from calves. *Journal of Protozoology* 34(4), 398–402.

Appendix

The effect of free chlorine on the viability of *Cryptosporidium* sp oocysts after 4 hours incubation at 5°C

Table A1.   Incubation at 5°C for 4 hours

Chlorine concentration (mg/l)	% excystation*		
	pH6	PH7	pH8
5	100.00	100.00	100.00
10	100.00	100.00	100.00
20	100.00	98.76	100.00
30	96.53	100.00	100.00
40	100.00	100.00	97.94
50	100.00	98.81	100.00
100	94.33	87.47	100.00
200	88.06	84.31	90.63
300	84.50	78.04	84.70
500	72.03	84.70	75.13
1,000	50.72	62.40	51.31
2,000	65.74	65.51	70.56
4,000	47.02	35.43	37.57
8,000	25.77	28.00	25.12
16,000	23.20	21.59	17.49

*The percentage excystation expressed as percentage of the mean control excystation.

Table A2.   Incubation at 20°C for 4 hours

Chlorine concentration (mg/l)	% excystation*		
	pH6	PH7	pH8
5	100.00	100.00	100.00
10	100.00	100.00	100.00
20	100.00	84.59	100.00
30	100.00	100.00	96.50
40	96.02	100.00	100.00
50	100.00	98.79	100.00
100	85.32	85.41	100.00
200	88.68	90.63	94.86
300	79.79	83.69	85.27
500	79.23	73.55	74.40
1,000	73.61	79.62	71.18
2,000	57.49	58.31	66.41
4,000	33.19	48.57	28.96
8,000	21.98	37.00	36.38
16,000	14.90	25.97	27.29

*The percentage excystation expressed as percentage of the mean control excystation.

Table A3.   Incubation at 5°C for 12 hours

Chlorine concentration (mg/l)	% excystation*		
	pH6	PH7	pH8
5	100.00	100.00	100.00
10	83.90	100.00	100.00
20	100.00	100.00	100.00
30	100.00	100.00	100.00
40	100.00	90.09	100.00
50	94.07	100.00	100.00
100	81.80	84.48	89.36
200	66.22	71.18	79.73
300	79.62	73.72	75.98
500	84.00	79.28	94.07
1,000	83.15	71.32	95.65
2,000	63.90	59.89	42.51
4,000	47.93	44.48	40.33
8,000	24.75	23.20	14.85
16,000	11.77	14.39	10.07

*The percentage excystation expressed as percentage of the mean control excystation.

Table A4. Incubation at 20°C for 12 hours

Chlorine	% excystation*		
concentration (mg/l)	pH6	PH7	pH8
5	100.00	100.00	100.00
10	100.00	100.00	100.00
20	100.00	100.00	100.00
30	100.00	95.96	100.00
40	100.00	100.00	100.00
50	80.64	100.00	100.00
100	77.62	86.54	89.36
200	64.47	79.62	86.90
300	75.25	83.69	74.85
500	100.00	88.09	94.00
1,000	66.70	72.31	76.57
2,000	40.33	50.21	42.00
4,000	45.78	44.51	39.89
8,000	32.91	34.49	14.86
16,000	12.84	15.80	10.08

*The percentage excystation expressed as percentage of the mean control excystation.

Table A5. Incubation at 5°C for 24 hours

Chlorine	% excystation*		
concentration (mg/1)	pH6	pH7	pH8
5	100.00	100.00	85.20
10	100.00	100.00	82.33
20	100.00	100.00	99.94
30	92.80	100.00	81.94
40	79.10	98.53	100.00
50	96.68	98.79	82.50
100	61.76	62.37	54.60
200	58.00	53.40	ND
300	50.41	50.07	48.85
500	55.32	54.22	51.31
1,000	38.10	46.03	51.82
2,000	52.61	31.61	30.51
4,000	21.87	17.78	35.43
8,000	0.00	0.00	1.50
16,000	0.00	0.00	0.00

*The percentage excystation expressed as percentage of the mean control excystation.

Table A6. Incubation at 5°C for 24 hours

Chlorine	% excystation*		
concentration (mg/1)	pH6	pH7	pH8
5	100.00	100.00	100.00
10	78.84	100.00	100.00
20	100.00	100.00	98.87
30	100.00	97.91	100.00
40	91.67	90.91	98.56
50	74.70	79.34	73.89
100	65.14	63.78	52.13
200	57.86	65.26	48.57
300	61.02	56.76	47.02
500	35.43	50.44	62.43
1,000	49.47	46.82	56.45
2,000	36.95	33.87	42.59
4,000	27.51	9.94	14.82
8,000	11.20	1.13	0.00
16,000	0.00	0.00	0.00

*The percentage excystation expressed as percentage of the mean control excystation.

Part II – Paper X

The Removal of Cryptosporidial Oocysts During Sewage Treatment

Edmund B Pike, BSc, PhD, MI Biol, C Biol, MIWEM.

Principal Microbioliogist, Water Research Centre, Henley Road, Medmenham, Marlow, PO Box 16, Buckinghamshire, SL7 2HD.

1. Cryptosporidia are excreted by infected persons and animals as the resistant oocyst stage within the faeces. If there are cases of cryptosporidiosis in the population, the oocysts will be present in the raw sewage. Since domestic and wild animals can also be hosts to species of cryptosporidium, surface water drainage may also carry the oocysts into sewage. Because cases of cryptosporidiosis are sporadic, whereas faecal indicator bacteria are always present in faeces, no correlation should be expected between presence of cryptosporidium and counts of faecal bacteria (eg the coliform group, faecal streptococci and sulphite-reducing clostridia). Indeed none was found in a study of the incidence of coliform bacteria and cryptosporidial oocysts in a watershed[1]. The correct statistical model is not correlation, but association.

Table X.1 The fractions of cryptosporidial oocysts surviving sewage treatment

Reference	Conditions of Treatment and Sampling	Mean count occysts/1 (and range)	Fraction Remaining
5	Sample size 3781:		
	Raw sewage	17	
	Activated-sludge effluent	5.9	0.35
6, 7, 8	Domestic Sewage:		
	Raw sewage (4 samples, 2 works)	5283(850–14 000)	
	Chlorinated activated-sludge effluent (9 samples, 9 works)	1374(140–4000)	0.26
	Sand-filtered, chlorinated effluent (2 samples, 2 works)	180(16–340)	0.13*

* Comparing sand-filtered and activated-sludge effluents.

Identical data are presented in References 6–8.

2. Sewage treatment involves a number of stages, ie pretreatment by screening and removal of gross solids and grit, primary sedimentation to remove much of the suspended solids as raw sludge and biological aerobic treatment by either biological filtration or by the activated sludge process. The biologically treated effluent is settled to remove suspended solids as secondary or biological sludge before being discharged. During treatment, many of the microorganisms in the sewage are removed either by sedimentation in the primary treatment or in the biological stage. In the biological stages removal may occur by physico-chemical adsorption to the biological filter slimes or to activated sludge flocs or by grazing by the microscopic and visible animal life. The net result of sewage treatment is the production of two process streams, the treated effluent which contains far fewer faecal organisms than the sewage and the sludge in which faecal organisms are concentrated, compared with sewage. There is a discrepancy caused by mortality, in that the total rate of input of faecal microorganisms is greater than the output.

Table X.2 Calculated free-falling velocities of resting stages of parasites in water at 15°C*

Organism	Diameter (μm)	Density g/cm³	Velocity (cm/h)	Reynolds' no (Rₑ)
Cryptosporidium	5	1.08	0.35	4.2×10^{-6}
Entamoeba histolytica	12	1.07	1.8	5.1×10^{-5}
Taenia saginata	40	1.3	83	8.1×10^{-3}
Ascaris lumbricoides	50	1.111	48	5.9×10^{-3}

See Appendix 1 for basis of calculation. For ovoid resting stages the diameter is the average for the three axes.

3.   There are two other processes in sewage treatment which are relevant when considering the release of faecal microorganisms into the aquatic environment. Raw and biological sludges are usually combined and given further treatment to remove water and to reduce putrescibility, thereby assisting disposal. More than half the sludge produced in Britain is given anaerobic digestion to stabilise it and to reduce the content of pathogens and more than 60 per cent of all sludge is used in agriculture or in landfill. Under existing and future guidelines to acccompany implementation of the EC Directive 86/278/EEC on agricultural use of sludge measures must be taken to avoid contamination of water courses and sources of abstraction. The second consideration is the arrangement for handling storm sewage. It is normal for sewage flows greater than three times the nominal dry-weather flow (3DWF) to be diverted to storm-water tanks, which hold 2 hours capacity at 3DWF. When these are full, storm sewage is diverted to a watercourse, otherwise the contents are returned to the normal flow after the storm event.

4.   Existing information upon the removal of cryptosporidial oocysts during sewage treatment is sparse and is confined to the work of Dr Joan B Rose and her colleagues at the University of Arizona, Tucson. There is apparently no information upon the rate of excretion of oocysts by patients. This must be expected to vary with the course of the disease and to lessen during convalescence. Because of the present shortage of information it will be necessary to assess the likely effects of sewage treatment upon oocysts by analogy with other parasitic organisms and by consideration of the physics of sedimentation processes.

5.   Table X.1 summarises the data which have been published by Rose and associates[2-5]. References 3–5 present the same data. The results show, as expected for a disease which tends to occur sporadically, great variability in counts detected in raw sewage. Neither of the surveys was conducted during a recognised outbreak, as far as is recorded. The percentages of oocysts remaining after activated-sludge treatment are relatively high at 35 and 26 per cent respectively. By contrast, activated sludge treatment can be expected to remove in excess of 90 per cent of enteric bacteria and enteroviruses. The treated effluents were chlorinated. This is practised in the Tucson area because effluents are used to recharge groundwater and are required to meet a viral standard. Chlorination of effluents can be assumed to have no effect at all upon viability of oocysts. Even after sand filtration, 3.4 per cent of oocysts remained. These conclusions must be qualified, since the data for References 3–5 are not matched.

6. Parallel examinations of raw sewage and chlorinated secondary effluents by Rose and colleagues[4, 5] appeared to indicate that cryptosporidial oocysts were less efficiently removed than cysts of the protozoan parasite giardia, which is also waterborne. The cysts of giardia are larger than the oocysts of cryptosporidium and thus may sediment more rapidly. Detailed information upon the removal of cysts of the protozoan parasite *Entamoeba histolytica,* which causes amoebic dysentery, has been collected by Feachem and others[6]. Primary sedimentation removed up to 64 per cent of cysts. Studies, quoted by these authors, from India, where this parasite is prevalent, showed the following percentage removals of cysts: primary sedimentation for 2 hours, 64 per cent, for one hour 27 per cent; full sewage treatment with biological filtration 71–94 per cent; full treatment with activated sludge 83 per cent.

7. A key parameter controlling the efficiency of primary sedimentation and secondary settlement tanks in removing suspended solids is the surface loading rate (ie the ratio of rate of flow of liquor to surface area of the liquid). The dimensions of surface loading rate are m/h and this represents the vertical component of the velocity of the liquid. During the initial phase of sedimentation, solid particles settle freely, unhindered by proximity of neighbouring particles and therefore attain a maximum free-falling velocity, as described by Stokes' Law (Appendix 1). It is conventional to design tanks to accommodate a surface loading rate of 0.5 m/h at DWF and a maximum rate of 1.5 m/h at 3DWF. It is obvious that a particle which is unable to attain free-falling velocities of this order cannot be removed by sedimentation, unless it is attached to a larger or more dense particle.

8. Table X.2 shows the average dimensions and densities of various parasitic resting stages and their maximum free-falling velocities calculated from Stokes' Law in water at 15°C. This temperature is a reasonable average over the year. In colder sewage the greater density and viscosity of water would reduce the velocities somewhat. Stokes' Law holds for Reynolds' numbers between 10^{-4} and 1. The table shows that Stokes' Law does not hold for the cysts of *E.histólytica* and oocysts of cryptosporidium, as their Reynold's numbers are below 10^{-4} and their settling would be hindered. On the other hand the value predicted for eggs of the beef tapeworm, *Tsaginata,* of 83 cm/h compares with a median settling velocity of about 1 m/h by experiment[10]. This indicates the applicability of Table X.2 and indicates that sedimentation alone, unassisted by coagulation or attachment to larger or denser particles, would fail to remove oocysts and cysts from sewage. It therefore confirms qualitatively the observations made in paragraphs 5 and 6.

9. The evidence presented above, although sparse, indicates that oocysts of species of cryptosporidium are poorly removed during sewage treatment, in comparison with faecal indicator bacteria, pathogenic bacteria and enteroviruses. Since resting stages of parasites are largely unaffected by mortality or grazing, it must be concluded that raw sewage, storm sewage discharges, raw sewage sludge and treated effluents must all be considered to be major potential sources of cryptosporidial oocysts in receiving waters, when the contributing community contains excretors.

Appendix 1.

Stokes' Law

The free-falling velocity, v, attained by spheres, radius r, density D, settling in water of density, d and dynamic viscosity n is given by Stokes' Law.

$$v = 2r^2 (D-d)g/9n \ldots \ldots \ldots 1$$

Where g is gravitational acceleration (981 cm/s^2) and where v has units cm/s when centimetre-gram-second units are used.

Water has a maximum density of 1.000 g/cm^3 at 4°C, when n = 0.01520 g/ cm/s. Corresponding values at 15°C are 0.9991 g/cm^3 and 0.01138 g cm/s.

Stokes' Law holds where the Reynolds' Number R_e of the particles ranges between 10–4 and 1. Reynolds Number is defined as;

$$R_e = Dv2r/n \ldots \ldots 2$$

References

1. ROSE, J. B., DARBIN, H. and GERBA, C. P. (1988). Correlations of the protozoa *Cryptosporidium* and *Giardia* with quality variables in a watershed. **Water Science and Technology** 20 (11/12), 271-276.
2. MUSIAL, C. E., ARROWOOD, M. J., STERLING, S. R. and GERBA, C. P. (1987). Detection of *Cryptosporidium* in water by using polypropylene cartridge filters. **Applied and Environmental Microbiology** 53, 687-692.
3. ROSE, J. B., CIFRINO, A., MADORE. M. S., GERBA, C. P., STERLING, C. R. and ARROWOOD, M. J. (1986). Detection of *Cryptosporidium* from wastewater and freshwater environments. **Water Science and Technology** 18, 233-239.
4. ROSE, J. B., MADORE, M. S., RIGGS, J. L. and GERBA, C. P. (1986). Detection of *Cryptosporidium* and *Giardia* in environmental waters. Proceedings, Water Quality Technology Conference, Portland OR, 16-20 November 1986. American Waste Works Association Denver Co, pp 417-424.
5. ROSE, J. B., KAYED, D., MADORE, M. S., GERBAS, C. P., ARROWOOD, M. J., STERLING, C. R. and RIGGS, J. L. (1988). Methods for the recovery of *Giardia* and *Cryptosporidium* from environmental waters and their comparative occurrence. In Advances in *Giardia Research*, ed P. M. Wallis and B. R. Hammond. University of Calgary Press, Calgary, pp 205-209.
6. FEACHEM, R. G., BRADLEY, D. J., GARELICK, H. and MARA, D. D. (1983). Sanitation and Disease. **Health Aspects of Excreta and Wastewater Management.** John Wiley and Sons, Chichester, pp 343-344.
7. PIKE, E. B. and CARRINGTON, E. G. (1986). Stabilisation of sludge by conventional and novel processes—a healthy future. In **Symposium, The Agricultural Use of Sewage Sludge—is there a future?**, Doncaster, 12 November 1986. Institute of Water Pollution Control, Maidstone, Paper C.

Part II – Paper XI

The Role of Public Bodies in Scotland in the Recognition and Control of a Waterborne Outbreak of Cryptosporidiosis

The Scottish Office, Edinburgh

Introduction

Chapter 12 of Part I of the Report outlines the general procedures to be followed in the event of an outbreak or suspected outbreak and gives guidance on prevention. It also applies to Scotland, but the administrative arrangements are different; this paper outlines the roles of the various bodies which may be involved.

Administrative bodies involved
Health Boards

The investigation and control of foodborne and waterborne disease is the joint responsibility of local authorities and Health Boards. The exercise of this joint responsibility is facilitated by the fact that the Chief Administrative Medical Officer of each Health Board is also the designated medical officer of the related local authorities for this purpose. One or more consultants in public health medicine may also be similarly designated.

Scottish Home and Health Department (SHHD)

The Scottish Home and Health Department is responsible in Scotland for policy and legislation on health matters including public health. It also provides advice to health boards and environmental health departments of district councils on outbreaks of disease and on health matters generally. The Department would wish to be informed of any suspected outbreak. Depending on the scale of the outbreak, the Department might also wish to be represented on any Outbreak Control Committee.

Scottish Development Department (SDD)

The Scottish Development Department is responsible for legislation on public water supplies, primarily the Water (Scotland) Act 1980 as amended by the Water Act 1989 together with the Water Quality Regulations 1990. It also gives advice to water authorities (the regional and islands councils), to the Central Scotland Water Development Board and to the river purification authorities. In view of Scottish Office concern for public health, it is essential that water authorities, district councils, and the river purification authorities inform the Department of any events which might pose a threat from water-borne disease.

As Scottish water authorities are already publicly accountable bodies there is no parallel to the Drinking Water Inspectorate of England and Wales.

River Purificiation Authorities (RPAs)	The Scottish river purification authorities – the 7 independent river purification boards and the 3 islands councils – are responsible for maintaining river quality, which they protect by a system of discharge consents and by monitoring. Pollution incidents will be investigated by the authorities to establish responsibility. Evidence may be offered to the procurator fiscal who will decide if prosecution is appropriate. River purification boards do not monitor for the presence of cryptosporidium. They would, however, investigate illegal discharges of effluent, for example slurry, which may pollute watercourses. Discharges of farm waste may contain cryptosporidial oocysts which would be unaffected by any treatment required by the river purification authority under the Control of Pollution Act. Thus even authorised discharges have the potential to spread cryptosporidia in the environment. Although it is unlikely that river purification boards would be able to play a major role in investigating, or giving early warning of, an outbreak they should co-operate with water authorities in drawing their attention to possible contamination routes.
Water Authorities (WAs)	The regional and islands councils, as water authorities, have statutory duties to provide wholesome water and to meet the Water Quality Regulations, including sampling supplies and providing information. Microbiological quality of potable water is a vital factor in safeguarding public health and the key responsibility must lie with water authorities. Liaison with other public bodies is also crucial however. Water authorities have a statutory duty to notify district councils (departments of environmental health) and health authorities of any event which is likely to give rise to a significant risk to the health of persons residing in the authorities' areas.
Central Scotland Water Development Board (CSWDB)	The Central Scotland Water Development Board provides bulk supplies of water to, and a strategic reserve for, authorities in the central belt. It does not supply consumers directly and the water authorities remain responsible for the quality of water supplied to consumers in their areas. Close liaison is, however, maintained with its constituent water authorities and the Board should co-operate fully in the investigation and control of a suspected outbreak.
Environmental Health Authorities – District and Islands Councils	The district and islands councils have a statutory duty, normally exercised through their environmental health departments, to monitor the quality of drinking water in their area. They have powers to apply to a sheriff to close down or restrict supplies where they are injurious to health (Section 27, the Water (Scotland) Act 1980). These authorities have a duty to keep themselves informed on the wholesomeness of water being supplied in their area. If they are not satisfied they have a duty to require the provision of alternative supplies. Should a water authority not comply with such a request, the district and islands councils have a duty to ask the Secretary of State to take enforcement action (Part VIA, the Water (Scotland) Act 1980).
Measures under consideration for implementation in the near future Outbreak Control Committee	It is proposed that in each health board area there should be an advisory committee known as the Outbreak Control Committee. Its main functions would be:

a. to advise the health board through the Chief Administrative Medical Officer (Director of Public Health) on matters relating to outbreaks of foodborne or waterborne disease;

b. to formulate control policies based on national policies for approval by the health board; and

c. to prepare plans for dealing with outbreaks of foodborne or waterborne disease.

The membership of the Outbreak Control Committee should comprise:

a. The Chairman of the Committee, who should be the Chief Administrative Medical Officer (Director of Public Health) or his nominee, normally the Consultant in Public Health Medicine (Communicable Diseases and Environmental Health).

b. The Secretary of the Committee, who should be an Administrative Officer appointed by the General Manager of the Health Board.

c. Other core members who would be —

i. the Directors of Environmental Health of District Councils within the health board area;

ii. a consultant microbiologist;

iii. an infectious disease physician or a clinician representative;

iv. the Area Control of Infection Nurse, and

v. the Director(s) of Water Supply.

d. The Committee would have power to co-opt other members and consideration should be given as appropriate to the following:

i. a veterinary representative,

ii. a public analyst,

iii. Director(s) of river purification boards, and

iv. other officers of local government, central government, CSWDB or the health board whose presence, in local circumstances, may be necessary.

Ideally, the Committee should have a membership not exceeding 12 persons. It would be the responsibility of the Chairman to convene meetings and of the Secretary to implement Committee decisions. The Committee should meet twice yearly. Additional meetings should be arranged if circumstances suggest that urgent action is required to implement a policy decision, to give rapid advice to the health board or to have an immediate response for the health board or the Scottish Home and Health Department, should an outbreak occur which affects more than one area. There would be considerable advantage in a very close relationship between the Outbreak Control Committee for foodborne and waterborne diseases and the Area Control of Infection Committee which deals with hospital infections.

The Outbreak Control Team

An outbreak control team would be established whenever the Consultant in Public Health Medicine (communicable diseases and environmental health), acting either independently or in consultation with the Chairman of the Outbreak Control Committee, considered that a serious outbreak situation existed. The Consultant in Public Health Medicine (communicable diseases and environmental health) would be the leader and principal investigator of the Team. In all instances it would be necessary for the Director of Environmental Health for the local authority district concerned, or his representative, to be closely associated with any outbreak of foodborne or waterborne disease. This equally applies to Directors of water supply if an outbreak of waterborne disease is being investigated.

Recognition and Control of an Outbreak
Background — Cryptosporidium in Scotland

In Scotland cryptosporidiosis has been classified as a reportable infection since 1 January 1989. This means that any laboratory identifying the organism causing the disease, or any physician who diagnoses the condition in a patient, should immediately notify the health board and the Communicable Diseases (Scotland) Unit. The number of cases of cryptosporidiosis recorded each year has risen considerably in the last few years. Whereas fewer than 50 cases were recorded in the early years of the 1980s, this number rose to over 500 in 1988 and over 1,200 in 1989, thus becoming the fourth most important gastrointestinal disease following salmonellosis, campylobacteriosis and rotavirus infections. In January 1989 a National Surveillance Officer was appointed for cryptosporidiosis and this allowed detailed epidemiological studies to be undertaken. Although it would appear that the majority of cases are sporadic, outbreaks of the disease have been associated with water supplies to the Stevenston/Salcoats area of Ayrshire, and with areas supplied by water from Loch Lomond.

Control of an outbreak

The methodology for the control of an outbreak of waterborne disease is recorded in detail in "The Investigation and Control of Foodborne and Waterborne Disease in Scotland" (a document in press). Although an outline of the administrative measures for control is given in this paper, for full details of outbreak control in Scotland reference should be made to the above document. In April 1989, the Scottish Home and Health Department wrote to Community Medicine Specialists and Directors of Environmental Health giving notes on the disease, what measures should be taken if an outbreak should occur and what routine preventative or monitoring arrangements should or should not be undertaken. The same guidance also stated what criteria should be met before a 'boil water' notice was issued. That advice still stands and is not modified in any way by what is said in this Report.

It would be the responsibility of the Outbreak Control Team to investigate outbreaks in accordance with the principles of outbreak investigation given in "The Investigation and Control of Foodborne and Waterborne Disease in Scotland" which includes a Code of Practice for the Scottish Health Service. The Team would also be responsible for recording adequately the details and management of the outbreak and for reporting accordingly to the Outbreak Control Committee.

In all outbreaks, close liaison should be maintained with the Communicable Diseases (Scotland) Unit, the Environmental Health (Scotland) Unit, and the Scottish Home and Health Department as necessary.

'Boil Water' Advice

'Boil Water' advice should only be given after very close consultation between health, environmental health and water authorities during which the various implications of such advice would be considered. When a consensus view has been arrived at, the Scottish Home and Health Department should be consulted for their agreement.

Summary

When an outbreak of cryptosporidiosis occurs, the above administrative actions should be brought into force. It is essential that there is close collaboration between health, environmental health and water authorities as each have their specific parts to play. There must be close and continuing contact between the Directors of each water authority and the health boards within that authority's area to ensure that outbreak procedures are fully understood.

Part III (I)

Interim group report on cryptosporidium in water supplies

From

Sir John Badenoch, Chairman of the Group of Experts to:

The Rt Hon Christopher Patten MP
Secretary of State for the Environment

and to:

The Rt Hon Kenneth Clarke QC MP
Secretary of State for Health

25 July 1989

Dear Secretaries of State,

PROGRESS REPORT ON THE WORK OF THE DoE GROUP OF EXPERTS ON CRYPTOSPORIDIUM IN WATER SUPPLIES

On 2 March 1989 the following an outbreak of cryptosporidiosis in that part of Oxfordshire and Swindon supplied by water from the Farmoor Reservoir, Michael Howard, QC MP Minister for Water and Planning, announced that an expert group had been set up, in consultation with the Department of Health, to advise the Government on the significance of cryptosporidium in water supplies.

The group was given the following terms of reference:

i. To examine the occurrence and extent of cryptosporidium in water supplies;

ii. To assess the significance for public health of cryptosporidium in water supplies;

iii. To assess methods of monitoring for cryptosporidium and to formulate advice to water undertakers upon monitoring strategies;

iv. To consider and formulate advice upon the protection of water supplies, treatment processes and the maintenance of distribution systems;

v. To report jointly to the Secretary of State for the Environment and the Secretary of State for Health and to produce an interim report by the end of July 1989.

From the outset it was clear that an assessment of the prevalence of cryptosporidium in water systems throughout the country, and therefore its significance as a waterborne pathogen for man, could not be made without further study. Further information was also needed about the ways in which the organisms gain entry into the water supplies and on the efficiency of water treatment processes in removing them. Some of the work is in hand and other projects are being planned. We consider that the most useful way to acquire the necessary information is through an adequately financed nationally co-ordinated programme of research by water undertakers, the Public Health Laboratory Service, other research organisations and Government departments.

This letter represents our interim report on measures that can be taken now to safeguard water supplies and discharges our remit to respond by the end of July. It also provides guidance on public health aspects of infection with cryptosporidium .

Later, we propose to report more extensively on the medical aspects of cryptosporidiosis and to formulate further interim guidance for water undertakers. This will be followed by a final report on the extent and significance of contamination of water supplies by cryptosporidium and on the methods which can be used for its control.

To date the group has held six meetings. It has taken oral evidence and studied a large number of scientific and technical papers.

I am greatly indebted to my colleagues for giving so much time and effort to the work of the group and to the Secretariat from the Department of Environment and the Department of Health for generous and effective support.

Cryptosporidium in water supplies

The organism cryptosporidium has a worldwide distribution. Although it has long been recognised as a parasite of animals, it was not until 1976 – a little over a decade ago – that it was shown to be capable of producing illness in man. Infected animals including man excrete the organism in their faeces in the form of minute oocysts which may cause infection if they are ingested.

Because of the organism's widespread distribution it must be assumed that from time to time oocysts will be present in all surface waters, including springs and shallow wells, and will be found intermittently in the effluent from sewage treatment works. Ground water from deep wells should theoretically be free from cryptosporidium but to confirm this further evidence is needed. Current methods of water treatment and disinfection properly carried out cannot eliminate entirely the risk of cryptosporidium passing into the water supply

Advice on water treatment

In the past, water undertakers had no reason to develop the capacity to test for cryptosporidium because it was not perceived as a public health risk. However, in the light of increasing knowledge of its role as a human pathogen they should now develop the capacity to monitor for it and ensure that they have access to a laboratory which has the necessary expertise for its isolation and identification.

The oocysts of cryptosporidia are difficult to kill. In particular they are unaffected by chlorine in the concentrations that can be used to treat drinking water. It is important that the use of ozone and other potentially effective disinfectants should be explored.

In water treatment, there is no evidence to suggest that the use of either aluminium or iron compounds in flocculation processes is superior in entrapping the oocysts of cryptosporidium.

Care should be taken in the operation of filter beds to avoid sudden surges of flow which may dislodge deposits including cryptosporidia. The use of turbidity meters, ideally on individual filter bed outlets, would provide a sensitive indication that such a surge has occurred and also indicate when a filter has been penetrated by particulate matter: their use is recommended.

In line with the advice given in the Department of the Environment's letter to water undertakers of 22 March 1989, we do not advocate routine monitoring for cryptosporidium in water supplies.

Cryptosporidium is most likely to be present in water sources in the spring and autumn. At these times of the year, when a treatment works is under strain, as in conditions of high throughput or when there has been a significant change in operating procedures, the water which has been used in the treatment process should be monitored. (This includes principally the water used for washing filters, and water associated with sludge from the flocculation process.) If oocysts of cryptosporidia are found in significant numbers, the disposal of this water should be carefully controlled and it should not be returned to the waterworks inlets untreated. Under similar operating conditions monitoring of the final drinking water should also be considered. If oocysts are found, the operation of the works should be reviewed, and the appropriate medical authorities informed.

It is important that the water industry maintains high standards in the maintenance and repair of distribution systems including service reservoirs to reduce the risk of contamination by oocysts of cryptosporidium.

Even in the most carefully regulated and supervised systems, occasional emergencies may arise when temporarily the water supply is considered unfit for drinking. Non-domestic users of water, especially hospitals, and including industrial users and members of the retail trade for food and drink should consider how they would respond to the notice of an emergency being declared.

Water undertakers should develop a close collaboration with local authorities and health authorities. They should develop arrangements for the regular exchange of information so that they can respond to a possible incident of waterborne disease. The importance of close collaboration is reinforced by the fact that first indication of a possible waterborne outbreak of cryptosporidiosis is likely to be a report to the Medical Officer for Environmental Health (MOEH) that there has been a sudden increase in the number of cases.

Public Health Aspects of Cryptosporidiosis

Although giving advice on matters of public health is not strictly within our terms of reference we thought this should be included in our interim report.

In man cryptosporidiosis is usually characterised by a self-limiting illness with diarrhoea, abdominal cramps, vomiting and sometimes fever that resolves in one to three weeks. It can affect persons of any age but is most common in children between the ages of one and five years. In patients with AIDS and others whose resistance to infection is impaired, it is much more serious and may lead to severe and lasting disability.

It is not a common cause of diarrhoea. National reporting began in 1984: between 1984 and 1988 the annual number of recorded cases in England, Wales and Northern Ireland varied between 1,700 and 3,500 but this is almost certainly an underestimate of the actual number. A study by the Public Health Laboratory Service showed that only between 1 per cent and 5 per cent of all cases of diarrhoea which were confirmed by stool culture were due to cryptosporidium.

The disease is contracted by ingestion of the infective oocysts and develops after an incubation period of usually 3 to 11 days, but which can be as long as 25 days.

It is spread by direct or indirect contact with the faeces of an infected person or animal. It passes readily from person to person, in the family, play groups or nursery schools and other institutions.

Those in contact with farm animals such as farmers, visitors to farms, veterinarians and workers in abattoirs are also at risk and need to take appropriate precautions. Domestic pets can spread the infection but the risk from them appears to be less than that from farm animals.

Medical staff and others caring for patients with cryptosporidiosis should be aware of the risk of contracting the infection and that cryptosporidiosis is one of the recognised causes of travellers' diarrhoea.

Spread from person to person and from animals to man can be minimised by strict attention to personal hygiene with routine washing of hands especially before eating and after using the lavatory.

Cases of diarrhoea occurring in play groups or nurseries or in school children, particularly those how have recently visited farms or have been in contact with young farm animals, should be reported to the MOEH without delay.

There is a potential risk that raw milk could become contaminated by cryptosporidia and the public are advised not to drink milk unless it has been pasteurised.

It is probable that cryptosporidia are present in small numbers from time to time in all surface waters, including springs and streams. It is our advice that the public should not drink from these.

Cryptosporidiosis and Drinking Water Supplies

Outbreaks of cryptosporidiosis due to contamination of drinking water supplies have been reported only rarely. To date there have only been six proven outbreaks: three in the United States of America and three in the United Kingdom.

An individual is much more likely to contract the infection if he comes into direct contact with the faeces of an infected person or animal. But the importance of contamination of the water supply is the potential that exists of giving rise to a very large number of cases. Where there has been an unusual incident involving gross contamination of the source of the water, existing water treatment procedures can not prevent cryptosporidia passing into the water supply.

When our studies are complete we will be reporting on measures designed to control the effects of such accidental contamination. In the interim surveillance should be continued by the water, local and health authorities, who will be responsible for advising the public should additional measures be required to safeguard drinking water.

We have received considerable help from the Scottish Home and Health Department and from other colleagues in Scotland. I am therefore copying this letter to the Secretary of State for Scotland.

SIR JOHN BADENOCH

Part III (II)

Oral and Written Evidence Submitted

Evidence, oral and/or written, has been received from the following experts and organisations:

Mr P Allen	Department of Environmental Health, Oxford City Council

Aluminium Sulphate Producers Association

Professor A Amirtharajah	Georgia Institute of Technology
Dr R Aston	Communicable Disease Surveillance Centre
Mr S Bailey	Agricultural Development and Advisory Service, MAFF
Mrs A H Biffen	Communicable Disease Surveillance Centre
Mr A Buck	Department of Public Health, Swindon Health Authority

Central Scotland Water Development Board

Dr J S Colbourne	Thames Water Utilities Ltd
Mr J V Dadswell	Public Health Laboratory Service, Reading
Mr E L Farmery	Department of Public Health, Swindon Health Authority
Mr R A Frankenberg	Department of Community Medicine, Oxfordshire Health Authority
Mr R Gilmour	Scottish Parasite Diagnostic Laboratory
Dr M Gregory	Central Veterinary Laboratory, MAFF

Johnson Filtration Systems Ltd Feltham, Middlesex

Dr G S Logsdon	US Environmental Protection Agency

London Borough of Hillingdon

Dr W J Masschelein	Compagnie Intercommunale Bruxelloise des Eaux
Dr R T Mayon-White	Department of Community Medicine, Oxfordshire Health Authority
Mr P McIntosh	Thames Water Utilities Ltd

National Rivers Authority

Dr J E Ongerth	School of Public Health and Community Medicine, University of Washington
Dr S R Palmer	Communicable Disease Surveillance Centre
Dr J W Parsons	Department of Public Health, Swindon Health Authority
Dr E B Pike	Water Research Centre
Mr R C Ramsay	Department of the Environment
Mr A J Richardson	Department of Public Health, Swindon Health Authority
Professor J B Rose	College of Public Health University of South Florida
Dr J Selkon	Public Health Laboratory Service, Oxford
Mr J Sexton	Public Health Laboratory Service, Oxford
Mr M P Upstone	Severn Trent Water Ltd
Dr C Waller	Thames Water Utilities Ltd
Dr D C Warhurst	London School of Hygiene and Tropical Medicine

World Health Organisation

Part III (III)

SELECTIVE BIBLIOGRAPHY

This bibliography lists some of the material considered by the Group. More comprehensive lists of references follow the Part II papers.

MEDICAL

ALPERT G, BELL LM, KIRKPATRICK CE *et al.* Outbreak of cryptosporidiosis in a day – care center. Pediatrics 1986; vol 77 no 2 (Feb): 152–157.

ANGUS KW. Cryptosporidiosis in man, domestic animals and birds: a review. J Roy Soc Med 1983; vol 76 (Jan): 62–70

ANGUS KW, BLEWETT DA. Cryptosporidiosis: Proceedings of the First International Workshop Animal Disease Research Association, Edinburgh 1989. 139pp.

ATTERHOLM I, CASTOR B, NORLIN K. Cryptosporidiosis in Southern Sweden. Scand J Infect Dis 1987; 19: 231–234

BAXBY D, HART CA, BLUNDELL N. Shedding of oocysts by immunocompetent individuals with cryptosporidiosis. J Hyg Camb 1985; 95: 703–709

CASEMORE DP. Educational farm visits and associated infection hazards. PHLS Communicable Disease Surveillance Centre. CDR 1989/19.

CASEMORE DP. Human cryptosporidiosis. In Recent Advances in Infection No. 3. Ed REEVES DS and GEDDES AM. Pub: Churchill Livingstone, Edinburgh 1989; 209–236

CASEMORE DP, JESSOP EG, DOUCE D, JACKSON FB. *Cryptosporidium* plus campylobacter: an outbreak in a semi-rural population. J Hyg Camb 1986; 96: 95–105

CHAPMAN PA, RUSH BA. The use of methods based on a monoclonal antibody to investigate the epidemiology of cryptosporidiosis. DMRQC Newsletter 1987; 2 (Sept): 1–4 (Obtainable from Chief Librarian, Central Public Health Laboratory Library, 61 Colindale Avenue, London NW9 5HT)

COOK GC. Small-intestinal coccidiosis: an emergent clinical problem. Editorial J Infect 1988; 16: 213–219

COOK GC. Intestinal parasitic infections. Curr Opin Infect Dis 1988; 1: 91–101

CURRENT WL. *Cryptosporidium:* Its biology and potential for environmental transmission. CRC Critical Reviews in Environmental Control. Vol 17 (1): 21–51

CURRENT WL, BICK PH. Immunobiology of *Cryptosporidium* spp. Pathol Immunopathol Res 1989; 8: 141–160

CURRENT WL, REESE NC, ERNST JV, BAILEY WS, HEYMAN MB, WEINSTEIN WM. Human Cryptosporidiosis in immunocompetent and immunodeficient persons: studies of an outbreak and experimental transmission. N Engl J Med 1983; May 26: 1252–1257

D'ANTONIO RG, WINN RE, TAYLOR JP *et al.* A waterborne outbreak of cryptosporidiosis in normal hosts. Ann Intern Med 1985; 103 (6 pt 1): 886–888

DEPARTMENT OF HEALTH. Review of law on infectious disease control: consultation document. Crown Copyright 1989. 87pp.

FAYER R, UNGAR BLP. *Cryptosporidium* spp and cryptosporidiosis. Microbiol Rev 1986; vol 50 no 4 (Dec): 458–483

GARCIA LS, BREWER TC, BRUCKNER DA. Fluorescence detection of *Cryptosporidium* oocysts in human fecal specimens by using monoclonal antibodies. J Clin Microbiol 1987; vol 25 no 1 (Jan): 119–121

GARCIA LS, BRUCKNER DA, BREWER TC, SHIMIZU RY. Techniques for the recovery and identification of *Cryptosporidium* occysts from stool specimens. J of Clin Microbiol 1983; vol 18 no 1 (July): 185–190

GRABOWSKI DJ, POWERS KM, KNOTT JA. *et al.* Cryptosporidiosis – New Mexico 1986. MMWR; vol 36 no 33: 561–563

HANNAH J, RIORDAN T. Case to case spread of cryptosporidiosis; evidence from a day nursery outbreak. Public Health 1988; 102: 539–544

HAYES EB, MATTE TD, O'BRIEN TR. *et al.* Large community outbreak of cryptosporidiosis due to contamination of a filtered public water supply. N Engl J Med 1989; vol 320 no 21 (May): 1372–1376

HOJLYNG N, HOLTEN-ANDERSON W, JEPSEN S. Cryptosporidiosis: a case of airborne transmission. Letter Lancet 1987; Aug: 271-272

JOKIPII L, JOKIPII AMM. Timing of symptoms and oocyst excretion in human cryptosporidiosis. N Engl J Med 1986; vol 315 no 26 (Dec): 1643–1647

KOCH KL, PHILLIPS DJ, ABER RC, CURRENT WL. Cryptosporidiosis in hospital personnel —evidence for person-to-person transmission. Ann Intern Med 1985; vol 102 no 5: 593–596

MATHAN MM, GEORGE R, VENKATESAN S, MATHEW M, MATHAN VI. Cryptosporidium and diarrhoea in Southern Indian children. Lancet 1985; Nov: 1172–1175

NIME FA, BUREK JD, PAGE DL, HOLSCHER MA, YARDLEY JHL. Acute enterocolitis in a human being infected with the protozoan Cryptosporidium. Gastroenterology 1976; vol 70 no 4 (April): 592–598

ONGERTH JE, STIBBS HH. Prevalance of *Cryptosporidium* infection in dairy calves in western Washington. Am J Vet Res 1989; vol 50 no 7 (July): 1069–1070

POHJOLA S, OKSANEN H, JOKIPII L, JOKIPII AMM. Outbreak of cryptosporidiosis among veterinary students. Scand J Infect Dis 1986; 18: 173–178

RENDTORFF RC. The experimental transmission of *Giardia lamblia* among volunteer subjects. Proceedings of a symposium September 1978. US Environmental Protection Agency Office of Research and Develoment, Environmental Research Centre, Cincinnati; EPA —600/9-79-001 June 1979

SOAVE R, ARMSTRONG D. *Cryptosporidium* and cryptosporidiosis. Rev Infect Dis 1986; vol 8 no 6 (Nov-Dec): 1012–1023

SOAVE R, DANNER RL, HONIG CL *et al.* Cryptosporidiosis in homosexual men. Ann Intern Med 1984; vol 100 no 4: 504–511

SOAVE R, JOHNSON WD. *Cryptosporidium* and *Isospora belli* infections. J Infect Dis 1988; vol 157 no 2 (Feb): 225–229

STERLING CR, ARROWOOD MJ. Detection of *Cryptosporidium* sp. infections using a direct immunofluorescent assay. Pediat Infect Dis 1986; vol 5 no 1: S139–S142.

STERLING CR, SEEGAR K, SINCLAIR NA. *Cryptosporidium* as a causative agent of traveller's diarrhoea. J Infect Dis 1986; vol 153 no 2 (Feb): 380–381.

SUNDERMANN CA, LINDSAY DS, BLAGBURN BL. Evaluation of disinfectants for ability to kill avian *Cryptosporidium* oocysts. Companion Animal Practice — Parasitology/Disinfection 1987; Nov: 36–39

TAYLOR JP, PERDUE JN, DINGLEY D, REED LA, GUSTAFSON TL, PATTERSON M. Cryptosporidiosis outbreak in a day-care center. Am J Dis Child 1985; 139 (Oct): 1023–1025

THOMPSON MA, BENSON JWT, WRIGHT PA. Two year study of Cryptosporidium infection. Arch Dis Child 1987; 62: 559–563

TZIPORI S. Cryptosporidiosis in animals and humans. Microbiol Rev 1983; vol 47 no 1 (March): 84–96

UNGAR BLP, SOAVE R, FAYER R, NASH TE. Enzyme immunoassay detection of immunoglobulin M and G antibodies to *Cryptosporidium* in immunocompetent and immunocompromised persons. J Infect Dis 1986; vol 153 no 3 (March): 570–578

WOLFSON JS, RICHTER JM, WALDRON MA, WEBER DJ, McCARTHY DM, HOPKINS CC. Cryptosporidiosis in immuno-competent patients. N Engl J Med 1985; May: 1278–1282

Part III (IV)

SELECTIVE BIBLIOGRAPHY

This bibliography lists some of the material considered by the Group. More comprehensive lists of references follow the Part II papers.

WATER TECHNICAL

AWWA Water Quality Technology Conference, Philadelphia, Nov 1989. Proceedings: in press.

CAMPBELL I, TZIPORI S, HUTCHISON G, ANGUS KW. Effect of disinfectants on survival of *Cryptosporidium* oocysts. Vet Rec 1982; 111: 414–415.

DEPARTMENT OF THE ENVIRONMENT STANDING COMMITTEE OF ANALYSTS. Isolation and identification of Giardia cysts, Cryptosporidium oocysts and free-living pathogenic amoebae in water etc 1989—HMSO Crown Copyright 1990. 30pp.

DICK TA. Report of an inquiry into water supplies in Oxford and Swindon following an outbreak of cryptosporidiosis during February-March 1989. Thames Water Utilities.

ENVIRONMENTAL PROTECTION AGENCY: National Primary Drinking Water Regulations; Filtration and disinfection, turbidity, Giardia lamblia, viruses, Legionella and heterotropic bacteria; Proposed Rule. Federal Register Part II 1987; vol 52 no 212.

GERTIG KR, WILLIAMSON-JONES GL, JONES FE, ALEXANDER BD. Executive Summary: Filtration of Giardia cysts and other particles under treatment plant conditions. Volume 3: Rapid-rate filtration using 1'X1' pilot filters on the Cache La Poudre River. AWWA Research Foundation: 9–15.

LIPPY EC, WALTRIP SC. Waterborne disease outbeaks 1946–1980: a thirty-five year perspective. Jour AWWA; 76: 60–67.

LOGSDON GS. Evaluating treatment plants for particulate contaminant removal. Jour AWWA 1987; Sept: 82–92.

LOGSDON GS. Comparison of some filtration processes appropriate for *Giardia* cyst removal. Advances in *Giardia* Research, University of Calgary Press 1988: 95–102.

LOGSDON GS, JURANEK D, MASON L et al. *Cryptosporidium*: a roundtable discussion. Jour AWWA 1988; vol 80 no 2: 14–27.

LOGSDON GS, MASON L, STANLEY JB. Troubleshooting an existing treatment plant. Proceedings of the AWWA Annual Conference, Orlando, Florida, June 1988.

MADORE MS, ROSE JB, GERBA CP, ARROWOOD MJ, STERLING CR. Occurrence of *Cryptosporidium* oocysts in sewage effluents and selected surface waters. J Parasit 1987; 73(4): 702–705.

MASON L. Experience with *Cryptosporidium* at Carrollton, Georgia. Proceedings of the AWWA Water Quality Technology Conference, Baltimore, 1987; Nov: 889–898.

MAYON-WHITE RT, FRANKENBERG RA. "Boil the Water." Lancet 1989; 2: 216.

MOSHER RR, HENDRICKS DW. Executive Summary: Filtration of *Giardia* cysts and other particles under treatment plant conditions. Volume 2: Rapid rate filtration using 2' × 2' field scale pilot filters on the Cache la Poudre River. AWWA Research Foundation: 21–27.

MUSIAL CE, ARROWOOD MJ, STERLING CR, GERBA CP. Detection of *Cryptosporidium* in water by using polypropylene cartridge filters. Appl Environ Microbiol 1987; vol 53 no 4: 687–692.

ONGERTH JE, STIBBS HH. Identification of *Cryptosporidium* oocysts in river water. Appl Environ Microbiol 1987; vol 53 no 4: 672–676.

PEETERS JE, MAZAS EA, MASSCHELEIN WJ, VILLACORTA MARTINEZ DE MATURANA I, DEBACKER EC. Effect of disinfection of drinking water with ozone or chlorine dioxide on survival of *Cryptosporidium parvum* oocysts. Appl Envion Microbiol 1989; vol 55 no 6: 1519–1522.

ROSE JB. Occurrence and Control of *Cryptosporidium* in Drinking Water. In Drinking Water Microbiology: Progress and Recent Developments. Pub: Springer–Verlag 1990; 14: 194–321.

ROSE JB. Occurrence and significance of *Cryptosporidium* in water. Jour AWWA 1988; Feb: 53–58.

ROSE JB, DARBIN H, GERBA CP. Correlations of the protozoa *Cryptosporidium* and *Giardia* with water quality variables in a watershed. Wat Sci Tech 1988; vol 20 no 11/12: 271–276.

ROSE JB, GERBA CP, JAKUBOWSKI W. Survey of potable water supplies for *Cryptosporidium* and *Giardia*. Environ Sci and Techn 1990: in press.

SCHULER PF, GHOSH MM, BOUTROS SN. Comparing the removal of *Giardia* and *Cryptosporidium* using slow sand and diatomaceous earth filtration. Proceedings of the AWWA Annual Conference, Orlando, Florida, June 1988.

Part III (V)

GLOSSARY

MICROBIOLOGICAL AND MEDICAL TERMS

This glossary is intended as a general aid to the reader of Part I of this Report and is not intended to be definitive.

ANTIBODY
A substance produced by the body's immune system in response to infection.

ANTIGEN
A substance which may provoke the production of an antibody or other immune response.

ANOREXIA
Aversion to food or loss of appetite.

ASYMPTOMATIC
Situation in which an infected person does not have symptoms.

BACTERIUM
A minute single-celled organism which may be harmless or pathogenic. Included among the pathogenic types are **salmonella** and **campylobacter.**

BILIARY SYSTEM
The network of ducts connecting the gall bladder, liver and intestine.

BIOPSY
A sample of body tissue taken during life.

BOWEL MUCOSA
The inner lining of the intestine.

CAMPYLOBACTER
A group of **bacteria,** some of which are **pathogenic,** found in man and other animals.

CASE CONTROL STUDY
An **epidemiological** study in which the characteristics of persons with a disease are compared with a matched control group of persons without the disease.

COLONISATION
A condition in which **microorganisms** live on or in a **host** without necessarily giving rise to clinical disease.

COMMUNICABLE DISEASE
A disease, the causative organisms of which are capable of being passed from a person, animal or the environment to a susceptible individual.

CORTICOSTEROID
A naturally occurring body hormone. A synthetic form is used as an anti-inflammatory agent.

CRYPTOSPORIDIOSIS
The illness produced by infection with **cryptosporidium.**

CRYPTOSPORIDIUM
The general descriptive term for the **parasite** (Greek for hidden spores).

CRYPTOSPORIDIUM PARVUM (C.parvum)
The only species of **cryptosporidium** known to cause disease in man and livestock.

CYTOPLASM
The material which is contained within a living cell.

DUODENUM
A part of the upper small intestine.

ELUTION
To recover by washing.

ENDOSCOPIC PAPILLOTOMY
A treatment process to relieve **biliary** obstruction.

ENTERITIS
Inflammation of the intestine.

ENTEROCYTE
A cell lining the intestine.

EPIDEMIOLOGY
The study of factors affecting heath and disease in populations and the application of this study to the control and prevention of disease.

EPITHELIAL CELL
A cell lining the intestine.

ESCHERICHIA COLI (E.Coli)
A type of **bacterium** normally found in the intestine.

EXCYSTATION
The process by which **sporozoites** are released from the cryptosporidial **oocysts** by the opening of a **suture** in the **occyst** wall.

FOOD POISONING
A notifiable illness normally characterised by acute diarrhoea and/or vomiting caused by the consumption of food or water contaminated with **pathogenic** organsisms and/or their toxins.

GASTROINTESTINAL INFECTION
Infection of the stomach and intestine usually resulting in diarrhoea and vomiting.

GASTROINTESTINAL TRACT
The stomach and the intestine.

GIARDIA INTESTINALIS (Giardia lamblia)
A **protozoan parasite** capable of infecting man and causing diarrhoea.

HOST
An animal (including man) in which **microorganisms** such as cryptosporidium can grow or multiply.

HYPOGAMMAGLOBULINAEMIA
A disease in man in which part of the immune system responsible for producing **antibody** is deficient.

IMMUNE
The state of being resistant to infection, hence immunity.

IMMUNOCOMPETENT
Having normal immune responses, as in a normal healthy person.

IMMUNOFLUORESCENCE
A laboratory technique (IFAT) employing fluorescent dyes linked to specific **antibodies.** A similar technique (ELISA) uses an enzyme-linked system.

IMMUNOSUPPRESSED
Having impaired immunity due to disease or therapy especially drugs.

INCIDENCE
The number of new cases of a disease occurring in a specified period of time (Usually expressed as a rate per 1000 or per 100,000 of the population at risk).

INCUBATION PERIOD
The interval between becoming infected and the appearance of symptoms of an illness.

IN-VITRO
In a culture tube i.e. not in an animal **host** (literally "in glass").

JEJUNUM
A part of the small intestine.

LAMINA PROPRIA
A part of the intestinal wall.

LUMEN
The cavity of the intestine.

MICRON (MICROMETRE)
One thousandth of a millimetre.

MICROORGANISM
An organism such as a **bacterium, protozoan or virus,** of microscopic size.

MONOCLONAL ANTIBODY (mAb)
An **antibody** cultured *in vitro* which recognises one highly specific **antigen.**

MONOXENOUS
A **parasite** which completes its life cycle in a single **host.**

OOCYST
The environmentally resistant transmissible form of **cryptosporidium** excreted in the faeces of an infected **host.**

OPPORTUNISTIC
Refers to an organism which is usually harmless in **immunocompetent** persons but which can cause disease in patients whose immune system is defective (for example, those with AIDS).

PARASITE
An organism that lives on or in another, **the host,** sometimes to the detriment of the **host** and which it obtains its nutrition.

PATHOGEN
A **microorganism (protozoan, bacterium, virus)** capable of causing disease.

PLASMA ELECTROLYTE
A naturally occurring chemical in the blood.

PREVALENCE
The total number of cases of a disease, irrespective of the time of onset, at any given point (point prevalence) or within any given period of time (period prevalence).

PRIMARY INFECTION
Infection which has been acquired by contact with a contaminated source and not by person to person spread.

PROTOZOAN
A single-celled **microorganism,** usually somewhat bigger than a **bacterium,** which may be free-living or **parasitic.** Includes **cryptosporidium** and **giardia.**

RESISTANCE
The ability of the **host** to withstand infection.

ROTAVIRUS
A type of **virus** causing diarrhoea, mainly in children and young animals.

SALMONELLA
A type of **bacterium** which can cause diarrhoea.

SECONDARY INFECTION
Infection which has been spread by person to person contact.

SEROLOGICAL STUDY
The diagnosis or study of disease by blood tests.

SHIGELLA
A type of **bacterium** which can cause diarrhoea.

SPECIES
A group of genetically related organisms having many features in common.

SPOROZOITE
The motile stage of **cryptosporidium** which is released from an **oocyst** after **excystation.**

SUTURE
The sealed aperture in an **oocyst** wall through which **sporozoites** are released.

TEMPORAL
Refers to clustering of cases of infection in relation to time – may or may not be seasonal.

VILLI
Finger-like projections of digestive tissue on the surface of the intestine; hence **villous blunting** when these projections are damaged.

VIRUS
A sub-microscopic **organism** of simple structure capable of replication only within a living host cell. Includes **rotavirus.**

ZOONOSIS
A disease which can be transmitted naturally between animals and man.

Part III (VI)

GLOSSARY

WATER TREATMENT TERMS

This glossary is intended as a general aid to the reader of Part I of this Report and is not intended to be definitive.

ABSTRACTION
The removal of water from a river or other source for treatment in a water treatment works.

AQUIFER
A porous rock through which water can percolate and collect.

BACKWASHING
The process of cleaning filters used in the treatment of drinking water by forcing water through the filters in the reverse direction.

BACKWASH WATER
Water resulting from **backwashing.**

BREAK-PRESSURE TANK
A tank connected to the delivery main in which the free water surface level creates a limited head or pressure of water.

COAGULANT
A substance (usually aluminium or ferric salts) added in water treatment processes to cause coagulation followed by **flocculation.**

COLIFORMS
Types of bacteria used as indicator organisms in the water industry.

FILTRATE
The water flowing out of a filter, having been filtered through the filter media.

FLOCCULATION
The aggregation of very fine **organic** or **inorganic** particles to form larger particles (floc) which can be removed by separation processes, such as sedimentation, flotation or filtration, as part of the treatment of drinking water.

GRANULAR ACTIVATED CARBON (GAC):
Carbon in the form of granules which have been steam and/or heat-treated (hence activated) to increase their adsorptive capacity.

GROUND WATER
Waters contained in underground strata (aquifers).

HUMUS
Solid material in suspension following sewage treatment by biological percolating filtration.

INORGANICS
Chemicals (mainly salts) which contain no organic carbon.

ION-EXCHANGE
The process by which unwanted ions in solution (for example, calcium) are exchanged for those available (for example, sodium) on small resin beads.

LIME PRECIPITATION
A chemical process by which hardness salts (principally bicarbonates) are combined with lime, to precipitate insoluble calcium carbonate, as a sludge.

mg/l
A measure of milligrams per litre equivalent to parts per million (mass per volume).

MICRON (MICROMETRE)
One thousandth of a millimetre.

MICROPOROUS
Permeable material in which the pores are of microscopic size.

MICROSTRAINER
An engineering process unit, utilising a very fine woven mesh with openings of 25, 35 or 60 **microns,** mounted in the form of a rotating drum.

mV:
A measure of electrical potential – one thousandth of a volt.

NEPHELOMETRIC TURBIDIMETER
An instrument which measures the amount of light scattered from very fine particles suspended in water.

NTU (Nephelometric Turbidity Unit)
A unit of turbidity, established by a standard haze created chemically in water, measured with a nephelometric turbidimeter.

ORGANIC POLYELECTROLYTE
An organic polymer, which may be natural or synthetic, which carries electrical charges along its length, which is added during water treatment to aid the process of **flocculation.**

ORGANICS
Chemicals which contain organic carbon, which may be of synthetic or natural origin.

pH
A measure of the hydrogen ion concentration, which reflects whether the water is acidic or alkaline (pH above 7 is alkaline, below 7 is acid; pH = 7 is neutral).

POLYMER
A substance which consists of long, chain-like molecules.

REVERSE OSMOSIS
A process which uses high pressure to force water through a membrane, from a concentrated to a more dilute solution. (This is the reverse of natural osmosis, in which water passes through a membrane from dilute to more concentrated solution).

SCHMUTZDECKE
Layer of bacterial and algal slime formed at the top of a slow sand filter which contributes to filter efficiency.

SLUDGE, ACTIVATED
The solids which are retained in suspension during aerobic biological treatment of sewage. Also called bioflocs as they comprise biologically active aggregates of **microorganisms.**

SLUDGE, PRIMARY
The solids which settle from sewage under gravity, as a first stage of sewage treatment.

SLUDGE, SECONDARY
The solids which settle from sewage, after it has undergone aerobic biological treatment, as a second stage of sewage treatment (see also **humus**).

SLUDGE, WATERWORKS
The sludge produced by processes of water treatment.

SLURRY
A mixture of livestock dung and urine with minimal amounts of bedding, often diluted with water.

SUPERNATANT
The clear liquid remaining after the process of **flocculation**, and/or sedimentation.

TURBIDITY
The cloudiness of the water.

Part III (VII)

LIST OF ABBREVIATIONS

The following abbreviations appear in this Report:

Organisations or individuals

CCDC	Consultant for Communicable Disease Control
CDSC	Communicable Disease Surveillance Centre
CEHO	Chief Environmental Health Officer
DH	Department of Health
DOE	Department of the Environment
DPH	Director of Public Health
FWR	Foundation for Water Research
MAFF	Ministry of Agriculture and Fisheries and Food
MOEH	Medical Officer for Environmental Health
NHS	National Health Service
NRA	National Rivers Authority
PHLS	Public Health Laboratory Service
SCA	Standing Committee of Analysts
SDD	Scottish Development Department
SERC	Science and Engineering Research Council
SHHD	Scottish Home and Health Department
SPDL	Scottish Parasite Diagnostic Laboratory
WRc	Water Research Centre

Medical or technical terms

AIDS	acquired immunodeficiency syndrome
l/min	litres per minute
mAb	monoclonal antibody
mg/l	milligrams per litre
mZN	modified Ziehl Neelsen stain
NTU	nephelometric turbidity unit
o/l	oocysts per litre—the mean number of oocysts present in each litre of a sample submitted for analysis.

Printed in the UK for HMSO
Dd292787 C20 7/90